BLACK DISABILITY POLITICS

DUKE UNIVERSITY PRESS
Durham and London
2022

BLACK
DISABILITY
POLITICS

SAMI SCHALK

© 2022 DUKE UNIVERSITY PRESS
All rights reserved
Printed in the United States of America on acid-free paper ∞
Designed by A. Mattson Gallagher
Typeset in Garamond Premier Pro and Folio
by Westchester Publishing Services

Library of Congress Cataloging-in-Publication Data
Names: Schalk, Samantha Dawn, author.
Title: Black disability politics / Sami Schalk.
Description: Durham : Duke University Press, 2022. |
Includes bibliographical references and index.
Identifiers: LCCN 2021054697 (print)
LCCN 2021054698 (ebook)
ISBN 9781478023258 (hardcover)
ISBN 9781478025009 (paperback)
ISBN 9781478027003 (ebook)
ISBN 9781478092681 (ebook other)
Subjects: LCSH: African Americans with disabilities—
Political activity. | African Americans—Political activity. |
Disabilities—Political aspects—United States. | People with
disabilities—Political activity—United States. | Disability
studies—United States. | Sociology of disability—Political
aspects. | BISAC: SOCIAL SCIENCE / Ethnic Studies /
American / African American & Black Studies | SOCIAL
SCIENCE / People with Disabilities
Classification: LCC HV1568.2.S35 2022 (print) |
LCC HV1568.2 (ebook) | DDC 362.4089/96073—dc23/
eng/20220404
LC record available at https://lccn.loc.gov/2021054697
LC ebook record available at https://lccn.loc.gov/202105469

CONTENTS

ACKNOWLEDGMENTS

So much has changed in my life over the course of writing this book, but some things, some people, have remained consistent. I would first and foremost like to thank my extended network of long-distance friends and chosen family who held and supported me through love, loss, grief, and transformation. Thank you to Britney Johnson, Julia Cadieux, Jina B. Kim, Sarah Grumet, Maeve Kane, Jim Mallek, Michael Patrick Burton, Sue Ellen Riegsecker, Darran Mosley, Aimee Bahng, Megan Albertz, Katie Hu, Kavita Patel, Sarah Hayward-McCalla, Eris Eady, and adrienne maree brown. Thank you also to my local Madison support network: Whryne Reed, Annie Menzel, Stephanie Selvick, Ruben Tabares, Shawna Lutzow, Ali Mulrow, Dana Pellebon, Lara Gerassi, Joshua Hargrove, Molly Clark-Barol, Jing Taylor, and Warren Scherer. I could not have completed this book without the many hugs, phone calls, texts, pep talks, dates, and meals these people have provided me. I want to especially acknowledge my cousins Sydney and Jonathan Schalk, who inspire me with their honest, brave selves. I love you so much, my little weirdos! Finally, thanks to everyone who has welcomed me into the Edwards family, especially Kevin and Shakira—I am so blessed to be your sister.

I am grateful for the support of my agent, Rolisa Tutwyler, who has dramatically improved my professional life, and my editor, Elizabeth Ault, who has been immensely supportive as this project shifted, encouraging me to write "the better book later" rather than rush something that wasn't ready yet. I know this book is better than what I could have done alone because of Elizabeth's support and insight along the way.

Research for this book began during a postdoctoral fellowship at Rutgers University under the mentorship of the late Cheryl Wall and continued under a Nellie McKay Fellowship through the Office of the Vice Provost for Faculty and Staff Programs at the University of Wisconsin–Madison.

Support for this research was also provided by the Office of the Vice Chancellor for Research and Graduate Education at the University of Wisconsin–Madison, with funding from the Wisconsin Alumni Research Foundation. I would like to thank Madelyn Sundquist, my research assistant for this book, as well as the librarians and archivists at the Sophia Smith Collection at Smith College and the Stanford University Special Collections and University Archives. I am also deeply indebted to the Black disabled activists and cultural workers who allowed me to interview them for this project—their names and words appear throughout chapter 5.

Further, I am forever grateful to my academic mentors who have continually taught me how to survive as a Black queer disabled woman in academia. Thank you to LaMonda Horton-Stallings, for continuing to guide and support me long past the dissertation; Alison Kafer, for always cheering me on and believing in my work; Margaret Price, for helping me learn to be more vulnerable and human in academic spaces; and Ellen Samuels, for being the most supportive faculty mentor and making my transition to working at the University of Wisconsin–Madison incredibly easy. I would also like to thank my other colleagues in the Department of Gender and Women's Studies, especially Annie Menzel, James McMaster, Anna Campbell, Jill Casid, Pernille Ipsen, LiLi Johnson, and Jenny Higgins. Thank you as well to my other colleagues across the country who have supported and inspired this work, particularly Jina B. Kim, Kathy McMahon-Klosterman, Marlon M. Bailey, Juliann Anesi, Ally Day, Lezlie Frye, Nirmala Erevelles, Julie Avril Minich, Susan Burch, Eli Clare, Moya Bailey, Alice Wong, Akemi Nishida, Anna Mollow, Robert McRuer, Mimi Khúc, Cassandra Jones, Aimee Bahng, Ayana Jamieson, Leah Lakshmi Piepzna-Samarasinha, and Rebecca Cokley.

Finally, thank you to Jess Waggoner for, well, everything you are and do in my life. I can't believe we hit the academic job jackpot. I look forward to many more colorful, glitter-filled adventures together—a heart don't forget something like this.

INTRODUCTION

Black Health Matters

The mandate for Black people in this time ... is to avenge the suffering of our ancestors ... to earn the respect of future generations ... and be willing to be transformed in the service of the work.
—MARY HOOKS, "The Mandate (Chant)"

Read the epigraph again.

If you're a Black person, read it out loud.

I am a Black person who seeks to avenge the suffering of my ancestors and to earn the respect of future generations. I have been and will continue to be transformed by this work. I am not the person I was when I began this book in 2017. Since that time I moved across the country, began a new job, started and ended major relationships, lost my longtime animal companion, published my first book, went on a yearlong book tour, gained tenure, twerked with Lizzo, discovered family I never knew I had, visited my homeland of Jamaica for the first time, stepped into my work as a public intellectual, became a local organizer for Black liberation work, and so much more.

Writing this book, learning about the incredible labor and sacrifices of activists who came before me in the Black Panther Party and the National Black Women's Health Project, as well as about the continued labor, care, and genius of Black disabled activists and cultural workers today, has changed me, fueled a fire in me that had gone quite dormant. This book that you hold (or scroll through on your screen or listen to) has become my own way of taking up Mary Hooks's mandate for Black people in this time. I began the project in order to understand how Black people have addressed disability as a political concern. The research process of finding how those freedom fighters addressed the way disability is experienced and, at times, inflicted on Black populations has helped me know that the only way I can understand my own experiences with disability, illness, and pain is through the lens of Blackness, of Black disability.

Through researching and writing this book, I have come to identify as disabled and to do so publicly more and more. At first, I said I had chronic pain stemming from a 2016 car accident. Then I stopped correcting people online who referred to me as disabled. I wasn't *not* disabled; I just—despite over a decade of investment in disability studies—wasn't sure if I was allowed to really claim disability yet. I already have so many marginalized identities; it felt excessive. As I developed arguments for how Black activists have long addressed disability and health as a political concern in ways that differ from the mainstream white disability rights movement, I began to see more clearly my own relationship to disability and the ways it is shaped by race, gender, and sexuality for me as a fat Black queer woman—a fat Black queer disabled woman. I will write more about this someday, in another space, but the short version is that as a person with depression, disordered eating, chronic pain, and anxiety, I am unquestionably disabled. What has prevented me from feeling that I can claim disability is the way my disabilities do not fit into the typical legal and medical models of disability and accommodations, the ways white disabled people especially have been dismissive of my understanding of how racism, sexism, homophobia, classism, and fatphobia have materially created, sustained, and exacerbated my disabilities. I cannot get on board with approaches to disability that do not understand it as inherently, inextricably tied to racism and other oppressions. I cannot and will not promote a disability-first or disability-pride-only analysis—and the research that undergirds this book has only solidified and clarified for me these beliefs that I once held more quietly and tentatively. In claiming this Black disability identity, I often use *we*, *ours*, and *us* when referring to disabled people, Black people, and Black disabled people. I refuse to use *they* as if I am separate from the communities I write about, live within, and learn from every day.

I write this personal narrative first to invite you, my readers and listeners, into this space. Are you willing to not only do the work but be transformed by it? Are you willing to read not only for historical information and social theory but for strategies and methods that you can take into your own work as a scholar, an activist, an artist, a person living in a world that desperately needs transformation? Take a moment to think about why you're reading this, what you want to take away from it, and how it might be useful to you and your people. I offer it as one part of a much larger conversation about collective liberation. I hope it helps. In particular, I hope it helps Black people.

This is a book written for Black people, especially Black disabled people. By this I mean that my primary audience is Black scholars, activists, writers, and artists who might take up this theory of Black disability politics in their work for Black liberation. Of course, I understand that this book will be read by non-Black people. I certainly hope that's the case, but this book is not for them. If you are a non-Black person, imagine that you have just walked into my living room, where I'm having a conversation with my Black family and friends. You are welcome to come in, listen, and learn from the conversation, maybe even contribute to it when appropriate, but the conversation, the space of this book, is not for or about you. For my Black readers: Welcome. Settle into this space. Mark the pages. Make it yours. Pass it along. If this book is helpful to you, meaningful to you, that is what matters here. If these ideas I've developed get us even slightly closer to collective liberation, then I've done what I set out to do.

On January 18, 2016, a Black queer liberation collective called Black.Seed shut down the Bay Bridge in San Francisco, displaying three large white banners with pink lettering across the roadway that read: Black Health Matters. Figure 1.1 is one helicopter view of the protest that captured my attention that day.

The protest sought to move the city away from "police murders, rising housing costs, rapid gentrification, and apathetic city officials" and toward "an increase in the health and wellbeing of all Black people in Oakland & San Francisco" by making a series of demands for divestment from policing, investment in affordable housing, and the resignation of several city officials and police officers.[1] The optics of the action were impressive: news-helicopter shots revealed hundreds of cars backed up on the bridge as the protesters remained chained to cars and each other. Police arrived approximately thirty minutes after the shutdown began, and twenty-five protesters were arrested.

I followed the protest via Twitter as it happened. Although at the time I was in the middle of revising my first book manuscript, I took a break from that work to read and watch the social media and mainstream news coverage, saving images and screenshots. At that time, the book you now hold in your hands (or read on your screen or listen to) was still just the germ of an idea, just an observation that disability often appears obscurely or at the

FIGURE I.I The pink Black Health Matters banners across the Bay Bridge during the Black.Seed protest on January 18, 2016.

margins of Black activism and cultural work, a hunch that there was more to Black approaches to disability politics than what existed in the academic literature. Later, when I returned to the Black.Seed bridge action to write this introduction, I found a video about the protest that featured an interview with Alicia Bell, a member of Black.Seed, who provided details about what the action entailed.[2] In line with Dr. Martin Luther King's radical legacy of disruptive nonviolent protest, Black.Seed coordinated dozens of members to shut down the bridge by stopping a single car in each lane of traffic and then chaining themselves to the cars and each other. In addition to the prominent Black Health Matters sign, which was most visible in helicopter shots of the protest, other signs on the bridge called for an end to the criminalization of Blackness and justice for Black people killed by police. Further, the organizers set up an altar with the names of people harmed by state violence, on which people placed offerings. The use of the altar within a nonviolent protest against anti-Black state violence underscores that Black.Seed and similar Black activist groups recognize the importance of not merely ending state and interpersonal violence against Black people but also promoting our health, healing, and well-being, physically, mentally, and spiritually.

The title of this introduction comes from the powerful image of Black.Seed's sign across the San Francisco Bay Bridge, blocking hundreds of cars from crossing. More broadly, the motivations behind this book, *Black Disability Politics*, connect directly with the approaches and demands of this particular act of civil disobedience. The protest explicitly included mention of not just Black lives but Black health and well-being—a suggestion that the deeper concern is not just the murder of Black people by police but all the ways Black people are harmed via housing, finances, and more. Black.Seed's statement, therefore, draws attention to not only Black death but also Black life and the conditions necessary for Black lives to not merely subsist or survive but thrive. *Black Disability Politics* takes inspiration from Black.Seed and other social justice movements and organizations led by Black people, especially Black disabled people, Black women, and Black queer and trans people. More specifically, *Black Disability Politics* analyzes how issues of disability, broadly construed, have been and continue to be incorporated into Black activism from the 1970s to the present. I define Black disability politics as anti-ableist arguments and actions performed by Black cultural workers. Black disability politics are often performed in solidarity with disabled people writ large, but the articulation and enactment of Black disability politics do not necessarily center traditional disability rights language and approaches, such as disability pride or civil rights inclusion; instead, they prioritize an understanding of disability within the context of white supremacy. The book therefore identifies and analyzes examples of Black disability politics in order to claim, celebrate, understand, and learn from this legacy in all its brilliance and imperfection. My hope is to provide a framework for understanding Black disability politics that benefits scholars, activists, and cultural workers who wish to engage in coalitional and intersectional liberation practices. We must learn from each other if we are to build a new world together.

Fields and Frameworks: Black Disability Studies and Disability Justice

Academically, this book contributes to the emergent field of Black disability studies. Merging scholarship, theories, and methods from disability studies and Black studies, as well as from postcolonial studies and feminist studies, especially Black feminist theory, Black disability studies explores both the lives of Black disabled people and the relationship between race and (dis)ability as systems of privilege and oppression.[3] Black disability studies scholarship traces how disability has appeared among Black people, how disability has been treated and understood within Black communities, and how Blackness and disability have been—and continue to be—discursively linked in various cultures. As this field continues to develop and expand beyond the boundaries of the United States, scholars such as Christopher Bell, Nirmala Erevelles, Therí A. Pickens, Moya Bailey, myself, and others have increasingly demonstrated the ways that disability, as an identity, an experience, and a political category, has been conceptualized and approached differently by Black activists and intellectuals than by white activists and intellectuals, thereby requiring changes in scholarly and activist methods and frameworks.[4]

For instance, there is a common narrative in disability studies that Black people have distanced themselves from concepts of disability and disability identity because of the way discourses of disability have been used to justify racist oppression. This narrative is often connected in the field with Douglas Banyton's frequently cited article "Disability and the Justification of Inequality in American History." The article's central thesis is that disability appears all over American history if we simply look closely enough. However, Baynton is often cited more specifically for his argument that marginalized groups, such as Black people, women, and immigrants, had discourses of disability foisted on them as justification for their exclusion from full rights and citizenship. In response, Baynton argues, these groups distanced themselves from disability as a means of accessing certain rights and freedoms. By distancing themselves from disability, he further contends, these other marginalized groups left unquestioned the notion that people with disabilities do not deserve full rights and citizenship, thereby passively accepting that disability is a justifiable rationale for discrimination and exclusion.

Baynton's article, which I myself frequently cite and teach, is incredibly important and useful; however, its narrative has become in some ways canon in the field of disability studies, used to explain why Black art, culture, and politics use disability merely as a metaphor for the impact of racism and often fail to incorporate disability politics, culture, or pride as typically understood in white disability studies and the disability rights movement. This narrative of Black distancing from disability is not wholly untrue, as much scholarship has demonstrated. However, disability studies scholars often use this narrative about Black people's relationship to disability without considering two key factors: first, the whiteness and racism of the disability rights movement and disability studies as a field, which often excludes or alienates Black disabled people; and, second, the possibility that disability politics may actually exist in Black activism and cultural work but manifest and operate in ways that do not look the same as disability politics in the mainstream movement. Recent work in Black disability studies demonstrates the multiple complex and nuanced ways that Black people, historically and contemporarily, have engaged with disability beyond simple distancing or denial.[5] Collectively, my colleagues in Black disability studies have made clear that the narrative of Black disavowal of disability is merely a convenient, partial narrative that has remained underquestioned and underexplored within disability studies as a whole. This book aims to contribute to this growing body of knowledge by developing a theory of what Black disability politics entail.

In addition to my intellectual foundations in Black disability studies, my work is also strongly influenced by the disability justice movement. Disability justice is a relatively new activist practice and framework developed in the mid-2000s by disabled people of color, disabled queer people, and disabled queer people of color, such as Patty Berne, Leroy Moore, Leah Lakshmi Piepzna-Samarasinha, and Mia Mingus as well as groups like Sins Invalid, the Disability Justice Collective, and Azola Story. Disability justice builds on and extends the work of the early disability rights movement, which was often very white and focused on the single issue of disability rights. Those involved with disability justice readily acknowledge that they appreciate and benefit from the advancements achieved by the early disability rights movement. However, not dissimilar from how the Black Panthers, discussed in chapters 1 and 2, were responding to the fact that Black Americans had achieved legal civil rights, yet were still socially and materially oppressed, disability justice practitioners seek a broader understanding of anti-ableism, one not limited to state-sanctioned individual rights, which often primarily benefit disabled people who are already relatively privileged by race, class, gender, sexuality, and/or citizenship status.

Further, disability justice is an inherently intersectional approach. Patty Berne writes that disability justice understands white supremacy and ableism as "inextricably entwined, both forged in the crucible of colonial conquest and capitalist domination."⁶ Disability justice values the leadership of those most impacted (i.e., multiply marginalized disabled people), anticapitalism, cross-movement organizing, sustainability, cross-disability solidarity, interdependence, collective access, and collective liberation.⁷ Practitioners of disability justice recognize that their work "already connects and overlaps with many movements and communities' work," especially work by feminist and queer people of color within reproductive justice, transformative justice, and healing justice movements.⁸ Disability justice work brings important knowledge, theory, and practices to contemporary antiracist activism. A disability justice framework also reveals how the disability rights movement has overlooked or dismissed Black activism around disability. Throughout this book I analyze how Black cultural workers have engaged issues of disability in the late twentieth and early twenty-first centuries from the perspective of disability justice, aiming to articulate a theory of what constitutes Black disability politics specifically. By taking up this research and analysis, I hope to help reclaim a legacy of disability justice work in Black liberation movements and develop a collection of methods, approaches, and lessons we can take away from this history in the name of continued quests for freedom.

In naming my primary fields and frameworks as Black disability studies and disability justice, I am inherently claiming an interdisciplinary, perhaps even undisciplined, approach in this book, breaking some norms of academic research and writing. My sites of analysis vary from the archives of Black activist organizations to interviews, social media, and blogs, while my scholarly influences span disciplines like history, literary studies, public health, and media studies. This is not a history of Black disability politics. Rather, this book is a historically informed analysis of a continually developing political theory that seeks to understand and dismantle ableist and racist oppressions. I turn to history because it benefits us as Black people to know and learn from what our ancestors did, to understand and honor them, and to continue their legacy of finding liberation. It is comforting to know we are not the first or the last, or alone, in our fight for Black lives, especially Black disabled lives. I am indebted to the historians whose work I build on, but in the process of researching and writing this book, I have let my subject and my political investments guide me more than my loyalty to the boundaries of any particular academic discipline or field. I write for a Black scholarly and activist audience first and foremost with the goal of helping us move toward collective liberation via scholarship and theory, and I use whatever disciplinary tools and approaches I find most useful in this work. *Black Disability Politics* refuses to be disciplined.

This undisciplined nature may be particularly evident in the way I talk about and define disability. A major intervention of Black and critical race disability studies is to expand our conceptualization of disability. This expansion draws on work in disability justice and crip theory, a strain of disability studies theorizing (inspired by queer theory) that encourages a move away from a primarily identity-based approach to disability and toward a theoretical approach that seeks to trace how disability functions as an ideology, epistemology, and system of oppression in addition to an identity and lived experience.[9] Relatedly, disability justice activists "are building an analysis that includes political and historical understandings of disability, bodies, ableism, pace, illness, care, cure, aging, the medical industrial complex and access."[10] Disability justice activists often include terms like *sick* and *chronically ill* to acknowledge and include people who may not identify as disabled, especially those who have been made sick or ill by white supremacist and heteropatriarchal violence and neglect. Similarly, crip theorist Alison Kafer describes disability as an expansive "political, and therefore contested and contestable category" and argues for recognizing the collective affinities among disabled, impaired, sick, ill, and Mad people, who are connected not by essential or inherent qualities but by the related oppressions we experience for our nonnormative bodyminds.[11] These two similar approaches to disability as a political and social concern matter because disability studies and the disability rights movement have each often focused on apparent physical and sensory disabilities rather than on cognitive and mental disabilities or chronic illnesses. As Kafer notes, this "oversight is all the more troubling given the fact that diabetes occurs disproportionately" among racial minorities and that "asthma is a common side-effect of living in heavily polluted neighborhoods, which, unsurprisingly, are more likely to be populated by poor people."[12] In other words, existing disability studies and disability rights frameworks for understanding and defining disability have been developed with little attention to the types of disability most common in poor and racialized communities. These white disability studies frameworks therefore are unable to fully account for the ways disability politics manifest in Black communities and activism.

The expansive understanding of disability I use in this book requires engagement with not only disability studies but also health science studies, medical humanities, and the history of science and medicine. I have argued elsewhere that scholars of race and disability should include issues of illness and health in their work because so many Black folks and other people of color experience disability as the impact of capitalism, interpersonal violence, state violence, and/or state neglect.[13] It is also important that scholars and practitioners of health science studies, medical humanities, and the history of science and medicine understand and engage with disability studies and disability justice in order to better theorize and respond to disability from an explicitly political and social position that centers the voices and experiences of disabled and ill people of color. As the individual chapters of this book show, we cannot understand Black disability politics without engaging histories of anti-Black violence, scientific and medical racism, health disparities, health activism, and environmental racism. We also cannot understand Black disability politics without exploring how Black people have conceptualized not only disability, illness, and disease but also health, wellness, and healing within our own communities.

This book, *Black Disability Politics*, aims to bring about a better understanding of its titular term by exploring how specific Black organizations and individuals have engaged the intersections of and relationship between Blackness and disability, or racism and ableism, in their work. My time period for this book spans from the 1970s to the 2010s, focusing on Black disability politics articulated and enacted alongside or in the wake of the contemporary disability rights movement.[14] I selected this period in order to assess how Black people have engaged issues of disability in moments when disability rights activism and legislation were already in existence, that is, moments when Black cultural workers could reasonably be expected to have some awareness of disability rights. This is not to say that Black disability politics or the disability rights movement began in the 1970s. There is clear historical evidence that this is not the case, but by the 1970s the disability rights movement was unquestionably in full effect.[15] Therefore, selecting this time period as my focus allows me to trace how Black people have engaged disability politics in comparison to the mainstream disability rights movement. Again, while this work is historically informed by archival research, it is not a comprehensive history of Black disability politics or even the Black disability politics of the organizations I focus on. This book is one part of a larger academic, activist, and cultural conversation that I want to bring more people into through my work so that we can collectively learn and know more in order to do and be better.

As this section has already indicated, I take a broad, interdisciplinary approach that uses disability studies as a method rather than an object-oriented area of study that would focus exclusively on the lives of disabled people and representations of disability.[16] This conceptualization of disability studies as a politicized approach to research entails critical exploration of how (dis)ability operates as a social system, historically, discursively, ideologically, and materially in our world. This matters for my theorization of Black disability politics because, at times, the articulations and enactments of Black disability politics I analyze are not performed exclusively by Black disabled people. This is important for activist readers to understand: you can do the work of disability justice without being disabled, though multiply marginalized disabled people's expertise and leadership should be centered. The role of nondisabled Black people specifically in the work of Black disability politics also matters because, as I demonstrate throughout the book, ableism and racism are so deeply linked that we cannot dismantle white supremacy and end its violence against us as a collective if we do not also understand and address the role of ableism in shaping Black lives.

While the articulations and enactments of Black disability politics explored in this book do not erase or trump those moments when Black cultural workers have distanced themselves from disability, better understanding other ways Black people have engaged with disability can help build the theoretical tools necessary for Black disability studies scholarship. Further, assessing both the accomplishments and missteps of Black disability political work can help activists, intellectuals, and artists today. We can neither uncritically romanticize nor trash our radical movements of the past, and I do my best to balance appreciation, honor, and respect for the work of those who came before me with a desire for more inclusive radical politics that leave no one behind. I aim to help us learn lessons from Black disability politics historically so that we may continue to cocreate better coalitional politics that remain attuned to how racism and ableism, often in conjunction with sexism, classism, queerphobia, and transphobia, collude in the lives of all Black people, disabled or not. Let me say that one more time: ableism negatively impacts all Black people, whether or not you consider yourself to be disabled. All Black folks need to know this and take it to heart. Understanding these cultural locations of Black disability politics allows us to sharpen our political and theoretical approaches as Black cultural workers in our quest for Black liberation.

Defining Black Disability Politics

What, then, are Black disability politics exactly? First, I define *disability politics* generally as engagement with disability as a social and political rather than individual and medical concern. Following Kafer, who encourages an "expansive approach to disability politics," my understanding of this term is not limited to policy or law.[17] I define *Black disability politics* as disability politics that are articulated (in text, speech, political platforms, and ideologies) or enacted (in activism, organizing, lobbying, art, and interpersonal dynamics) by Black cultural workers—an umbrella term for activists, artists, writers, scholars, intellectuals, and others whose work directly responds to and influences culture. In other words, *Black disability politics* is my term for how Black folks engage with disability from a liberation and justice perspective. Black disability politics can be understood as part of both disability justice and Black liberation movements writ large, providing lessons for people within both movements, whether or not individuals are Black or disabled. Black disability politics are developed, articulated, and enacted by Black people, but this work may influence or be influenced by the disability politics of other racial groups.[18]

In addition to articulating this primary definition of *Black disability politics*, this book also identifies and analyzes four common qualities of Black disability politics. Based on my research, I argue that when Black cultural workers engage with disability, their approaches tend to be intersectional but race centered, not (necessarily) based in disability identity, contextualized and historicized, and holistic. By identifying and analyzing qualities of Black disability politics, I provide a theoretical framework for interpreting articulations and enactments of Black disability politics—one that acknowledges, seeks to understand, and accounts for the distinct ways that Black people have experienced, engaged, and encountered the (dis)ability system. My hope is that my identification and analysis of the major qualities of Black disability politics here will prove useful to Black and disability studies scholars researching Black engagement with disability and to other Black cultural workers seeking to better integrate disability politics into their work. Further, I hope that my theorization of Black disability politics may be adaptable in form, if not substance, for other critical race and disability studies scholars exploring how racialized populations have articulated and enacted their own forms of disability politics.[19] In what follows, I briefly explain each of the central qualities of Black disability politics, which are further explored and analyzed through concrete examples in the chapters to come.

Intersectional but Race Centered

In researching Black engagement with disability politics across multiple cultural locations, I found that the work is always intersectional, but the emphasis tends to be on race/racism as the major analytic lens. By *intersectional*, I mean that the work is grappling with the relationship of multiple oppressions, not that the focus is on the intersection of specific identities, as I explain further in the next quality.[20] By *intersectional but race centered*, I mean that articulations and engagements of Black disability politics tend to be most concerned with the material impact of racism as it intersects with disability and overlaps with ableism, though the words *disability* and *ableism* may never be used. Disability is included and addressed, but this is often done within larger racial justice topics rather than as the main investment or concern. Black disability politics are often also feminist, anticapitalist, and anti-imperialist, but generally they are first and foremost antiracist politics operating in solidarity with disabled people. There are both benefits and pitfalls to this first quality. I apply the label of Black disability politics to Black cultural work even when it is imperfect or conflicting, even when solidarity and coalition are intended but falter. My interest is less in attempting to locate or dictate the perfect marriage of anti-ableist and antiracist movements and more in highlighting how investment in Black lives by Black people has often necessitated grappling with disability and ableism, whether or not the Black cultural workers involved or white leaders in disability rights and disability studies claim or recognize such work as disability politics. I argue that anti-ableism may be incorporated into antiracist work in a variety of ways that differ from what is typically expressed or prioritized within traditional disability studies and mainstream disability rights activism. One key method in locating Black disability politics, therefore, is understanding how the political and cultural work can be intersectional but race centered and still operate in solidarity with disabled people.

Not Necessarily Based in Disability Identity

The second major quality of Black disability politics is that the work is not necessarily based in disability identity. As already mentioned, although the work is conceptually intersectional in that it addresses the relationships of ableism/disability and racism/Blackness as well as of other oppressions and social categories, it is not necessarily intersectional in regard to the identities of the cultural workers involved. This manifests in two ways. First, Black disability politics are not exclusively enacted by Black disabled people. Although Black disabled cultural workers appear frequently throughout my research, I argue that Black disability politics can be expressed and performed by any Black person who interrogates the intersection of racism and ableism and attempts to combat both of these oppressions. Second, I include "not necessarily based in disability identity" as a central quality of Black disability politics because some Black people with impairments, disabilities, or illnesses do not claim disability as an identity for a variety of reasons. These reasons may include lack of access to official disability diagnoses, services, and resources (in other words, not being legally or medically recognized as disabled); the traumatic or oppressive circumstances of their disablement; internalized ableism; identification with disability-specific rather than disability-general communities (i.e., Deaf, autistic, Mad, etc.); the potential for a disability label to further their marginalization; or identity development within communities of color and families of origin in which politicized or celebratory concepts of disability did not exist.[21] In short, Black disability politics are not necessarily based in disability identity because the work tends to be more race centered, as already discussed, and because disability identity is contentious for many Black people.

Contextualized and Historicized

Given the complex nature of disability within Black communities, the third quality of Black disability politics is that the work is typically contextualized and historicized. That is, Black cultural workers engage with disability with critical attention to the sociopolitical contexts of race, class, gender, religion, and geography in a given time period as well as to the historical circumstances, events, and legacies that have shaped experiences and understandings of disability within Black communities. As disability studies scholars have argued, the line between disabled and nondisabled is unstable, permeable, and socially, historically, and contextually defined. Black disability politics are intently attuned to how race shapes understandings and experiences of disability and vice versa. Various scholars have also demonstrated how race has shaped perceptions of what is and is not a disability, who is and is not disabled, and, at times, who does and does not warrant accommodation and inclusion.[22] Others have explored how racial, gender, and class oppression and violence produce the material circumstances of increased disability, illness, and disease among Black and other marginalized populations.[23] This existing scholarship makes clear that we cannot understand Black disability politics without understanding the specific racial context and history of Black experiences of disability. Black cultural workers frequently perform such contextualization and historicization within their articulations of Black disability politics.

Owing to this importance of context and history, Black disability politics are often articulated in conversation with what Julie Livingston calls *debilitation*.[24] Jasbir Puar, building on the work of Livingston, argues that debilitation should be understood as distinct from disablement because it emphasizes "the slow wearing down of populations instead of the event of becoming disabled."[25] Puar therefore uses debility as "a triangulation of the ability/disability binary," further noting, as I already mentioned, "that while some bodies may not be recognized as or identify as disabled, they may well be debilitated, in part by being foreclosed access to legibility and resources as disabled."[26] This context of debilitation, the slow wearing down by racial violence—psychological, emotional, financial, and physical—is essential to understanding Black disability politics, as Black disability political work often occurs at sites of or in response to the debilitation of Black people.

While I am conceptually influenced by Livingston's and Puar's work, I still primarily use the word *disability* in this book because of the key role disabled people and oppression against disabled people play in this project. I also choose to use the word *disability* because, while disability identity is not essential for Black disability politics, disability studies and disability justice are central frameworks for my thinking. My use of *disability* as a central term, therefore, honors and prioritizes the preferred terms of the communities within which I have developed this research as well as my own chosen term of identification. Further, this book aims to highlight the ways Black and other antiracist cultural workers can identify the relationship of their work to disability rights, disability justice, and anti-ableism. I use the word *disability* because of its recognition and value in the wider world beyond the academy, a world in which I hope this work will prove useful. I value accessibility in my writing and language choices here. I want a wide audience because I believe that many different populations can learn a lot from the way Black cultural workers have engaged issues of disability. I hope that by mining the past and present for these examples, providing a framework of analysis, and offering critiques of (and alternatives to) missteps and failures of solidarity, this book can participate in increasing and improving intellectual, political, and artistic engagement with disability justice by Black people and all those who operate in solidarity with us.

Holistic

Last, as a result of the other three central qualities, Black disability politics are ultimately quite holistic. By using the term *holistic*, I mean, first, that the work tends to address whole bodyminds and is not predominantly focused on physical disability as disability studies and disability activism have been historically. I use the term *bodymind* after Margaret Price and expand on it more in depth in my previous work.[27] Briefly, *bodymind* refers to the inextricable nature of body and mind, insisting that one impacts the other and that they cannot be understood or theorized as separate. In fact, the separation of the body and the mind, also referred to as the *Cartesian dualism*, has been used against people of color and women to claim that we are primarily or exclusively controlled (and therefore limited) by our bodies. The term is particularly appropriate for my work on the Black Panther Party and the National Black Women's Health Project, as both organizations attended to Black people's well-being with attention to physical, psychological, and emotional needs, or "body and soul," as the Panthers put it. *Bodymind* as a term best represents the holistic nature of Black disability politics, and I refer to mind and body separately only when analyzing discourse that uses such separation. Second, I also use *holistic* to refer to the work itself because it attends to social and political change at both micro (individual and community) and macro (societal, national, and international) levels. In short, I use *holistic* to refer to the wide range of bodymind topics addressed within Black disability politics as well as the diversity of tactics and approaches employed within Black disability political work.

Topically speaking, Black disability politics operate holistically because they are not limited to physical disability nor even to official legal or medical definitions of disability. Throughout this book Black cultural workers employ Black disability politics to attend to the physical, mental, emotional, and spiritual health and well-being of Black people as political and social concerns. This means, as my discussion of contextualizing and historicizing Black disability already suggests, that Black disability politics include engagement with health, illness, disease, and medicine even as these topics may not be considered disability issues as defined by the state, the medical industrial complex, or the disability rights movement. Since Black disability politics so often intersect with health activism and health-care reform, analyzing this work at times requires challenging ableist assumptions about health and wellness within Black activism, especially health activism, where disability is often used as a specter, a symbol of racial violence. For instance, when disabled children are used as examples of the failures of the medical industrial complex to care for Black mothers, disability is used simplistically as the negative result of racist neglect, drawing on ableist reactions to disability to produce empathy for Black mothers, who are implicitly positioned as nondisabled caretakers burdened by disabled children. In this book I attempt to identify when Black cultural workers have resisted this sort of ableist move, and when they have not, I propose alternative rhetorical, theoretical, and activist approaches that might move us away from using disability in this reductive and oppressive way. I offer such critiques in the praxis interludes of *Black Disability Politics* with acknowledgment of the difficult tensions and conflicts involved in intersectional work, the deep roots of ableist assumptions in American culture, and the fact that none of us operate outside oppressive systems of power.

By approaching the (dis)ability system holistically, Black disability politics can be applied to a wide range of issues, even those that do not necessarily seem to be directly or obviously *about* disability. This quality of Black disability politics topically parallels conflicts between the early Black feminist movement and the civil rights, Black Power, and women's liberation movements in which Black men and white feminist activists often dismissed Black feminist concerns as not properly or sufficiently about race or gender, respectively.[28] Similar to how Black feminists covered a wide range of topics in their organizing and publications, work in Black disability politics frequently entails countering the combined impacts of racism and ableism in a variety of political and social arenas.[29] These parallels are important because the intersectional thinking and organizing developed by Black feminists and other feminists of color in the 1960s and 1970s led the way for the intersectional thinking and organizing of Black disability politics, and several of the examples of Black disability political work examined in this book were and are performed by Black feminists.

This quality of being holistic also applies to the tactics of Black disability politics. Black disability politics focus simultaneously on micro (individual and community) and macro (societal, national, and international) change. This aspect of Black disability politics is common to many activist movements historically. Many cultural workers understand individual intellectual change to be the foundation for collective movement toward systemic change, recognizing that without addressing our individual and interpersonal habits of internalized oppression and lateral aggression, true freedom is impossible. In the specific case of Black disability politics, the concurrent focus on micro- and macrolevel change differs from predominantly rights-based organizing, which heavily depends on and trusts the state to be the arbiter of liberation and protection. This move away from rights-based discourses is reflected in much disability justice work today and is also apparent in the Black Power movement, which sought to move beyond civil rights alone when it became clear that changes in laws would not be enough to counter systems of oppression.

In practice, the holistic nature of Black disability politics means that this political work can take a variety of forms, from patients' rights advocacy and health-care reform protests to the creation of community-support systems and individual consciousness-raising and empowerment. Black disability politics provide a framework for understanding the wide variety of ways that systems of race and (dis)ability intersect in our world and the many avenues one might take to fight these oppressive systems.

Book Overview

This book contains this current introduction, five chapters, two praxis interludes, and a conclusion. The first four chapters are historical in orientation. The praxis interludes serve as contemporary bridges to draw lessons for social justice work today from the work of Black activists in the past, building on their successes and learning from their missteps. The praxis interludes aim to demonstrate some practical applications of the Black disability political theory developed in the historical chapters.

Chapters 1 and 2 explore the Black Panther Party's engagement with disability within their larger antiracist, anticapitalist, anti-imperialist revolutionary liberation ideology, relying primarily on the BPP's own representation and explanation of their involvement in their weekly newspaper. Chapter 1, "'We Have a Right to Rebel': Black Disability Politics in the Black Panther Party," discusses the 504 sit-in, the party's most direct engagement with disability rights, followed by a shorter discussion of the Panthers' Oakland Community School to demonstrate how Black disability politics can be articulated and enacted in ways that are often overlooked or misunderstood in disability studies and Black studies alike. Chapter 2, "Fighting Psychiatric Abuse: The BPP and the Black Disability Politics of Mental and Carceral Institutions," then focuses on the BPP's activism against various forms of psychiatric abuse in prisons, mental institutions, and psychiatric hospitals, especially the return of psychosurgery. Following these chapters, praxis interlude 1, "Anti-ableist Approaches to Fighting Disabling Violence," explores and critiques how the Panthers' work on psychiatric abuse at times missed the mark and perpetuated ableist language and tropes in their fight against disabling violence. Within my critique I offer alternative rhetorical approaches for cultural workers to use in discussing and combating such violence.

The next two chapters focus on the National Black Women's Health Project (NBWHP), positioning its Black feminist health activism in the 1980s and 1990s as a prime example of Black disability politics. Chapter 3, "Empowerment through Wellness: Black Disability Politics in the National Black Women's Health Project," introduces the history of the NBWHP and then analyzes the NBWHP's holistic, cultural, and political approaches to health and wellness, highlighting the ways disability is included and addressed in both explicit and implicit ways. Chapter 4, "More Than Just Prevention: The NBWHP and the Black Disability Politics of HIV/AIDS," assesses how the NBWHP's approaches to health were enacted in programming and publications regarding HIV/AIDS among Black women and Black communities. I use the NBWHP's work on this specific disability concern to demonstrate how health activist work that promotes prevention or reduction of potentially disabling diseases and conditions can still be anti-ableist. After these two chapters on the NBWHP, praxis interlude 2, "Approaches to Disability Identity in Black Disability Politics," critiques the NBWHP's general avoidance of explicitly politicized disability identity and draws heavily on the knowledge of contemporary Black disabled cultural workers to consider how we can critically engage disability identity within Black communities today.

Finally, in chapter 5, "Black Disability Politics Now," I shift fully to the twenty-first century and discuss my interviews with eleven contemporary Black disabled cultural workers. In this chapter, I argue that Black disabled cultural workers are using their articulations of Black disability politics to change how we organize for social justice. I analyze their contemporary Black disability political work and make connections to the qualities of Black disability politics I identify in the historical work of the previous chapters, arguing that these qualities remain similar or have only slightly shifted. This final chapter also identifies some of the ways that Black disability politics are being incorporated into other Black-led activist movements.

For this part of the research project, I received an institutional review board waiver to perform interviews with Black disabled cultural workers, particularly activists.[30] I began with reaching out to members of the Harriet Tubman Collective and expanded my search based on recommendations from participants. In total, I interviewed eleven people, seven of whom are members of the Harriet Tubman Collective. All of the participants identify as both Black and D/disabled. Some capitalize the *D* in Disabled when referring to their identity, and some do not; therefore, both spellings appear in chapter 5. Not all of the interview participants called themselves *activists*. Some preferred other words, like Talila "TL" Lewis's term *social justice engineer*.[31] As a result, I refer to the interview participants collectively as Black disabled activists and cultural workers, though the questions I asked focus more on activist and political work than artistic work. I name each interview participant here because each of them matter immensely. This is how they asked to be identified:

* T. S. Banks (he/him): poet, facilitator, organizer, mental wellness advocate, and board member for Disability Pride Madison
* Patrick Cokley (he/him): administrator of the Lead On Update and founding member of the Harriet Tubman Collective

- * Candace Coleman (she/her): community organizer for Access Living (Chicago) and founding member of the Harriet Tubman Collective
- * Dustin Gibson (he/him): founding member of the Harriet Tubman Collective
- * Lorrell Kilpatrick (she/her): advocacy services coordinator and founding member of the Harriet Tubman Collective
- * Talila "TL" Lewis (no pronouns): social justice engineer, movement lawyer, community organizer, educator, codeveloper of Disability solidarity praxis, volunteer director for Helping Educate to Advance the Rights of Deaf communities (HEARD), and founding member of the Harriet Tubman Collective
- * Tiara Simmons Mercius, JD (she/her): family law clerk and creator of the hashtag #DisabilityAblesplained
- * Tinu Abayomi-Paul (she/her): author, disability advocate, and creator of the hashtag #EverywhereAccessible
- * Kayla Smith (she/her): Black autistic disability rights advocate and creator of the hashtag #AutisticBlackPride
- * Vilissa Thompson (she/her): social worker, founder of Ramp Your Voice, and founding member of the Harriet Tubman Collective
- * Heather Watkins (she/her): disability advocate, writer, mother, consultant, speaker, creator of the blog *Slow Walkers See More*, and founding member of the Harriet Tubman Collective

There were other people I was unable to interview owing to scheduling conflicts, the pandemic, and time constraints for the project. I want to make clear that the goal of this work is to uplift their voices and make connections with my archival research, but more comprehensive interviews with these and other Black disabled cultural workers would be of immense value. I hope someone reading this takes on that particular task to contribute to the conversation and the movement.

My goal in taking on the methodological and temporal shifts in this book is to break from the typical disciplinary academic monograph mode and create something that is more clearly emerging through shared political community and useful for cultural workers outside of academia, especially activists. In my interview with TL Lewis, Lewis states, "Most disability studies or whatever it is called—I don't know who it's for, but I certainly can't access it and I'm literacy privileged—if that shit's for the academy, y'all can have it. Disability justice, disability solidarity, Black disability politics is about: this is for us." The inclusion of interview quotes at various moments throughout the book brings us back to the overarching goals of not just this book but the larger work of collective liberation. I am immensely grateful not only for the time, knowledge, and expertise of each of the participants but also for the way doing these interviews has forever changed me, bringing me into my own new relationship to disability identity and Black disability politics even after years of researching and writing on this subject. For any of us who are involved in the work of liberation, whether our role is artist, organizer, writer, educator, healer, thinker, or policy maker, we need to be in conversation with one another. I have learned so much from talking to the eleven Black disabled cultural workers here. I have learned so much from reading the work of other contemporary Black disabled cultural workers. Black feminists have a long lineage of creating work that bridges academic and activist communities, and I do my best to honor and participate in that legacy here.

Finally, the book ends with "(Not a) Conclusion: The Present and Futures of Black Disability Politics," where I return to my own narrative voice to reflect on the process of writing this book in the midst of national and global upheaval. This final section addresses both scholarly and activist audiences, summarizing the arguments and ideas of the book while also attempting to imagine what comes next. I wrote the first draft of this nonconclusion in the midst of a global pandemic as COVID-19 forced a worldwide slowdown like nothing we have ever experienced before. I began writing the last part of this book while participating in social distancing in my home in Madison, Wisconsin, while on leave from teaching. I finished it several months later after participating in the Black liberation uprisings of the summer of 2020 as an on-the-ground organizer and activist. In the nonconclusion I reflect on how my research influenced my approach to these direct actions and how these experiences transformed my understanding of the purpose of this book (and forced me to finally finish it).

For over a year before finishing the first draft of *Black Disability Politics*, I knew that the book I had originally set out to write had changed into something else, something more interdisciplinary, more activist oriented, but I struggled to envision the full structure. In the spring and summer of 2020, with a pandemic and uprisings altering life as we know it, I realized that so much was going to change, so much would never be the same. There was no point in trying to write the book I had originally envisioned because the world I had started to write this book in was gone. What you hold in your hand (or are reading on a screen or listening to) is the book that I needed to write in and for this moment. It has been a labor of love but labor nonetheless. This is the knowledge I have been able to acquire with the privilege of my position as an academic and with the risks of my positions as an activist. I hope it is useful now and in the future for us, for Black people, especially Black disabled people, as well as for anyone who claims to love and support us. In accord with Mary Hooks in the epigraph that began this introduction: in this new world, may we avenge the suffering of our ancestors, earn the respect of future generations, and be willing to be transformed by the work again and again and again.

Let's begin.

1

"WE HAVE A RIGHT TO REBEL"

Black Disability Politics
in the Black Panther Party

Content note: Quoted archival material
contains racist and ableist language.

On May 7, 1977, the cover story of the *Black Panther*, the weekly newspaper of the Black Panther Party (BPP), read, "HANDICAPPED WIN DEMANDS— END H.E.W. OCCUPATION." The page included three images. The first photo features two Black men: a wheelchair user, Brad Lomax, and his fellow Panther member Chuck Jackson, who stands behind Lomax's chair. The second image is of a blind Black man named Dennis Phillips holding up a protest sign that says, "You don't have to see to know."[1] The third picture is of a crowd of people of various races outside of a building with a seemingly non-Black woman wheelchair user in the center of the frame. Cover stories are reserved for the most important or pressing news of a particular moment. The choice to place a disability rights activist win on the cover of a Black activist newspaper is undeniably symbolic. This cover reflects the BPP's belief that the success of the occupation of the Department of Health, Education, and Welfare (HEW), now more commonly referred to as the 504 sit-in or the 504 demonstration, was not merely important news but news relevant and connected to the Panthers' own antiracist, anticapitalist, and anti-imperialist work. The placement of the success of the 504 demonstration on the cover of the *Black Panther* is in many ways the height of explicitly visible disability politics within the BPP. It is the most significant moment of coalition and solidarity with disabled people in the entirety of the paper's

CONTINUED ON PAGE 6

FIGURE I.I Cover of the *Black Panther* on May 7, 1977.

publication between 1967 and 1980 and thus provides a launching point for my analysis of Black disability politics within the BPP.

The Black Panther Party was a revolutionary, antiracist, anticapitalist, anti-imperialist organization started in Oakland, California, in 1966 by Huey P. Newton and Bobby Seale. The Panthers originally focused the bulk of their activities on armed self-defense and patrol of police within Black communities, rapidly obtaining national and international membership and influence. Although the BPP is most known for the image of Black men wearing black berets and carrying guns, for the bulk of its existence, the BPP had a majority of women in its membership, and several women, such as Elaine Brown, Ericka Huggins, and Katherine Cleaver, took on major leadership roles.[2] In December 1968 the BPP had offices in twenty cities, and by the height of the BPP's membership and influence in 1970, sixty-eight cities had party chapters of varying sizes.[3] In 1969 the director of the Federal Bureau of Investigation (FBI), J. Edgar Hoover, referred to the BPP as a "violence-prone black extremist group" and declared that the BPP, "without question, represents the greatest threat to the internal security of the country."[4] Over the course of several years, the FBI, via its covert counterintelligence program (COINTELPRO), targeted members and suspected members of the BPP, men and women alike, for surveillance, harassment, incarceration, and violence with the aim of disrupting and discrediting the organization among the public, its allies, and its members.[5] Despite this explicit governmental suppression of the BPP and the chaos that it caused within the organization, the BPP adapted and continued its cultural, political, and community work in a somewhat smaller though *nonetheless influential and radical* form until 1982.[6]

I emphasize "nonetheless influential and radical" because the period of the BPP's history I discuss in this chapter is often considered a period of "rapid decline" for the Panthers, one some scholars and activists do not recognize as radical or revolutionary.[7] Scholarship on the Panthers predominantly focuses on the time between their founding in 1966 and the early 1970s, with many scholars considering the period of decline as beginning somewhere between 1972 and 1974.[8] *Decline* here refers to a reduction in size and membership but is also used by some scholars to indicate a shift in the radical nature of the BPP after 1972. However, owing in large part to the work of scholars like Alondra Nelson and Robyn C. Spencer, more scholars are exploring the differently revolutionary work of the BPP from the mid-1970s to their official close in 1982.[9] I believe a major reason that previous scholarship has ignored this period or considered it no longer radical is that the BPP at this time was predominantly led and run by women, and their focus was on local survival programs that attended to the health and well-being of the people, especially children, the elderly, and the disabled. Despite the fact that even BPP founder Huey Newton wrote about the survival programs as inherently part of the revolutionary agenda because they provided the basic conditions necessary (food, housing, medical care, education, and so on) for people to begin to organize and act for change, the value of the survival programs and the overall work of the Panthers between 1972 and 1982 is glaring underdiscussed in scholarly assessments of the BPP.[10] There is, of course, much to say about those early militant years, but there is also significant value in the work of the Panthers after 1972, and we can learn critical lessons from how they organized for change *after* organizational splits, membership decline, and governmental suppression.

I contend that, in addition to the federal smear campaign that influenced mainstream perceptions of the BPP, sexist and ableist attitudes within academia have also strongly shaped our understanding of the revolutionary nature of the BPP throughout its existence. My work here aims, in concert with the above-mentioned newer scholarship, to help shift this understanding of the BPP. I argue that the Panthers' revolutionary ideology understood the relationship of racism, classism, and ableism, but their approach to disability politics did not always align with the language and tactics of the white mainstream disability rights movement. As a result, their work has been overlooked and underappreciated in disability studies, while the importance of disability and health to the Panthers in this latter period and the revolutionary nature of their work at this time have been similarly overlooked and underappreciated in Black studies.

The shift in the form and function of the BPP in the wake of governmental repression was reflected in changes to their ten-point platform, a document that defined the demands, beliefs, and investments of the Panthers. The first version of the BPP's platform, drafted in October 1966, focused on freedom and the "power to determine the destiny of our Black Community" via calls for full employment, "land, bread, housing, education, clothing, justice and peace."[11] In March 1972, however, the platform was revised in two key ways that reflected changes in the ideology and activities of the BPP. First, point 1 was changed to call for freedom and the "power to determine the destiny of our Black *and oppressed* communities."[12] Second, the ten points were expanded to include a call for "completely free health care for all Black and oppressed people."[13] These two significant changes to the political platform set the stage for increased and more explicit engagement with disability politics.

I base the majority of my claims in this chapter and the next on the way disability and health were discussed in the *Black Panther*, the BPP intercommunal newspaper, published from 1967 to 1980. The paper served as one of the BPP's main political tools, providing a way to inform and politically educate members while also raising money. The ten-point platform, for example, was published at the end of every issue. The *Black Panther* included a wide range of news stories about injustices done to Black, Brown, and poor people across the country, from police brutality and unfair legal proceedings to discrimination in employment, housing, and health care. The paper also featured advertisements for Panther programs, political cartoons, educational and theoretical articles on social issues, and international news from other revolutionary anti-imperialist movements. At its height, the BPP printed 150,000 copies of the *Black Panther* weekly, with national and international circulation.[14] By the late 1970s, the focus of this and the next chapter, the *Black Panther* had a circulation of around 5,500 copies per week and was distributed nationally in select major cities, such as Los Angeles, Chicago, Detroit, and Milwaukee.[15] By this period in the BPP's history, however, the bulk of the copies were distributed in California, especially in the Bay Area, where the BPP was headquartered.

This distribution information about the *Black Panther* matters substantially to my arguments about the BPP because even though by the mid-1970s the BPP's on-the-ground community work was happening almost exclusively in the Oakland area, the Black disability politics expressed within the paper still had a wide reach and influence. Archival records of inner-party memorandums indicate that members were expected to read the paper in full weekly.[16] It matters that all members nationally as well as other Black people and non-Black supporters of the BPP read about disability rights and disability politics in the *Black Panther* as being integral to collective liberation. This framework likely influenced future Black activist approaches to and understandings of disability and health as political concerns. As Jane Rhodes argues, "The Panthers' goal was often consciousness-raising rather than a particular set of actions; they sought to mobilize the frustrations of the black American underclass and turn these simmering emotions into a critical mass movement."[17] Thus, the ideas and values promoted via the BPP's consciousness-raising apparatus, the *Black Panther* newspaper, matter substantially to our understanding of the BPP's Black disability politics.

During the 1970s, as the BPP shifted from a primary focus on community-controlled, armed self-defense against police to community survival programs, the Panthers began to enact Black disability politics. This chapter begins the work of tracing how Black activists incorporated disability into their work and how they articulated the reasons for this incorporation. To make my arguments, I first discuss the 504 sit-in, the most explicit engagement of the BPP with disability rights, using the BPP's own explanation of their involvement to argue that disability politics were part of their revolutionary liberation ideology. The 504 sit-in will likely be familiar to disability studies readers, which is why this chapter also includes a less explicitly disability rights–focused example of the Panthers' Black disability politics: the Oakland Community School. This second, shorter example of how the Panthers integrated disability politics into their work demonstrates that Black disability politics are often enacted in ways that go under the radar for disability studies and Black studies scholars alike without a critical framework for understanding how Black cultural workers have engaged disability as a political concern. Together these two examples support my claim that the Panthers integrated disability into their revolutionary liberation ideology in a period typically considered less radical and in decline for the

BPP. This chapter then sets the stage for a more focused discussion of the Panthers' antipsychiatry activism in the next chapter as another example of their Black disability politics.

The 504 Sit-In

The 504 sit-in was a major milestone in the disability rights movement. It was a twenty-five-day occupation of the San Francisco regional office of the HEW during which over a hundred protesters refused to leave until the national HEW secretary, Joseph Califano, signed into effect regulations for Section 504 of the 1973 Rehabilitation Act. The Rehabilitation Act of 1973 was the first piece of federal legislation dictating civil rights for disabled people. Section 504 specifically stated that programs receiving federal funds, such as public schools, universities, and hospitals, could not discriminate against or exclude people on the basis of disability. While the Rehabilitation Act was signed by President Richard Nixon in 1973, Section 504 remained ineffective without written, published regulations that defined who was disabled and what constituted discrimination. After years of delays, lawsuits, and broken promises, disability rights activists nationwide organized and created the American Coalition of Citizens with Disabilities to agitate for official regulations for Section 504 to be drafted and approved. When newly inaugurated President Jimmy Carter took office, his HEW officials attempted to create different regulations than those drafted under President Gerald Ford. In response, the coalition warned that if the regulations were not signed as is, the organization would stage sit-ins at HEW offices across the country on April 7, 1977. While the protests in Atlanta, Boston, Chicago, Denver, Los Angeles, New York City, Philadelphia, and Seattle lasted for a few hours, and the relatively large protest in Washington, DC, lasted just over a day, the protest in San Francisco continued for weeks, thanks to careful planning and organizing by disabled activists in the Bay Area. The occupation of the HEW building in San Francisco garnered extensive local and national news coverage and has taken on legendary status within the disability history and disability activist communities for its innovation and power. The sit-in ended only when the regulations were finally signed. It remains the longest nonviolent occupation of a federal building in US history.

In most scholarly accounts of the 504 demonstration, the role of the Panthers is relegated to a brief mention that the BPP provided food throughout the twenty-five-day occupation of the San Francisco HEW regional office building.[18] Though several scholars of the BPP have written about the

Panther's community survival programs and health activism in the 1970s, I found no Panther scholarship that discusses their involvement in the 504 sit-in. Only two articles, Susan Schweik's "Lomax's Matrix: Disability, Solidarity, and the Black Power of 504" and Keith Rosenthal's "The Intersections and Divergences of Disability and Race," provide extended scholarly engagement with this history. However, recent publications by disability activists (some of whom were at the sit-in) and the Longmore Institute's *Patient No More* traveling and digital exhibit on the 504 demonstration have added new details on the role of the BPP as well.[19] This section builds on that work and further assesses the BPP's engagement with the 504 sit-in, arguing that the Panthers supported the demonstration because disability rights and anti-ableism fit within their existing revolutionary ideology. As a major Bay Area activist group, the Black Panthers were involved with the 504 demonstration from start to finish, participating via the most commonly cited activity of providing daily food deliveries. The Panthers also, however, sent representatives to give speeches, put out a press release endorsement, supported two members of the BPP inside the protest, and published numerous articles in the *Black Panther*. I discuss each of these activities in turn.

Nearly all accounts of the sit-in note that a major part of its success was due to extensive coalitional support. This support came in the form of volunteers, donations, and endorsements from a variety of other activist groups and organizations focused on not only disability rights but also gay rights, women's liberation, civil rights, and more.[20] The organizers of the 504 demonstration secured this support in the planning stages of the protest and expanded their reach throughout the duration of the sit-in. While the BPP was not listed as part of the "504 Emergency Coalition" in the first press release issued by protest organizers, according to HolLynn D'Lil, who acted as insider photographer and press for the protest, BPP member Ellis White spoke at a rally on the first day of the demonstration.[21] D'Lil quotes White as later saying, "We've always been involved. We've had reps here from the beginning. The issue is self-determination. More human rights. Whether handicapped people have a right to survive. Whatever they do to ensure survival, we support. Califano threw drug addicts and alcoholics out of the handicapped group. They belong too. The issue is money. It's in keeping with our principles—survival."[22] Here White insists on not only the early involvement of the Panthers in the 504 demonstration but also how their involvement was directly in line with their principles, that is, the ten-point platform, which first and foremost called for freedom and self-determination for all oppressed communities. The BPP understood disabled people, along with other people of color, people in poverty, women, and gays and lesbians, to be fellow oppressed members of society who had to fight for survival in an oppressive capitalist system. Indeed, despite having a cultural reputation for being sexist, masculinist, and homophobic, by the mid-1970s the BPP had explicitly and publicly supported the women's rights movement and was the first major Black organization to come out in support of gay rights.[23]

The BPP's solidarity with disabled people in general and with the 504 protesters specifically is further articulated in their April 8, 1977, press release, written and delivered by Michael Fultz, editor of the *Black Panther*.[24] The statement reads, "Along with all fair and good-thinking people, The Black Panther Party gives its full support to Section 504 of the 1973 Rehabilitation Act and calls for President Carter and HEW Secretary Califano to sign guidelines for its implementation as negotiated and agreed to on January 21 of this year. The issue here is human rights—rights of meaningful employment, of education, of basic human survival—of an oppressed minority, the disabled and handicapped. Further, we deplore the treatment accorded to the occupants of the fourth floor and join with them in full solidarity."[25] Like White's statement, the BPP's official public endorsement also emphasizes human rights, survival, and solidarity among oppressed groups. The BPP's role, however, was not limited to being a supporter in name alone; the Panthers also contributed in key material ways.

First, two members, Brad Lomax and Chuck Jackson, the disabled and nondisabled Black men featured together on the May 7 cover of the *Black Panther*, were on the inside as part of the sit-in and also acted as two of the representative delegates to Washington, DC, for the 504 coalition. According to the *Black Panther*, Lomax "first discovered he had the symptoms of M.S. in 1969, when his legs collapsed from under him while selling Black Panther newspapers in the community. Despite the best medical attention available, Brad's condition grew steadily worse, to the point where he is now both wheelchair-confined and legally blind. In spite of his medical problems, however, he has remained a member of the Black Panther Party."[26] As a disabled Panther, Lomax worked to incorporate disability politics into the efforts of the BPP by making connections with the Center for Independent Living along with Donald Galloway.[27] Because Lomax was a rank-and-file member, however, his work still had to align with the goals and ideology of the BPP.

According to former BPP leader Elaine Brown, Lomax's participation in the 504 demonstration and his work at the Center for Independent

Living were considered part of his work for the BPP. Brown states that while Lomax and Ed Roberts, leader of the Center for Independent Living, brought awareness of disability rights to the Panthers, the BPP's existing ideological position of focusing on systemic change for all marginalized groups meant that further transforming their thinking to include disability politics "wasn't hard."[28] In fact, soon after being made aware of disability politics, BPP leadership ordered all BPP buildings to install wheelchair access ramps.[29] This work, which Lomax took the lead on, is documented in the Dr. Huey P. Newton Foundation Inc. Collection in a handwritten report from Lomax to program coordinators on September 3, 1977, a few months after the 504 sit-in.[30]

In the report Lomax provides an update on his progress with getting ramps installed in the BPP's main office and grab bars installed in the bathrooms of the Oakland Community Learning Center, which also housed the Oakland Community School, discussed later in this chapter. He notes a future appointment he has with Judy Heumann (a white disabled leader of the 504 demonstration) and lists contacts he has made with disabled people and disability/accessibility professionals who might serve as volunteers for the BPP's accessibility work.[31] Lomax is therefore an example of how multiply marginalized individuals play a key bridge leadership role between groups due to his work to foster the further development of disability politics within the BPP *after* the 504 sit-in.[32]

The archival material on Lomax and his ideas about the intersection of Blackness and disability is likely limited in part by his role as a rank-and-file member (Panther leadership work is far more frequently documented) but likely also due to his multiple marginalized identities. Multiply marginalized people in any movement are more likely to get burned out, have fewer resources (including time) to spare, have their intersectional concerns ignored, and, consequently, not rise to the levels of leadership that leave extensive historical evidence. For multiply marginalized people to lead, their needs and concerns must be centered and supported within the organization at all levels. As Mary Phillips writes in regard to women in the BPP, their hard work "deprived them of the luxury to debate and write about theory. Women acted on the ground as soldiers ready to die for the liberation just like the men. [Ericka] Huggins commented, 'We didn't have the time to write.'"[33] Lomax likely had little time or support to write as well. And yet, despite the limited direct historical evidence he left behind, he is an essential figure for Black disability politics who undoubtedly fostered the BPP's support of the 504 sit-in—their most direct involvement with disability rights. The

Panthers' involvement in the 504 demonstration could not have occurred, however, without the existing revolutionary ideology that undergirded all of their work. Lomax himself was politicized via the BPP before he became disabled, and it is likely his political understanding of disability was influenced by the radical liberation ideology he embraced as a Panther. In writing about Lomax, therefore, I want to at once recognize and honor his important historical role and acknowledge, as the rest of my work on the BPP will show, that the Panthers' disability politics did not start, end, or rest entirely on the shoulders of one individual.

As most accounts of the Panthers' involvement in the demonstration state, the BPP also contributed materially by donating food. More specifically, once it became clear that the sit-in was going to continue beyond a day or two, the Panthers began bringing daily hot dinners, such as fried chicken and meatloaf.[34] The BPP also brought in mobile showers for the protesters and supplied a form of security as well.[35] While the exact form of this security is unclear, it is apparent that members of the BPP, familiar with the tactics of federal agencies and the police, ensured that supplies got through the door. For example, one *Black Panther* article stated that more than a week into the sit-in, "with all incoming telephone service abruptly cut-off, and all food denied entry—Party members saw to it that a sympathetic guard 'discreetly' allowed the breakfast foods they had brought upstairs to the demonstrators."[36] Similarly, in her memoir Corbett O'Toole writes, "I happened to be in the lobby the first night that the Black Panthers brought us dinner. The FBI blocked them and told them to leave. The Panthers, being extremely sophisticated about how to manage police interactions, merely informed the FBI that they would be bringing dinner every night of the occupation. They would bring the food, they would set it up, and they would leave. If the FBI prevented them from doing that they would go back to Oakland and bring more Black Panthers until the food got delivered to the protesters. The FBI soon backed down."[37] Elsewhere, O'Toole more explicitly asserts: "I think the secret history of the 504 sit-in is that we never, ever would have made it without the Black Panthers. The Black Panthers fed us dinner—they fed 150 people of which only one was a Panther—every single night for the whole demonstration. *We never would have survived without them.*"[38] Clearly, the material support provided by the Panthers in the form of members on the inside, food, and supplies was essential to the longevity of the protest. Additionally, the BPP provided extensive coverage of the demonstration in their newspaper, coverage that reveals the way the Panthers linked their existing revolutionary ideology with disability rights to form their Black disability politics.

The *Black Panther* provided the most national coverage of the 504 protest—only a local paper, the *San Francisco Chronicle*, covered it more often. The BPP published ten articles and announcements of varying lengths about the demonstration between April 16 and July 7, 1977.[39] After the demonstration ended, the 504 sit-in was mentioned an additional eight times in the paper in related stories, such as "Protest Systematic Exclusion: Disabled Sue A.C. Transit" and "Disabled Score Victory over Supermarket Barriers: Blind Mother Fights Bias for Custody of Children," which typically featured events in which former 504 protesters were involved.[40]

The *Black Panther* coverage of the demonstration is significant because it meant that thousands of Black people were frequently informed of disability rights over a period of several months in a way that framed disability politics as directly connected to Black community concerns and liberation for all oppressed communities. The impact of a major Black activist organization directly supporting and increasing awareness of disability rights among Black Americans cannot be directly calculated. The paper was mailed to homes and to organizations and was sold directly on the street. Each of the approximately 5,500 copies was likely read by multiple individuals.[41] What did it mean, then, for Black disabled activists, intellectuals, and young people across the country who read the *Black Panther* to read about Brad Lomax and Dennis Phillips? What was it like to see their pictures on the cover, learn of their activism, and read about them each proudly claim Blackness and disability as identities? How did the paper's coverage of the 504 sit-in influence nondisabled Black people's thinking about disability rights and identity in ways historical records can never capture? How did it resonate and reverberate in ways we can feel today? The national distribution of the *Black Panther*'s coverage is incredibly important to our understanding of Black disability politics in large part because it is a moment in which, rather than distancing themselves from disability, as is so often the narrative about communities of color and disability, Black people embraced and understood disability politics as a necessary part of collective liberation.

The articles in the *Black Panther* portrayed the sit-in as an important act, calling it "a powerful and significant protest for human and civil rights of handicapped and disabled people."[42] The rhetoric in the paper makes clear the connections between the disability politics being enacted in the sit-in and the work the BPP had already been doing to increase the freedoms of oppressed people. In the first article on the demonstration, for example, the paper noted that "despite stereotypes and stigmas, real and very much alive," protesters "have embarked upon a serious drive to control and transform the oppressive conditions of their lives."[43] The emphasis on oppression, stereotypes, stigma, and other sociopolitical concerns in the *Black Panther*'s representation of the 504 sit-in presented readers a social model of disability that paralleled the BPP's own understanding of race and class oppressions.[44] The social model of disability emerged from disability activism in the 1970s, particularly that of the Union of the Physically Impaired against Segregation in the United Kingdom.[45] The social model proposes that disability is primarily a social issue resulting from the refusal of society to accommodate and include people with disabilities. A common explanation of this model was included in a *Black Panther* article via a quote from an unnamed 504 protester who stated, "If they'd take away the handicaps (like stairs, and others barriers for wheelchair-confined and otherwise disabled people), then we wouldn't be handicapped."[46] As this quote indicates, the social model of disability—posed in contrast to the medical model, which understands disability as a purely mental or physical problem to be cured or treated— suggests that *impairments* (one's mental or physical differences) become *disabilities* only when bodyminds interact with inaccessible environments. While disability studies scholars have since critiqued and adapted this model to better account for pain, nonphysical disabilities, and attitudinal and behavioral (rather than just physical and sensory) access barriers, the BPP was clearly engaged with and influenced by the then-cutting-edge theorizing around disability as a social and political concern.

I contend that the Panthers took quickly to the social model of disability because it paralleled their own understanding of race and class oppression as stemming from the biases and failures of larger society rather than from the shortcomings of any individual or marginalized group. Throughout the *Black Panther* coverage of the 504 sit-in, the BPP regularly made connections between racism and ableism in an attempt at articulating solidarity. For instance, in an address at a victory rally after the end of the demonstration, a leading member of the BPP, Ericka Huggins, made the connection of oppressions explicit. Huggins is a former political prisoner who was denied adequate medical care during her incarceration and whose work with the BPP I discuss further in the next section.[47] At the victory rally, she stated that "the United States has always had its niggers.... And they come in all sizes, shapes, colors, classes, and disabilities.... The signing of 504, this demonstration, the sit-in, this beautiful thing that has happened these past weeks, is all to say that the niggers are going to be set free."[48] To the BPP, therefore, disability rights were an obvious part of their goal to obtain freedom and self-determination for all oppressed communities; here "niggers" was abstracted into a synecdoche for all those excluded and exploited within the United States rather than used as a term specifically tied to Blackness and race. As several scholars of race, gender, and disability have argued, oppression analogies (those in which one oppression is compared to another), while often intended to promote connection or identify similarity, can easily end up reifying one oppression in the name of fighting another, erasing the presence of people located at the intersection of multiple oppressions or appearing to rank one oppression as worse or more prevalent than the others.[49] In the case of Huggins's speech, however, I would argue that her use of *nigger* does not negate nor rank racism or ableism but rather leaves space for the intersection of Blackness and disability.

Additionally, in line with the Black Panthers' frequent critiques of the federal government, the newspaper also highlighted the Ford and Carter administrations' failures to follow through with implementing the 504 regulations. Unlike other nationally distributed papers, which often mentioned 504 regulations' implementation costs and the rationales for resistance to it alongside coverage of the protest, the *Black Panther* focused on rights, access, and empowerment.[50] The one time the newspaper did discuss the costs of mandating accessibility, it was in order to critique a cost-benefit model of decision-making. The editorial article sarcastically asks, "How much will it cost us for 'you people' to have your human rights?" before detailing the estimated costs alongside the profits "the newly-employed disabled people will add to the gross national product." The article estimates that "to allow 35 million Americans to have an equal access/barrier-free environment necessary to live full and decent lives" will cost "a little over 8 ½ cents per disabled person. Not very much at all." The editorial continues by stating, "How much? Well, from the human point of view, a great deal more than the racists and reactionaries are willing to give up without a fight. If the rednecks and the others don't have 'cripples' to hate and make fun of anymore; if 'niggers' and the rest of the oppressed in this society aren't the enemy anymore, then who will all that anger and frustration built up within the 'silent majority' be turned against?"[51] Here once again, the BPP makes direct connections between the operation of racism and ableism, but in this article, with its overall supportive arguments and use of scare quotes around *cripples* and *niggers*, these connections are made in ways that seek not to compete or compare but rather to connect.

As with oppression analogies, one of the concerns when analyzing how marginalized groups discuss "other" forms of oppression is that those who are multiply marginalized are sometimes erased from the conversation. In the *Black Panther*'s coverage of the 504 sit-in, however, Black disabled people and disabled people of color were prioritized. In addition to the direct involvement of Black disabled Panther Brad Lomax, the newspaper published an interview with Dennis Phillips, the blind Black man pictured on the May 7 cover. In the interview Phillips encouraged his "brothers and sisters that are Black and that are handicapped" to "get out there, we need you. Come here, we need you. Wherever you are, we need you."[52] The interview with Phillips was edited, so the choice of what to include was purposeful. It is particularly important that the editors included the following statement from Phillips: "I'm not a member of the Black Panther Party. I'd like to join the Black Panther Party. I am a member of the Black Panther Party as far as my own initiative and soul is concerned. They have fed us. They have given us respect. They have treated us as human beings."[53] This quote not only places the BPP in a positive light, emphasizing their coalitional work, but also suggests that the BPP wanted to highlight the potential for (more) Black disabled involvement and inclusion within their work via Phillips's statement.

The *Black Panther* interview with Phillips and a later interview with Lomax together acknowledge the particularity of the lives of Black disabled people and other disabled people of color, demonstrating the centrality of intersectionality to their Black disability politics.[54] A decade before the coining of the term *intersectionality*, Lomax referred to being Black and disabled as "multi-disabilities," while in another article on the congressional hearings at the San Francisco HEW office, the *Black Panther* made sure to mention a minority panel of four people, "all of whom eloquently expressed the 'double whammy' experienced by handicapped minorities."[55] Throughout their coverage of the demonstration, the *Black Panther* interviewed, quoted, and named several other individual protesters, often protesters of color, alongside the main white disabled leaders of the protest, such as Judy Heumann, Kitty Cone, and Ed Roberts, who, along with HEW officials and politicians, were most often interviewed and quoted in other papers. The inclusion of so many rank-and-file protesters in the newspaper's coverage of the sit-in reflects the BPP's emphasis on the "power of the people" and the role that every individual has to play in a revolutionary agenda.[56]

Further, the choice to include so many explicit representations of disabled people of color in their coverage of the 504 sit-in demonstrates the

BPP's commitment to intersectional thinking, even as their work prioritized race and class as central concerns. Indeed, in much of the BPP's work and in *Black Panther* articles like the above-quoted pieces using the terms *multi-disabilities* and *double whammy*, we can see the influence of feminist-of-color theorizing of the period, particularly Third World feminism and Black feminism. For instance, Frances M. Beal wrote about the "double jeopardy" of being a Black woman in 1969 in a pamphlet for the Third World Women's Alliance that was later republished in Toni Cade Bambara's groundbreaking 1970 anthology *The Black Woman*.[57] Further, in April 1977, the same month as the 504 sit-in, the Combahee River Collective wrote their foundational Black feminist statement.[58] The overlap and likely mutual influence are more apparent when we consider that Combahee River Collective member Demita Frazier had been a member of the Chicago chapter of the BPP, and, of course, iconic Black feminist Angela Davis had been involved with the BPP as well.[59] By the mid-1970s, women dominated Panther membership and leadership. Former Panther women have since written and spoken about the role of gender and feminism in their work.[60] When I write here about the intersectional disability politics of the BPP, therefore, I am also fundamentally writing about a Black disability politics informed by Black feminist theorizing and organizing.

My claims throughout this section about the radical, intersectional ideology of the Panthers as an example of Black disability politics are not intended to suggest, however, that there was no ableism within the BPP or within its representations of disabled people and disability rights. The *Black Panther*'s coverage of the 504 demonstration occasionally used ableist language, that is, language that promotes negative and oppressive attitudes toward disabled people, such as describing the protest as "inspiring" or "most poignant" and repeatedly referring to Lomax as being "victimized by multiple sclerosis."[61] Terms like *inspiring* and *poignant* are often perceived as patronizing, suggesting that disabled people are an inspiration to nondisabled people for existing with their differing bodyminds or for "overcoming" their disability to become political actors. These concepts present disability as a personal rather than political or social issue and obscure the role of inaccessible environments and attitudes. The term *victimized* would be read by most disability studies scholars similarly as suggesting that one is always a victim, suffering from or harmed by disability, rather than a person living with a disability—even if that disability may cause pain or difficulty. Disability studies scholar Susan Schweik, for instance, argues that this language in the *Black Panther* reveals "a general lack of disability consciousness" within the BPP.[62] Schweik's choice of the term *disability consciousness* here is essential because it highlights that the Panthers were not yet fully aware of how language was being used and transformed within predominantly white disability rights communities even as they used a social model of disability and supported the work emerging from disabled activists.

While I agree that the use of this type of language suggests that writers and editors for the *Black Panther* had not fully divested themselves of ableist thinking, I am interested in a closer interpretation of the language used in the BPP's coverage of the 504 demonstration. Within the overall rhetoric used in articles about the sit-in, the language leans toward being progressive for its time, such as using both *handicapped* and *disabled* as descriptors. Furthermore, the intent predominantly aligned with a disability rights approach rather than with a medical model of disability. Of course, intention cannot be the sole basis for assessing ableist (or otherwise oppressive) language—harm can occur regardless of intention. Nonetheless, when analyzing potentially ableist language among people attempting to work in solidarity with disability communities, there is political and scholarly value in reading closely and in context, analyzing the intention of the overall text as well as the frequency, severity, and style of use of potentially ableist language. While disability studies scholars and disability rights and justice activists may want to eliminate words like *retard* or *vegetable* (I address the latter term in praxis interlude 1), other words, like *inspiring*, are not ableist in and of themselves but rather are often used in ableist ways.[63] There is a need, therefore, for analyzing more closely how language is being used in a specific racialized context rather than merely identifying the existence of certain potentially ableist words (in the case of disability studies) or leaving such language undiscussed or eliminated from quotes (in the case of Black studies).

In the *Black Panther*'s coverage of the 504 sit-in, *inspiring* was almost always used in conjunction with another adjective: "inspiring and powerful" protest, "tremendous, inspiring victory," or "spectacular and inspiring victory."[64] While this does not completely negate the potentially ableist implications, these quotes suggest that what was inspiring was the protest's power, length, and success more than merely the fact that it was done by disabled people. Importantly, the words *inspiring* and *inspiration* were never used to describe any disabled individual but rather were used exclusively in reference to the protest, the victory, and, once, the way the Black civil rights song "We Shall Overcome" was used as "an unofficial theme song" and as a "source of hope and inspiration" by the protesters.[65] Reading the use of *inspiring* and *inspiration* in these specific contexts, then, and within the larger scope of the BPP's involvement with the 504 demonstration, I would not consider the use of these words ableist. I would consider the repeated references to Lomax as a victim of his multiple sclerosis representative of latent ableist beliefs in the BPP even as Lomax seemed to be clearly supported and respected as a member. That said, I nonetheless propose that, like *inspiring*, the word *victim* may not always be ableist, or at least not ableist in the way it is typically understood in disability studies thus far. Again, the term *victim* in disability studies is typically interpreted as implying one is always suffering from a disability (as I think the use of *victim* in reference to Lomax in these articles ultimately does). However, in the context of disabling racial violence, referring to a disabled person of color as a victim may be intended to draw attention to the way marginalized people are subjected to violence and neglect in ways that disable and debilitate their bodyminds. I would strongly advise against using the term *victim* today and encourage instead a focus on the systems and behaviors producing harm—an argument I flesh out further in praxis interlude 1. But when interpreting texts from the past, it behooves scholars of race and disability to pay attention to the nuances of the way *victim* is used in regard to disability as well. These rhetorical claims are not to deny the ableism that undoubtedly existed in the BPP. Instead, I want to encourage interpreting potentially ableist language within its specific racialized context to help us understand how Black disability politics might diverge at times from approaches to disability politics in white and wealthy communities whose experiences of disability are less likely to come from experiences of state violence and neglect.

The success of the 504 sit-in depended on a number of factors: the planning, tenacity, and creativity of the protesters; the extensive media coverage's pressure on politicians; and even the ableism of employees at the HEW office, who deeply underestimated the resolve and capabilities of disabled people, notoriously patronizing the protesters the first day by serving punch and cookies.[66] The occupation could not have lasted as long and as safely as it did, however, without the extended network of supportive groups and organizations, such as the BPP. Schweik argues that this support is often framed as coming from "other" activist groups in a way that erases the connections and overlaps between social justice organizations and individual identities. Taking up an expansive approach to identifying and analyzing Black disability politics addresses this potential erasure. Taken as a whole, while the *Black Panther* was perhaps imperfect in aspects of its rhetorical execution, the BPP strongly supported the 504 demonstration in material and ideological ways because of their existing revolutionary agenda seeking freedom and self-determination for all oppressed people. The BPP's support of the demonstration, in the form of public endorsements, member participation in the sit-in, delivery of food and other supplies, and extensive coverage in their newspaper, is representative of how the Panthers' ideology included space for disability and more specifically of how they were articulating and enacting Black disability politics. The creation and management of their Oakland Community School represents another key example of this development of Black disability politics within the BPP, this time far removed from the explicit disability rights movement connections of the 504 sit-in.

The Oakland Community School

In 1973, four years before their explicit involvement in disability rights via the 504 demonstration, the Black Panther Party opened the Oakland Community School (OCS), a tuition-free, not-for-profit, community-organized child development center and elementary school for children ages two through twelve. The school was an evolutionary outgrowth of the BPP's preexisting Intercommunal Youth Institute.[67] The OCS was a nontraditional radical education space that used a culturally relevant, experience-based curriculum and a dialectical teaching method in which students were encouraged to ask questions, engage in discussion, make critiques, and find solutions in order to develop their critical thinking skills.[68] The school had "no traditional grade levels, only group levels based on their academic performance," so that each of the 50–150 students per year received "an education tailored to his or her specific needs and learning styles" in subjects such as "math, science, language arts (Spanish and English), history, art, physical education, choir and environmental studies."[69] The OCS was recognized for its innovations and achievements in education and was a training ground for many local educators. The school was in high demand; the waiting list for entry sometimes included pregnant women's unborn children.[70] The OCS closed its doors nearly a decade later, in 1982, in alignment with the formal end of the BPP.

Although the OCS does not seem to be directly or explicitly about disability, evidence shows that children with disabilities were included in the school.[71] Former OCS director Ericka Huggins and BPP scholar Angela D. LeBlanc-Ernest write that at the school "a student's ethnicity, economic class, learning style, *or physical ability* was never a criterion for entrance or retention" and that "OCS attracted the attention of other educators and community representatives who saw it as an effective educational program for all children *regardless of ability*, ethnicity, or geographic location."[72] In regard to children with disabilities more specifically, the authors discuss an interview with a former BPP member who worked at the school who "recalled working with a group of students with reading difficulties. Curriculum and community combined to solve the problem when a special education consultant visited the school specifically to make an offer to help assess any student with reading and/or cognitive difficulties. These children were tested and determined to have different learning styles. Consequently, the plan for their individual learning was adjusted, as was the instructor's teaching strategy."[73] This method of adapting teaching strategies to fit the educational needs of the students was based on the BPP's ideological investment in providing empowering education for all youth, which would prepare them to be leaders and change makers in their communities. The OCS's pedagogical methods also parallel approaches in universal design for learning, an anti-ableist educational framework developed in the 1990s that encourages a flexible, multimodal learning environment that supports various learning and communication styles.

While the exact number of children with disabilities at the school each year is unknown, the Black Panther Party's OCS was founded to "challenge the concept of 'uneducable youth'" and establish "a replicable model for education that was designed to empower whole communities."[74] JoNina M. Abron writes, "Some children who came to OCS had been expelled from Oakland public schools, or were labelled hopelessly incorrigible or uneducable by teachers and officials."[75] While the BPP primarily understood the label of "uneducable" as tied to racist interpretations of Black children's capabilities, communication styles, and behaviors in school, this term is also materially and discursively connected to disability. More specifically, the label of uneducable was used at this time to filter poor and racialized students into underfunded, segregated classrooms for the disabled, which demonstrates how disability gets racialized, how racialization can be disabling, and how the freedom of all of our communities, particularly for Black disabled people, depends on collectively resisting these mutually constitutive, mutually dependent oppressions. The BPP did just that in their work with the OCS and elsewhere.

For instance, although tests were used in the above example for assessing students struggling with reading, educators at the OCS resisted the use of standardized testing, except to prepare students for transitioning to public school for middle school. The OCS also completely rejected IQ testing, which was used in many public schools nationwide in a way that often lumped disabled children, nondisabled Black children, and children with English as a second language into undersupported, overcrowded special education classrooms where children sometimes had few to no educational lesson plans.[76] In fact, in 1977 and 1978 the *Black Panther* published a number of articles on the overrepresentation of Black children in special education classes owing to culturally biased IQ testing. The articles primarily focused on testimonies and arguments from the class-action lawsuit *Larry P. v. Riles*, in which a group of Black parents sued on behalf of their children who were improperly labeled "mentally retarded" and segregated into special education classrooms.[77] Although these parents were not directly involved with the OCS, the paper's extensive attention to this lawsuit connects with the BPP's existing work with the school.

Contemporary research continues to show the relationship of race, (dis)ability, education, and, increasingly, the prison industrial complex for Black youth.[78] Yet asserting that Black children are being over- or misdiagnosed as disabled without rhetorically positioning disability as inherently negative remains difficult for contemporary activist work in this arena. The Panthers provide a potential model for this. The BPP was paying attention and responding to the impact of poverty, the educational system, and the prison industrial complex on disabled and nondisabled Black youth long before scholars were writing about the school-to-prison pipeline and the role of race and disability within it. The BPP's Black disability politics involved clear arguments that public schools were failing Black, disabled, and Black disabled youth and that new teaching methods were required to address these failures of a one-size-fits-all educational model that centered white, middle-class, and nondisabled youth.

At the OCS, the BPP aimed to counter the violence and neglect in the public school system by educating children at their individual level, style, and pace in a way that also affirmed their cultural and racial identities, histories, and experiences. While the OCS was never conceived of as a school *for* disabled children nor promoted as a school inclusive of children with disabilities, the OCS did include disabled children, providing them concrete material assistance as needed and adapting to their educational needs, as the example of the students who had trouble with reading suggests. The OCS therefore is an example of how Black disability politics have been enacted by including issues of disability within intersectional Black activist work without necessarily explicitly naming or centering disability and anti-ableism. An understanding of the mutually constitutive nature of race and (dis)ability therefore undergirds how Black cultural workers contextualize and historicize their work on disability and health issues.

The Panthers' OCS is also an example of the importance of multiply marginalized individuals who create connections between communities and encourage solidarity. One of the major reasons the OCS incorporated the learning needs of disabled students so well is the knowledge and labor of Ericka Huggins, who directed the school. Huggins has a long history of investment in disability politics and the education of disabled children in particular. In an oral history, Huggins states that she attended college in order to become a teacher. More specifically, she "wanted to open a school for disabled children" because her first boyfriend had a disabled brother, named Theophilis, or "T." T had been institutionalized in a state home "because his parents couldn't take care of him.... They didn't have money, and his mother couldn't work full time and take care of him, and they couldn't afford child care." Huggins explains that she would visit T with her boyfriend on weekends, and they

> would drive back crying, because T was always under cared for. His
> clothes weren't right, he was mixed in with kids who had different dis-
> abilities but certainly not the one he had. Everybody was all clumped
> together. It was like a jail for disabled kids, it didn't make any sense.
> And I said, "That's it, I'm going to start a school.... [W]hen I get old,
> when I go to college I'm going to get my education. I'm going to start a
> school. You can't put birth defective children and emotionally harmed
> children and mentally disabled children in the same dorm and give them
> the same treatment."

Huggins further describes the conditions of T's institution, explaining, "Some of the children were just there because they couldn't walk. How could they be stimulated in the same environment with T? And T could walk, but he needed social contact to stimulate him. He wasn't getting it. The staff were overworked, there weren't enough of them. It went on and on, kids didn't get baths. I mean, it just was a disaster." This early firsthand experience of the failures to support the education and development of disabled children was impactful for Huggins. She states that she had an "epiphany in seeing that school where T went" and vowed to go to college in order "to serve people," especially children. Huggins put this vow to serve into practice in her work with the BPP and was able to follow through with her investment in education for disabled children through the OCS.[79]

In addition to being the director of the OCS, in 1976 Huggins became "both the first woman and the first Black person to be appointed to the Alameda County Board of Education, which serves children with cognitive, emotional and physical disabilities and incarcerated youth in the county's many school districts."[80] During her tenure on the board of education, Huggins advocated for improvements in the education programs for disabled and incarcerated youth in the county. In a three-part interview for the *Black Panther* after her first year on the board, Huggins explains that when first elected she had to "beg ... to be shown the special education programs."[81] Once introduced to these programs, Huggins identified several problems, such as the "horrendous" Deaf education program located in a "back hallway" room "only large enough for two small people" and the plans to build "the proposed North County Development Center for severely handicapped and mentally retarded children" on an earthquake fault line.[82] In the interview Huggins notes that "educationally handicapped and occupational therapy classes are usually filled with young Black males, regardless of the ethnic breakdown in a particular community," and she critiques "the abuse of drugs on children, such as speed drugs and amphetamines like Ritalin," explaining:

> Officials in the county schools deny that children are given drugs. They say that if a child takes Ritalin or another drug, it is because his or her own family doctor has recommended it. I was told that there are some children who really need drugs. The prevalent attitude of school officials favors drug usage.... They just want to get the "problem" off their hands and move the child out of the way. Let him or her nod out on Ritalin. Who cares, as long as the child won't be a problem in the classroom. This is the general attitude.[83]

Like the ocs concern with and resistance to the notion of uneducable children, in her work on the board of education Huggins pushed back on the racist disability rhetoric used against Black children. At the same time, Huggins used her position to advocate for improved educational conditions for disabled children of all races.

Huggins's work is an example of Black disability politics. In the interview she critiques the improper labeling of Black kids as disabled but does not engage in distancing from disability. Instead, she argues that both nondisabled Black children placed in special education and disabled children need better educational assistance and resources rather than the racist, ableist educational isolation and warehousing to which they were being subjected. In her work on the Alameda County Board of Education and as director of the Panthers' ocs, Huggins played an essential role in the articulation and enactment of Black disability politics by the BPP. Further, the publication of Huggins's perspective in the *Black Panther* once again demonstrates not only how the ideology of the BPP included disability politics but also how their specific approach to Black disability politics was circulated nationally to other Black activists and cultural workers, likely including some working in educational spaces outside of Oakland. The BPP's newspaper therefore critiqued the collusion of racism and ableism in the public education system and promoted the radical educational approach of the OCS, which was remarkably similar to universal design for education and other anti-ableist, inclusive educational models.

On the surface, the OCS and Huggins's work do not seem to be about disability at all. The existing scholarship on the OCS and Huggins pays little to no attention to issues of disability. And yet evidence suggests the school's individualized education style was inclusive of disabled children, and Huggins, who pursued a degree in education in the hopes of opening a school for disabled children, infused disability politics into her work as director as well as into her position on the Alameda County Board of Education. This work was then documented in the *Black Panther* so that the enactment of Black disability politics in the school and the articulation of Black disability politics in Huggins's rhetoric regarding what she learned in her role on the school board were distributed widely to BPP members and allies nationwide. It is important to interpret the OCS's educational approach, founded in response to racist and classist school systems, as an example of Black disability politics even as the language of disability access and rights is mostly absent from primary and secondary sources on the school. I discuss the OCS and Huggins here because their work illustrates how Black disability politics are often articulated and enacted in spaces not marked by explicit disability rights rhetoric and in spaces removed from the medical industrial complex. Further, the rhetoric employed in the *Black Panther*, particularly in Huggins's three-part interview about her first year on the school board, demonstrates how Black people have not simply distanced themselves from disability but rather have at times understood disability and the treatment of disabled people as deeply political concerns inherently tied to racism and classism. Indeed, the OCS is another example of what can be missed in Black history if we do not learn to identify Black disability politics as different from how disability politics have typically been understood in the context of the white mainstream disability rights movement. Black cultural workers like Ericka Huggins, Brad Lomax, and others make clear that attention to Black political approaches to disability model radical intersectional thinking that is useful for scholars and activists alike as we continue to study and fight back against the collusion of racism, ableism, classism, and other oppressions.

Conclusion

The Black Panther Party's involvement with the 504 demonstration in 1977 was their most explicit engagement with the disability rights movement. The importance of the 504 sit-in and the iconic nature of the BPP, particularly among leftists, progressives, and radicals, mean that this specific moment of engagement with disability politics has been recognized in the historical lore of the disability rights movement, though scholarship on the Panthers almost never mentions their role in the demonstration. Detailing the BPP's material and rhetorical support of the sit-in, particularly the role of Black disabled protesters like Brad Lomax and Dennis Phillips, is important for the historical record. To actually understand how the BPP incorporated disability politics into their work, however, we must look beyond this singular moment in history and examine how the Panthers engaged with disability less explicitly, such as within the OCS, where the BPP developed an alternative model of learning that centered the needs of disabled and nondisabled children of color, and in the *Black Panther*, where they critiqued the racism and ableism of the public school system.

To truly understand how Black cultural workers have articulated and enacted Black disability politics, we cannot limit ourselves to studying explicit engagement with disability rights by Black activists. Black disability politics are most often enacted within and alongside other, not-disability-exclusive concerns, in specific relationship to race, class, gender, and other major social issues without explicit or focused engagement with the methods and languages of the mainstream disability rights movement. This is apparent, for example, in the Panthers' health activism via free clinics and awareness-raising ad and testing campaigns for sickle cell anemia. Indeed, Black activism within and against the medical and psychiatric industrial complexes, the subject of the next chapter, is perhaps the most obvious location within which to locate Black disability politics because the medical industrial complex has long been a primary battleground for disabled people. Importantly, however, the power of the (dis)ability system and the medical and psychiatric industrial complexes extends far beyond the explicit confines of doctors' offices, clinics, and hospitals, into law, prisons, media, education, and other cultural arenas in which disability politics may be enacted, as the example of the Oakland Community School demonstrates.

A scholarly understanding of Black disability politics requires expanding the locations within which we search for Black engagement with disability and adapting our parameters for how disability politics can be defined, articulated, and enacted. This includes interpreting engagement with disability by Black cultural workers within the historical, racial, and cultural contexts of the communities from which these Black disability politics emerge. Black studies scholars can contribute to this work by bringing their knowledge of Black history, Black activism, and Black culture into conversation with the politics and theories of disability studies to better understand where these fields overlap as well as where they might clash—and explore what such clashing might mean for both fields. Disability studies has long acknowledged it has a race problem, but Black studies has been far less likely to address its own ableism. We cannot have a deracinated disability studies, and we cannot have a discussion of Black activism and Black communities that does not consider disability, gender, class, or sexuality anymore. We cannot have a disability rights movement or an antiracist movement that does not closely and explicitly attend to intersecting systems of oppression. To move forward, we, as scholars, activists, and cultural workers, must continue to fight for critical, intersectional approaches to history, theorizing, scholarship, justice, and change.

In the next chapter, I continue my analysis of the BPP from a Black disability studies perspective. There I investigate the BPP's fight against psychiatric abuse as another important historical example of Black disability politics. Further removed from the mainstream disability rights movement than the Panthers' involvement in the 504 sit-in, and yet closer to issues of medicine and health than the OCS, the Panthers' resistance to psychiatric abuse, such as psychosurgery and forced pharmaceutical treatment, was greatly informed by disabled activists and undertaken in solidarity with disabled people. The arguments published in the *Black Panther*, however, were primarily articulated through an understanding of the violence of racism within the medical, psychiatric, and prison industrial complexes. Like the examples of Black disability politics introduced in this chapter, the BPP's battles against psychiatric abuse aid us in mapping the nuances of Black disability politics historically. Understanding these nuances benefits scholars, activists, and other cultural workers who seek to strengthen our contemporary approaches to studying, articulating, and enacting Black disability politics specifically and cross-movement solidarity more generally.

FIGHTING PSYCHIATRIC ABUSE

The BPP and the Black Disability Politics of Mental and Carceral Institutions

Content note: This chapter contains extended discussion
of psychiatric abuse in prisons and psychiatric hospitals.

On December 31, 1977, the *Black Panther* published a guest commentary article titled "Principles of Radical Psychiatry" by Claude Steiner, a white founder and practitioner of radical psychiatry. The article opens with a quote by Malcolm X and then asserts that "psychiatry is a political activity" because "the psychiatrist has an influence in the power arrangements of the relationships in which he intervenes." Steiner argues that psychiatry and the psychiatrist can never be neutral because "when one person dominates or oppresses another, a neutral participant—especially when he is seen as an authority—becomes a participant in the domination." Steiner goes on to state that psychiatry's false and oppressive claim to neutrality makes marginalized people rightfully avoid psychiatric services. He then offers the alternative of radical psychiatry, writing, "A radical psychiatrist will take sides. He will advocate the side of those whom he is helping. The radical psychiatrist will not look for the wrongness within the person seeking psychiatric attention: rather, he will look for the way in which this person is being oppressed."[1]

The Black Panther Party (BPP) believed that overmedicalization of disability, illness, and disease depoliticized and individualized these experiences in ways that obscured the effect of the social and political on people's bodyminds, especially those from oppressed groups, who are more likely to be subject to state violence. This critique of overmedicalization was not limited to the physical alone but included the mental and psychiatric. In "Principles of Radical Psychiatry," Steiner uses language and frameworks with which BPP members and other *Black Panther* readers would already have been familiar. For instance, he discusses internalized oppression and refers to the inner voice of internalized oppression as "the Pig," the same term used by the Panthers to refer to police and others complicit in racist imperialist capitalist oppression. Further, Steiner writes that within radical psychiatry, anger is understood as "a healthy first step in the process of liberation rather than an 'irrational,' 'neurotic,' or otherwise undesirable reaction" and that "violence, not equivalent with anger, may be a product of demystification [the process of understanding one's oppression], when anger is discounted."[2] This framing of anger as an appropriate reaction to oppression and of violence as a valid response to the dismissal of anger produced by oppression aligns directly with arguments made by the BPP that framed Black anger as justified and in need of productive expression.[3]

In his concluding paragraphs, Steiner argues that rather than being "the art of soul healing...[t]he practice of psychiatry has been usurped by the medical establishment."[4] In contrast to this medical usurpation of mainstream psychiatry, Steiner asserts that "radical psychiatry is community control of soul healing. It has as its goal to demystify the oppressive practices of establishment psychiatry and the artificially generated scarcity of psychiatric resources. Radical psychiatry proposes to make psychiatric skills available to large numbers of people, so that it will be possible for people to heal each other's alienation without needing to resort to the mystified oppression and isolation promoted by establishment psychiatry."[5] Once again, Steiner's rhetoric here parallels many of the ideological positions of the BPP, such as advocating community control (of police, of clinics, of schools), serving people "body and soul," and providing education, skills, and tools to individuals who will continue to help improve and uplift their communities—including through improving their personal well-being. This article is one concrete example of how the BPP raised awareness about and fought against psychiatric abuse, thereby participating in Black disability politics.

In the previous chapter, I argued that the BPP supported disability rights during the 504 demonstration because they understood disabled people as one of the oppressed communities, as mentioned in their ten-point platform, for which they sought freedom. As a result, the incorporation of disability into the BPP's work, as Elaine Brown states, "wasn't hard" because it fundamentally fit within the BPP's overall radical liberation ideology.[6]

While the Panthers' support for the 504 sit-in marks the most direct engagement with disability rights in the BPP's history, it was neither the first nor the last time the BPP worked on issues of disability, as my discussion of the Oakland Community School in chapter 1 demonstrates. Studying the intersectional, complicated, and often obscured ways in which the BPP enacted disability politics helps document how Black disability politics have been articulated and enacted in the United States. Understanding disability politics in the work of the BPP definitively requires a disability justice approach because issues of disability within the Panthers' activism were often interlaced with issues of police brutality, access to health care, housing, incarceration, food access, and more.

This chapter addresses the Panthers' critiques of psychiatry, particularly their fight against psychiatric abuse. I use *psychiatric abuse* here as an umbrella term for oppressive or violent practices within the psychiatric industrial complex, including, but not limited to, involuntary commitment, forced pharmaceutical treatment, psychosurgery, electroshock therapy, prolonged restraint, solitary confinement, coercion, and a variety of other harmful conditions and practices within institutions, such as forced unpaid labor or the denial of access to food or human contact. Psychiatric abuse is more likely to be targeted at marginalized populations, especially people with diagnosed or assumed mental disabilities. I use *mental disability* after Margaret Price, who employs it "as an umbrella term to encompass cognitive, intellectual, and psychiatric disabilities, mental illness, m/Madness and a/Autism, as well as brain injury or psychiatric survivorship. Mental disability is not intended to replace any of these more specific terms or erase differences, but rather to enable coalition."[7] Both of these terms are purposefully wide and inclusive because the BPP's work on these issues overlapped and intersected with the prison industrial complex, the military industrial complex, white supremacy, and state violence.

The BPP protested psychiatric abuse on a variety of fronts throughout the 1970s. On multiple occasions the Panthers worked with and/or supported mental disability and psychiatric activist groups to protest abuses within mental institutions, hospitals, and wards, including those associated with prisons. The BPP collaborated at different times with the Network against Psychiatric Assault (NAPA), the Coalition against Forced Treatment (CAFT), the Committee Opposing Psychiatric Abuse of Prisoners, and the California Mental Health Coordinating Council.[8] The *Black Panther* also published numerous articles detailing mental disability and antipsychiatry activist work on issues like forced pharmaceutical treatment, unpaid labor inside of mental institutions, and involuntary commitment.[9] Although the deinstitutionalization movement to reform, downsize, or close institutions for mentally (and sometimes physically) disabled people began in the late 1960s in the United States, the movement gained more public recognition, prominence, and success in the 1970s as journalists, former (ex-)patients, consumers, survivors, and their family members exposed and spoke out against the often inhumane conditions, abuses, and neglect occurring at many state and private facilities.[10] The *Black Panther* followed suit, along with other major papers during this period, by publishing stories about conditions in and lawsuits against a variety of institutions nationwide, from mental hospitals to nursing homes.[11] The Panthers also worked with lawyer Fred J. Hiestand on several "public interest lawsuits," including *Black Panther Party v. Kehoe* in 1974, in which the BPP "successfully sued Oakland area nursing homes and convalescent hospitals to compel them to make public certain information about health code violations."[12] Through political action, activist collaboration, and the publication of consciousness-raising articles and news reports, the BPP worked against the proliferation of psychiatric abuse in multiple arenas.

The most prominent matter within the Panthers' fight against psychiatric abuse was their protest of psychosurgery. *Psychosurgery* is another umbrella term, this time referring to surgical procedures on the brain intended to have therapeutic mental and behavioral effects. The most infamous form of psychosurgery is lobotomy, which was first used in the United States in 1936 and remained a popular and respected medical practice for nearly twenty years.[13] However, owing to botched procedures, growing lay concern, and the advent of modern psychiatric pharmacology, lobotomy specifically ceased to exist as an American medical practice by the late 1950s. Nonetheless, psychosurgery more generally continued to be used in research as well as in experimental and therapeutic procedures, notably experiencing a resurgence in the late 1960s and early 1970s.[14] As Jenell M. Johnson notes in her rhetorical history of lobotomy in American culture, during this resurgence neuroscientists proposed that certain areas of the brain housed violent impulses and therefore sought "to use psychosurgery as a way to mitigate aggression and violence." In creating these arguments, medical researchers often used racially coded language about "urban" people and used riots occurring in predominantly Black cities and neighborhoods as illustrative examples.[15] The racialized nature of this language was not lost on the BPP, whose members kept up with publications in a variety of academic, scientific, and medical journals in order to share developments and new knowledge via their intercommunal newspaper, the *Black Panther*. The paper was one of the main venues the BPP used to raise awareness about and protest psychosurgery and other forms of psychiatric abuse.[16] The *Black Panther* responded strongly to the return of psychosurgery and often did so in relation to the prison industrial complex and race.

In this chapter, I detail how the BPP enacted Black disability politics via questioning the power of the psychiatric-medical industrial complex and its violent, coercive practices, especially among poor, racialized, and/or incarcerated populations. The BPP's Black disability politics entailed protesting the immense power of psychiatric and medical professionals over their patients and making important intersectional connections between institutionalized and incarcerated populations. I begin with an exploration of how the BPP made connections between prisons and mental institutions in solidarity with mentally disabled people, followed by a discussion of the BPP's arguments against psychosurgery specifically. The conclusion links the work of the BPP with the work of Black cultural workers today, in the hopes that we can affirm, learn from, and build on the Panthers' legacy.

Making Connections: Prisons and Mental Institutions

While disability studies and prison scholars have started to trace the relationship of institutionalization and incarceration historically and contemporarily, the Panthers understood this connection intimately in the 1970s because of the regular incarceration of members, who witnessed and/or experienced the use of psychiatric drugs in prisons as a means of control.[17] Of particular importance is the *Black Panther*'s June 26, 1971, story "Vacaville—America's Headquarters for Medical Genocide," which detailed the medical and legal abuses occurring at the Vacaville Medical Center, part of the California state prison system. The detailed and relatively lengthy article argues that "Vacaville is reminiscent of the medical centers at the infamous Nazi concentration camps during WWII, in which bizarre 'scientific experiments' were conducted upon Nazi victims," citing specific drugs and dosages being forced on prisoners. The article further contends that "these drugs and lethal chemicals can and do permanently impair and damage the minds and bodies of its prisoners, and are administered in an attempt to destroy the revolutionary potential or the will to resist in any of the brothers who have been courageous enough to speak out against the injustices in this society.

Most men are shipped to Vacaville because they are considered 'discipline problems' at other penal institutions."[18] Here the BPP directly argues that psychiatric medications are used in prisons and prison medical centers as a means of control targeted at activists and revolutionaries who protest the circumstances of their incarceration as well as the overall state of oppression in the United States, an argument repeated in later articles as well.[19]

The BPP's arguments are supported by historical research in the history of science and medicine such as Johnson's work cited above and Jonathan Metzl's *The Protest Psychosis: How Schizophrenia Became a Black Disease*. Metzl's book traces the political and cultural circumstances that caused members of the American Psychiatric Association to change the diagnostic criteria for schizophrenia, redefining it from a relatively benign condition common among white housewives to a violent mental disability often directly associated with Black men, especially those involved in civil rights activism. The Panthers were astutely aware of the racialized norms of able-mindedness, which constructed "appropriate" behavior, mental states, emotions, and reactions based on white male middle-class norms.[20] The BPP's approach to this fight against psychiatric abuse and forced pharmaceutical treatments consistently emphasized the relationship between prisons and mental institutions, while centering the voices of those most impacted by psychiatric abuse and the prison industrial complex.

In 1976 the *Black Panther* published several letters to the editor that reasserted the similarities of and connections between prisons and mental institutions. These letters are worth quoting at length because they provide direct statements from Black individuals being held in psychiatric institutions whose voices and perspectives are too often absent from the historical record and academic writing. Importantly, in this same year, the *Black Panther* also published two articles that provided some state and federal legal context for the claims of the letter writers detailed below. One article explained the CAFT's proposed California state bill to mandate the right to refuse "psycho-organic procedures" such as psychiatric medication and psychosurgery, while the other article reported on the congressional National Commission for the Protection of Human Biomedical Behavioral Research's decision to allow the continued use of psychosurgery as an experimental research procedure.[21] These articles demonstrate that the BPP was aware of and promoted the more macrolevel policy and political work of antipsychiatry, Mad pride, and consumer/survivor/ex-patient (C/S/X) movements while still attending to the microlevel experiences of individual Black people who were incarcerated and institutionalized by publishing their letters in the paper.

In the first letter to the editor on these issues, published on January 24, 1976, the author, Kevin Crockett, refers to himself as "currently incarcerated in the Chester Mental Health Center" in Chester, Illinois, after being "found incompetent to stand trial for robbery in Chicago."[22] Crockett's use of the word *incarcerated* rather than terms like *committed* or *treated* provides an initial association with prison rather than therapeutic psychiatric/medical care. Crockett continues by describing the forced treatment at the Chester Mental Health Center, explaining, "I am compelled to take medication four times a day, medication that is supposed to modify my behavior because the psychiatrist said that I have an explosive personality. I am supposed to be schizophrenic. We, the patients of Chester, have to take the medication orally, and if we refuse it, we are, through the use of force, compelled to or given a shot."[23] Note that the particular designation of "schizophrenic" in association with an "explosive personality" for a Black man mirrors Metzl's work on the history of schizophrenia in the United States. Crockett's rhetoric of "supposed to be" encourages readers to question or doubt this diagnosis. He then argues against the widespread and compulsory use of psychiatric medication, contending that "mental patients confined in security hospitals who are not violent in their actions and reactions to the people in their environment should have the right to appear in court every 90 days to appeal their cases before a psychiatrist appointed by the court to review patients in general to determine if a patient needs medication.... [B]ecause many of us who are waiting to go to trial are competent and don't need medication, we should have mandatory hearings every 90 days by a court appointed attorney and psychiatrist [to determine competency for trial]."[24] Here Crockett clearly lays out a proposed plan based on his experiences at Chester. The plan—to reevaluate a prisoner's/patient's need for medication and their competency for trial on a regular basis—acknowledges that some people may indeed need or desire medication, temporarily or permanently. It does not deny the reality of mental disability nor distance Blackness from it. Rather, Crockett's proposed plan for individuals deemed incompetent to stand trial insists on the possibility of changes in mental capacity or stability and the need to frequently assess who is being forcibly confined and medicated and why. Doing so, Crockett implies, would prevent people like himself from being permanently held in psychiatric, medical, and prison institutions under the assumption that they are incompetent and therefore, apparently, not worth close attention and care. Crockett's first letter therefore clearly reveals how people, particularly marginalized people with limited resources, can be lost and forgotten in these intersecting institutions.

In a second letter on May 1, 1976, written by Crockett and cosigned by five other patients, Crockett charges the Chester Mental Health Center with mental health code violations and requests legal assistance from the BPP.[25] He reiterates the patients' experiences of forced pharmaceutical treatment, emphasizing that "medication is the only therapy we receive here as treatment."[26] Crockett then states, "Many of the patients are nonviolent and do not act out, but yet we are subjected to chemotherapy. Most of us patients have criminal charges pending against us and were found incompetent to stand trial by the psychiatrist and the court, and in need of mental treatment. The charge aides treat the Black patients with contempt."[27] The experience of Crockett and the other patients of being held and forcibly medicated in the Chester Mental Health Center against their wills in lieu of trial, potentially indefinitely, further demonstrates how mental hospitals and institutions work in conjunction with the prison industrial complex to segregate, confine, and control Black people with and without disabilities. In the earlier-mentioned Vacaville article, the *Black Panther* noted that even once people were put on trial and convicted, the time during which they were held at the Vacaville Medical Center in California "for these 'medical observations and treatments' does not count in the overall time served by an inmate in prison. For example, there is documented evidence of an inmate who was arrested in 1963 for parole violation and was immediately shipped to Vacaville. He has remained there since that time. None of this time is applicable to his record. So that in fact, according to prison records, he has yet to begin finishing his time in prison for violation of parole."[28] Together these stories indicate how psychiatric and medical treatment can collude with the carceral and judicial system to both indefinitely suspend the trial process for people like Crockett and extend prison sentences for people like the man who violated parole. The psychiatric industrial complex therefore emerges as a space in which to permanently contain those initially confined via the prison industrial complex under the auspices of care, performing what Eunjung Kim calls *curative violence*. Kim uses this term to describe "the physical and material violence against people with disabilities that are justified in the name of cure."[29] *Cure* here refers broadly to any attempt to lessen or eliminate illness or disability. Thus, curative violence recognizes that society's ableist obsession with curing disabled and chronically ill people can often be damaging, resulting in further disability, debilitation, or even death. In the case of the Chester Mental Health Center, curative violence was enacted on prisoners/patients who were medicated without their consent and without regard to how the medication could impact their ability to stand trial in the future or otherwise advocate for themselves. By understanding the *Black Panther*'s publication of these letters as public documentation of curative violence against Black people, we can recognize how the BPP's critiques of psychiatry align strongly with those in disability studies and disability rights even as their language does not always reference disability explicitly.

The connections between mental and criminal institutions are made further explicit in another letter published in the *Black Panther* on August 7, 1976. Within, the author, Rayford Anderson, writes:

> So far the circumstance of "political or just plain prisoner" has been limited to prisons and jails. I will not attempt to give you a complete comparative study of life style similarities or dissimilarities of mental institutions and prisons. What I do have to say is that Atascadeso State Hospital (prison) is not a shade different from the joint. The only difference is that we don't have a gun tower overseeing the yard. Yet on second thought security is so tight they don't need a gun tower. They got the staffing gun of psychotropic medication and the brainwash tactic of institutionalization.[30]

Here Anderson directly compares prisons and mental institutions, seemingly influenced by the BPP's position on the role of prisons as a means of social control for marginalized people. Historical evidence shows that the *Black Panther* was delivered to people in some prisons as a means of connection, education, and empowerment. There was also an official chapter of the BPP inside the Louisiana State Penitentiary at Angola. Crockett's and Anderson's letters suggest that the paper was also distributed to or sold near state hospitals and prison hospital wards.[31] Anderson's letter indicates that the revolutionary, typically race-focused, framework regarding prisons provided by the *Black Panther* was useful in developing his own critical perspective on his confinement in a mental hospital.

While antipsychiatry, Mad pride, and C/S/X movements were already active at this time, as a Black man, Anderson was drawn more toward—or perhaps had easier access to—the political arguments of the Panthers instead. Existing studies of and books emerging from antipsychiatry, Mad pride, and C/S/X movements provide limited but clear evidence of the involvement of people of color.[32] According to Linda Joy Morrison, the "core leadership" of the C/S/X movement in the 1970s were all white activists, the majority of whom were "still considered active leaders, twenty-five and thirty years later."

Writing based on her interviews with C/S/X activists in the late 1990s and early 2000s, Morrison notes that this overwhelming whiteness has continued "at the highest levels of visibility [of the movement], while at the local levels more racial and ethnic diversity is apparent."[33] Existing scholarship, activist literature, and the letters analyzed here make clear that Black people and other people of color participated in antipsychiatry, Mad pride, and C/S/X movements. They simply were not considered leaders as often. This relative absence in the movement's literature further underscores the historical, scholarly, and ideological importance of the *Black Panther*'s attention to Black experiences with psychiatric abuse and their particular Black disability political perspective.[34]

As a whole, the letters of Crockett and Anderson make three things clear. One, the operations and effects of prisons and mental institutions have significant overlap. Two, the BPP's political positions and newspaper were important for developing the critical consciousness of Black men held in psychiatric institutions and shaping their individual articulations and enactments of Black disability politics from within the prison and psychiatric industrial complexes. Finally, the publication of these letters by the BPP represents their own enactment of Black disability politics. By putting these letters in the *Black Panther*, the BPP helped Black and allied readers understand and respond to this shared oppression within these institutions. As I argued in the previous chapter, there is immense value in the distribution and influence of these ideas for Black people and allies across the United States who received the paper. By sharing Crockett's and Anderson's experience-based Black disability political thinking, the BPP therefore implicitly supported and advocated for people who were institutionalized or being given forced treatment. That this expression of disability solidarity is contextualized within the experience of Black people, particularly Black men, in carceral institutions only further demonstrates how Black disability politics qualitatively differ from mainstream disability rights politics and thus require a change in our scholarly and activist approaches. In other words, the BPP's approach to disability politics looks different from much disability political work because it emerges directly from the experiences of Black people, both disabled and nondisabled, experiencing the effects of racism and ableism. To study, articulate, or enact Black disability politics, therefore, we as scholars and cultural workers must similarly ground our work in the mutually constitutive relationship of Blackness and disability as it is experienced by Black people, particularly Black disabled people, in social institutions like the law, schools, prisons, and psychiatric hospitals.

I have spent significant time emphasizing the connections the letters and articles in the *Black Panther* made between prisons and mental institutions because they collectively underscore the intersectional, multi-issue approach that the Panthers took to disability politics. Understanding the BPP's work on psychosurgery and institutions as Black disability politics means grappling with the deeply racialized, gendered, and classed dynamics of psychiatry and its role within the prison industrial complex. It is important for disability studies scholars and critical race scholars alike to not read the rhetoric in these articles and letters as merely oppression analogies.[35] The BPP was not using disability as a metaphor for racial oppression; rather, the Panthers understood mental disability, race, prison, and forced psychiatric treatment as inextricable, materially connected issues that could not be dealt with separately. As a result, they partnered with and published about mental disability activist groups like the NAPA, the CAFT, the Committee Opposing Psychiatric Abuse of Prisoners, and the California Mental Health Coordinating Council without needing to distinguish between what was most properly in the realm of antiracist versus anti-ableist activism. As I detailed more extensively in the previous chapter, the BPP was invested in freedom and the "power to determine the destiny of our Black *and oppressed communities*," including access to "completely free health care."[36] These issues were fundamentally inseparable to the BPP within their overall revolutionary ideology. In other articles the *Black Panther* focused on protesting psychosurgery more specifically, but the role of the prison industrial complex remained central to the BPP's Black disability politics.

Fighting the Return of Psychosurgery

In 1971, the same year that the article "Vacaville—America's Headquarters for Medical Genocide" appeared in the *Black Panther*, doctors from Vacaville's Psychiatric Diagnosis Unit applied for federal funds to support a psychosurgery program aimed at prisoners deemed to be "biologically violent."[37] When news of the planned program reached the public, Vacaville attracted national attention, becoming one of the programs that raised mainstream alarm over the potential for abuse in the return of psychosurgery.[38] The Black Panthers reported on this planned program in two stories titled "Burn Your Brains Out" and "Vacaville 'Medical' Facility," each of which exhorted readers to write to the facility's warden, L. J. Pope, to "let him know that we will not allow him to turn our incarcerated brothers into mindless men."[39] While neither of these stories used the words *psychosurgery* or *lobotomy*, discussion of potential psychosurgery is nonetheless present. For example, "Burn Your Brains Out" details how doctors diagnosed "rebellious" inmates with "Temporal Lobe Epilepsy" and proposed that if their "serious psychological disorder" proved resistant to forced pharmaceutical treatments, then the prisoners would undergo a procedure during which "long electrode needles are inserted into the man's brain. These needles will search out and locate that part of the brain, that lobe, which is causing the 'seizures.' When it is located, that portion will be burned out, electrically."[40] This description likely refers to the psychosurgery procedure amygdalotomy. Although the funding was denied and the program never officially initiated, "it was later revealed that in 1968, three inmates at Vacaville had received amygdalotomy to treat 'violent' seizures," just as the *Black Panther* article describes.[41] Undoubtedly, the BPP's accusations and fears about the Vacaville Medical Center, which coincided with the center's attempts to begin an experimental psychosurgery program for prisoners, were far from unfounded.

Importantly, the BPP's awareness of the injustices within Vacaville arose from the imprisonment of several members who reported back, including Black Panther leader David Hilliard.[42] In his autobiography Hilliard describes Vacaville prisoners, stating, "Prolixin-medicated HVP—high violence potential—inmates shuffle down the halls, the drug leaving them palsied, their hands and legs constantly shaking. In some way the hold of the authorities over you here is more insidious than the brute force displayed in Folsom [State Prison]."[43] Later in the same chapter, the autobiography includes two brief mentions of disabled prisoners at Vacaville. First, Hilliard shares how he asked the Panthers to help ensure that a diabetic prisoner would be kept at Vacaville rather than sent to San Quentin, where he would receive no support for his chronic illness. Second, Hilliard quotes Sandy Turner, his "spiritual advisor" while he was in prison, who recalls Hilliard telling her about a newly paraplegic prisoner who had been shot in the spine during a shootout. The man was locked alone in a maximum-security cell and provided no assistance with eating, bathing, using the bathroom, or going into the yard. Hilliard personally carried the man into the yard and eventually helped get him into a nearby hospital program for paraplegics that taught bladder control.[44] Though brief, these descriptions of disability in Vacaville reveal that BPP members witnessed how disabled people, particularly Black disabled people, were at increased risk of harm and neglect within prison facilities. They also saw how psychiatric labels were used to justify medically unnecessary pharmaceutical treatment of nondisabled "high violence potential" prisoners with drugs like Prolixin (fluphenazine), which is used to treat schizophrenia and psychosis. BPP members' experiences with prison, like Hilliard's, undoubtedly grounded and shaped the BPP's Black disability politics, particularly their fight against psychiatric abuse. For the BPP, the issue of psychosurgery was inherently tied to the racial and carceral logics of the United States. The BPP critiqued the excessive control exercised by the combined psychiatric, medical, and prison industrial complexes over Black people deemed too aggressive, violent, rebellious, or resistant for white colonialist middle-class social norms. The Panthers' legal, political, and social battles over psychosurgery occurred over several years in a variety of venues, which I now discuss in turn.

The *Black Panther*'s first article to actually use the word *psychosurgery* was published on January 6, 1973. The article, titled "Tearing Out Our Thoughts: Psychosurgery and the Black Community," states directly in the second sentence, "If it is not blatantly exposed, psychosurgery could become a major tool of repression."[45] The article proceeds to provide relatively neutral, detailed information on what psychosurgery is, how the operations are performed, how it had been used on animal and human subjects in the past, and what results it had. In its final two paragraphs, the article shifts to contemporary use of psychosurgery and funding for psychosurgery research, especially among Black and poor populations, stating, "Today psychosurgeons are homing in on revolutionaries and other people who struggle against the massive oppression we are faced with. Psychosurgery could become the primary weapon used by prison wardens *and hospital administrators*."[46] I have emphasized "hospital administrators" in this sentence to highlight the obscured yet nonetheless present disability politics of this statement. In this and other early articles on psychosurgery, the *Black Panther* focuses heavily on its potential use as a means of genocide and social control targeted at so-called violent Black people, especially radical activists.[47] However, as the inclusion of hospitals in the above statement suggests, the BPP did not ignore or overlook psychosurgery's potential for abuse of disabled and sick people of any race subjected to the control of medical practitioners, who could similarly use resistance to treatment as a sign of mental disorders requiring psychosurgery. The BPP was aware of the racist, classist, *and ableist* dynamics of psychiatric treatment and the heightened potential for abuse among marginalized groups, especially those already under state control via prisons and hospitals.

Later in 1973, the BPP took their concerns to a public, quasi-legal battle when the Panthers, represented by their lawyer, Fred J. Hiestand, addressed the California State Senate in hearings about the potential creation of the

Center for the Study and Reduction of Violence at the University of California, Los Angeles (UCLA). The details of the BPP's fight against the creation of the center have already been deftly charted by Alondra Nelson in her important book *Body and Soul: The Black Panther Party and the Fight against Medical Discrimination*. As a result, here I briefly summarize the events Nelson discusses more fully and place them within my own argument about how we can read the Panthers' work as enacting Black disability politics. The Center for the Study and Reduction of Violence was a proposed UCLA research center that was publicly supported by Governor Ronald Reagan in his state of the state address in January 1973. While the proposal for the center underwent several revisions in response to increased public scrutiny, its creators generally sought to use psychiatric and neuroscientific research to discover causes of and treatments or cures for supposedly biologically driven violent behaviors. Drafts of the proposal included planned research projects focused on urban populations, mental hospital patients, prisoners, and women.[48] The BPP, along with several other organizations such as the Committee Opposing Psychiatric Abuse of Prisoners and the California Mental Health Coordinating Council, formed a coalition to protest the creation of the center and to block its state funding. Hiestand testified as a representative of the coalition in State Senate hearings and filed an administrative complaint against the center on behalf of the coalition as well. Hiestand's testimony was directly informed by the work and ideology of the BPP. He highlighted the vagueness of the proposal, the potential for abuse among marginalized populations, and the problems with the biologization of violence. The coalition, in concert with much public outcry as well as with student and faculty protests at UCLA, was successful in preventing funding for the center, which stopped its creation entirely. In this moment the BPP actively worked with disability rights groups and women's rights groups to fight against the pathologization of oppressed communities, promoting instead a social and political approach to addressing violence, poverty, and more. This particular success, however, was not the end of the BPP's fight against psychosurgery and other psychiatric abuse.

The Panthers' final articles on psychosurgery appeared in 1977, published concurrently with stories about the 504 sit-in. These final three articles echoed the situation of Crockett and others at the Chester Mental Health Center but focused on the story of Lou Byers. The first article about Byers in the *Black Panther* was published on April 30, 1977, as a reprint from another Black newspaper, *Black Thoughts*. This first article warrants extensive quoting to relay Byers's narrative and to allow for more in-depth analysis of the BPP's arguments and rhetoric surrounding Byers in the two subsequent articles.

Lou Broadus Byers of Oakland, California, had joined the army at age seventeen. According to the first article on Byers, "Before entering the military, Lou had not known or experienced the bitter prejudices of overt racism and prejudice. But he was rudely awakened when he got to Germany and discovered that the military was perpetuating racism at a level much more accelerated than that in the United States."[49] Disillusioned and angry, Byers began writing and calling home expressing suicidal ideation. Although his mother's calls for assistance from the Red Cross yielded no results, eventually Byers was dishonorably discharged on account of "apathy towards the military and his inability to adjust."[50] Once back in the United States, the then nineteen-year-old "expressed an obvious hatred and resentment for all Whites. Several times this resentment and U.S. military-induced hatred was displayed in minor public altercations which led to subsequent incarceration."[51]

In the fall of 1976, Byers violated his parole, and "to avoid being sent to prison he asked to be committed to the psychiatric ward of the American Veterans Administration Hospital in Menlo Park, California."[52] While under observation in the psychiatric ward, Byers complained of pain in his leg, arm, jaw, and abdomen, and the doctors contacted his mother, Margarite Wallace, to ask "for parental consent to perform a spinal tap" for suspected meningitis, which was later diagnosed as herpes encephalitis.[53] Shortly afterward, however, the doctor also "requested permission for an experimental brain operation," explaining "that if Lou recovered he would live as a vegetable." Byers's mother asked for time to consult with family members and "at no time gave either written or verbal permission for the Veterans Hospital to perform this 'experimental brain operation' and was shocked to find him already in surgery when she got down to the hospital minutes later!"[54]

The story continues by explaining, "After the operation, Lou remembered no one and referred to his mother as 'you.'"[55] Byers received little to no postoperative follow-up or treatment. Upon visiting later, his mother found Byers sitting alone by a door, "beating his head against the wall and muttering incoherent language."[56] Eventually Byers was discharged, and the article concludes, "Today, Lou lives as a vegetable unable to pronounce his own name or communicate with his family. A caseworker from the clinic used to pay occasional visits to the Wallace home in an effort to pacify and console them, while subtly discouraging any legal actions against the hospital."[57]

FIGURE 2.1 *Black Panther* story on May 7, 1977, about psychosurgery and with a photo of Lou Byers and his mother.

After reprinting this initial story on Byers, the following week the *Black Panther* published their own article based on an interview with Byers's mother, Margarite Wallace, titled "Mother of Psychosurgery Victim Appeals for Community Help." This article, pictured in figure 2.1, includes a photo of Wallace and Byers standing together. Wallace is in a black shirt and light-colored pants on the left, standing with her lips pressed together in a straight line. Positioned slightly more forward, with his arm and shoulder covering part of Wallace's body, Byers wears an abstractly patterned collared button-up shirt, khakis, and a belt. He holds his hands low in front of his body with his head tilted down as he looks up toward the camera, unsmiling, with a mustache and trimmed beard. The image, which appears to represent the mother and son at the time of the article, depicts the two as solemn, yet put together—neither rich nor poor. Their expressions and poses do not evoke strong emotion, neither pitiful nor angry. Positioned at the top of the second column of text, directly below the title, this image humanizes Byers and Wallace, but it does not give any strong visual cues as to how the reader/viewer should feel before reading the article, despite the use of the words *victim* and *appeals* in the title.

In terms of content, the article briefly recaps the previous week's story and then provides new details from Wallace. The article explains that after the surgery Byers was treated poorly and ignored by staff, who allowed him to wander the hospital; at one point he even left the building entirely, only to be returned by the police. The article highlights specific details of Byers's new mental impairment, such as being unable to count above twenty or identify many everyday objects, such as a lamp. Wallace reiterates her son's threat to kill himself and expresses her belief that he was suicidal as a result of racism specifically. She states, "Lou told me it was hell there.... He had to fight the Ku Klux Klan in the Army and against racist Germans in the area."[58] The article concludes by noting that "the probation department is threatening to revoke his parole" and his mother is seeking "competent and concerned legal and psychiatric help" for Byers.[59]

This second article emphasizes race and racism as coconstitutive of disability and disablement in three ways. First, Byers's experience of racism in the army is framed as a cause for Byers's suicidal ideation and severe mental distress, a claim that research now supports.[60] Second, Byers's race is represented as a key factor in his treatment at the hospital, both in that surgery was performed without his or his mother's permission and in that he was ignored after the psychosurgical operation. Third, Byers's mental disability resulting from the psychosurgery is framed overall as having been produced and sustained (via lack of follow-up treatment) by multiple racist and ableist social structures: the military industrial complex, which subjected him to various forms of racism and placed his bodymind at increased risk for violence; the medical industrial complex, through which doctors operated on and then abandoned him; and the prison industrial complex, which Byers sought to avoid by going to a veterans hospital for psychiatric treatment but which nevertheless remained a threat via the potential revoking of parole. In multiple ways, therefore, this interview, performed and edited by Panther members working for the paper, exemplifies the necessarily complex nature of Black disability politics in a violently racist and ableist society.

A week later the *Black Panther* published a third and final article featuring Byers called "v.a. Hospital Pays for Human Guinea Pigs: Performs Psychosurgery on Black Oakland Youth." The story first describes a classified ad from the *San Francisco Chronicle* seeking healthy male veterans for a paid research study that would involve two spinal taps over two days. The article then introduces an abbreviated version of Byers's story from previous weeks before bringing the two examples together, arguing, "Byers' case and the *Chronicle* ad raise serious questions about practices at the v.a. hospital. It is noteworthy that the hospital is seeking veterans for its human experimentation. The majority of Vietnam era veterans, in particular, are unemployed, thereby likely candidates for human guinea pigs."[61] Here the *Black Panther* again addresses the specific intersection of the military industrial complex, the medical industrial complex, and, now, class to highlight the potentially coercive or abusive practices of medical research and experimentation among veterans, especially those who are unemployed.

Furthermore, this article's focus on the predatory nature of medical research studies advertising to marginalized and oppressed populations highlights a continued concern within the medical industrial complex. Harriet A. Washington writes that "geography, tradition, and culture intersect to make blacks likely research subjects for new technologies, but race and economics tend to place them outside the marketplace for these same technologies when they are perfected."[62] Even today people of color are more likely to be the paid participants of phase I clinical trials that test the safety of a drug or device, volunteering because of financial need, whereas white people are most likely to be the participants of phase III clinical trials that test effectiveness, volunteering because of medical need.[63] While not explicitly or exclusively about disabled people (though many people in later-phase clinical trials are disabled by illness and disease), the Panthers' argument about medical research reflects a larger issue in regard to the relationship of race and disability: that developments in medicine have historically relied on the bodyminds of people of color for testing in order to primarily benefit the health and well-being of white and wealthy people. Take, for example, the development of modern gynecological methods through testing on enslaved women by Dr. Marion Sims, the use of poor and racialized populations as living educational tools at teaching hospitals, the historical reliance of medical schools on Black bodies as cadavers, or the use of Henrietta Lacks's cells in medical research.[64] Each of these examples demonstrates that in articulating and assessing Black disability politics, we must think about not only the ways that racism and ableism collude and collaborate to target disabled, Black, and Black disabled populations but also the ways that certain disabled subjects at times benefit from the debilitation, impairment, and disablement of people of color by the medical industrial complex, even if that benefit is decades or centuries removed.

Throughout all of its articles on psychosurgery and psychiatric abuse, the *Black Panther* primarily focused on the harm and potential harm to the bodyminds of people of color, especially to the bodyminds of disabled people of color, created by the convergence of the medical, prison, and military industrial complexes. The BPP encouraged a wariness and critical stance toward medical professionals while raising awareness about existing wrongs and centering the voices and narratives of Black disabled people. The newspaper did not argue that psychosurgery or pharmaceutical treatments were wrong because they were used on Black people who were not actually disabled; rather, the BPP contended that psychosurgery and forced pharmaceutical treatments were problematic because they were primarily being done in coercive and nonconsensual ways among prisoners, mental hospital patients, and veterans while also largely targeting Black and other people of color for experimental purposes. In other words, the BPP did not distance Blackness from disability in their fight against psychiatric abuse. The BPP did not discount the realness of psychiatric disability or the need and desire among some people for psychiatric care—a move possibly attributable to their various collaborations with the NAPA, the CAFT, the Committee Opposing Psychiatric Abuse of Prisoners, and the California Mental Health Coordinating Council. What the BPP emphasized most in their newspaper coverage of psychiatric abuse was the danger and potential harm in forced treatment, especially irreversible treatment like psychosurgery. This emphasis echoes the arguments of psychiatric disability activist groups, but in the *Black Panther* articles, psychosurgery, forced pharmaceutical treatment, and institutionalization were always discussed within the framework of race and the prison industrial complex, with additional intersections with class and the military industrial complex in the multiarticle coverage of Lou Byers. This intersectional but race-centered approach to fighting psychosurgery and other forms of psychiatric abuse distinguishes the BPP's Black disability politics from much of the work by white disabled activists of the same period. The BPP offered nuanced, contextualized, intersectional critiques that are being more widely circulated in the twenty-first century, though rarely with recognition of how the BPP was engaging the relationship of race, disability, psychiatry, and prisons in the 1970s.

Conclusion

As a whole, the Black Panthers' activism around psychiatric abuse is an excellent example of Black disability politics. The BPP collaborated with multiple mental disability activist groups, remained attentive to the relationship of mental institutions and prisons, and often centered the voices and experiences of Black men subjected to psychiatric abuse and control. The Panthers' work in this area was intersectional but race centered, not based in disability identity, but contextualized (within the prison and medical industrial complexes) and holistically articulated by attending to both micro- and macrolevel change. From the numerous newspaper articles on psychiatric abuse in prisons to their involvement in the fight against the proposed UCLA Center for the Study and Reduction of Violence, the work of the BPP discussed in this chapter demonstrates that Black disability politics are also often necessarily coalitional, requiring alliances among nondisabled Black, non-Black disabled, and Black disabled people. The Panthers emphasized the connections between psychiatric facilities and prisons not to create analogies or comparisons but to build and encourage these alliances and coalitions, to trace larger operations of power, and to identify the relationships between systems of oppression in order to dismantle them. Like their work on the 504 sit-in, the Panthers' approach to protesting psychiatric abuse demonstrates how Black disability politics have been articulated in ways that do not necessarily center or explicitly name disability and yet nonetheless work in solidarity with disabled people, especially Black disabled people, and people at high risk of disablement by the violence of oppression.

In concluding here, I want to note that despite the BPP's relatively recent existence—with former leaders and members still living and several still imprisoned—the Black Panthers are often relegated to the place of lore in the mainstream. The BPP is consistently misunderstood and misrepresented in the US cultural imagination as a group of unequivocally violent, sexist/masculinist Black thugs with black berets and guns.[65] Take, for example, the conservative backlash to Beyoncé's 2016 Super Bowl performance of her song "Formation," in which the singer and her dancers wore black leotards, afros, and black berets reminiscent of the Panthers' attire, at one point raising their fists in the air. In response, conservative news outlets denounced the performance, perpetuating skewed, selective, and at times outright incorrect information about the BPP. On Fox News, former New York City mayor Rudy Giuliani claimed Beyoncé used the halftime show "as a platform to attack police officers," while Milwaukee County sheriff David A. Clarke Jr. compared the BPP to the Ku Klux Klan, referring to the Panthers as "a subversive hate group."[66] The conservative outrage resulted in social media calls to boycott Beyoncé and plans for a protest demonstration outside of the National Football League headquarters, the online component of which asked potential attendees, "Are you offended as an American that Beyoncé pulled her race-baiting stunt at the Superbowl? Do you agree that it was a slap in the face to law enforcement? Do you agree that the Black Panthers was/is a hate group which should not be glorified?"[67] Although the demonstration ultimately had almost no attendees and Beyoncé's career continued to soar after the performance—she even sold ironic "Boycott Beyoncé" shirts and phone cases on her Formation world tour and website—the strong reaction to her performance's homage to the Black Panthers demonstrates a continued gross misunderstanding among many Americans about the totality of the BPP's sixteen years of work, nationally and internationally.[68]

The two chapters on the BPP in this book represent one small part of a larger effort to correct this societal misunderstanding. In particular, I align myself with scholars who seek to move away from a predominant focus on the most recognized men of the organization and the BPP's work before 1972 and toward investigations of the work of rank-and-file members and leading female members of the Panthers, like Elaine Brown and Ericka Huggins, particularly in the later years of the BPP's existence. This work is being done by scholars like Alondra Nelson, Robyn C. Spencer, Angela D. LeBlanc-Ernest, and Joshua Bloom and Waldo E. Martin, as well as by cultural workers like Stanley Nelson, who directed and edited the documentary *The Black Panthers: Vanguard of the Revolution.*[69] This cultural reassessment of the Panthers is especially important in the wake of the Black Lives Matter movement, which emerged initially in response to police brutality against Black people. In 2017 a leaked Federal Bureau of Investigation (FBI) report on the movement warned about "premeditated, retaliatory lethal violence against law enforcement" by "black identity extremists" (BIE) within "the BIE movement" influenced by "BIE ideology."[70] The parallels between the FBI's label of "black identity extremists" in the twenty-first century and that same organization's claim in 1969 that the Panthers were the greatest internal threat to US security are striking. History, it seems, is repeating itself right in front of us. Therefore, learning from both the successes and the failures, the admirable attributes and the faults, of earlier Black activism is essential to our collective future liberation.

In the next section of this book, praxis interlude 1, I critically engage the failure of the BPP to avoid ableist language and sentiments in their fight against psychiatric abuse. Once I critique the Panthers' ableist language in this arena, I draw on the knowledge of my contemporary interview participants as well as on disability studies scholarship to provide alternative rhetorical approaches for future Black disability political work.

Anti-ableist Approaches
to Fighting Disabling Violence

Cultural representations can condemn violence while reaffirming the ideology of ability that provides its support.
—JULIE AVRIL MINICH, *Accessible Citizenships*

> Content note: This praxis interlude contains a brief description and discussion of police violence as well as an extended engagement with ableist language.

While the Black Panther Party (BPP) generally avoided distancing Blackness from disability to emphasize shared concerns with disability rights groups about forced treatments, their rhetoric was not without issue. Most prominently, the *Black Panther* articles on psychosurgery and psychiatric abuse repeatedly use the word *vegetable* to describe the potential result of psychosurgery and forced pharmaceutical treatments. The paper's use of this term differs from the use of *inspiration*, discussed in chapter 1, because *vegetable* is used in a clearly ableist way whereas the BPP's use of the words *inspiration* and *inspiring* in their coverage of the 504 sit-in is not actually ableist in the way these terms are frequently used regarding disabled people. This distinction warrants a closer engagement with the term *vegetable*. Across twenty-two articles on psychiatric abuse, forced pharmaceutical treatment, and/or psychosurgery published in the *Black Panther* between June 1971 and October 1977, the word *vegetable* is used seven times total. Four of the seven uses of *vegetable* specifically refer to Lou Byers, and two of those four uses occur in the first article on Byers, which was a reprint of an article originally published in *Black Thoughts* and thus not written by a member of the *Black Panther* staff. While the term *vegetable* is not overwhelmingly prevalent, the word's repeated use indicates a disconnect between the Panthers' intentions and their rhetoric around disability politics, despite their connections and collaborations with various disability activist groups. The Panthers' use of *vegetable* as an ableist term for a disabled person warrants more extended exploration because it reflects a larger issue in cross-movement organizing and solidarity with disabled people: how to protest disabling violence without making disability into a frightening, sad, or dangerous specter that exemplifies the injustice of that violence. This first praxis interlude takes a critical look at the ableist language the BPP used in its fight against psychiatric abuse and offers alternative rhetorical approaches that can be taken up by activists today as well.

To analyze the ableism within the *Black Panther*'s use of the term *vegetable*, I first place this term in its historical, medical, and linguistic context—a key practice of Black disability politics. Figurative uses of the word *vegetable* to refer to a person date back to the seventeenth century; however, these early uses of the word primarily described "one who leads an uneventful or monotonous life, without intellectual or social activity" and were generally devoid of medical or disability connotations. It was not until the mid-twentieth century that the second figurative use of *vegetable* emerged, defined as "one who is incapable of normal mental or physical activity, esp. as a result of brain damage."[1] One might imagine, as I myself did initially, that this use of *vegetable* derives from the medical term *vegetative state*, coined in 1972 to refer to a brain-damage condition in which a person appears awake, with limited ability to move, but is considered to not be aware or conscious.[2] Figurative and colloquial uses of *vegetable* or *human vegetable*, however, occurred in medical and popular debates about the potential impact of psychosurgery and lobotomy in the 1940s and 1950s, well before the existence of *persistent vegetative state* as a medical term.[3] *Vegetable*, therefore, had a clear history of decades-long use as an ableist term in mainstream US society in the 1970s.[4] The BPP was not necessarily out of the norm in using it; nonetheless, their ableist rhetoric warrants retrospective analysis and critique so we may do better in the present and the future.

The *Black Panther* first used *vegetable* in the figurative sense, as detailed above, occurred in January 1973 in their first article on psychosurgery; the article stated that psychosurgery would be used to save money on prisons by sending people "back into society as vegetables" rather than paying to incarcerate them.[5] As this example suggests, the Panthers' use of *vegetable* appears more aligned with its use in midcentury debates about psychosurgery, which were reemerging in the 1970s, than with the medical language coined around this same time.[6] The use of the word *vegetable* mars the overall solidarity the BPP exhibited with disabled people subjected to psychiatric abuse by drawing on ableist fears of disability to increase the rhetorical and emotional effect of their arguments. While identifying, critiquing, and eliminating ableist language is important in and of itself, understanding and analyzing the underlying logic of this tactic the Panthers employed is equally important to understanding and enacting Black disability politics.

The *Black Panther*'s figurative use of *vegetable* exemplifies a common larger issue in activist organizing efforts: how social justice movements sometimes use disability produced by oppressive violence as a seemingly self-explanatory symbol for how horrible and wrong such violence is. This tactic is commonly used by charity and nonprofit organizations in the form of the disabled poster child, but it also appears among social justice activist groups as well, especially in regard to environmental hazards, poverty, and social neglect.[7] Alison Kafer, writing about environmental activism, argues that we need "analyses that recognize and refuse the intertwined exploitation of bodies and environments without demonizing the illnesses and disabilities, and especially the ill and disabled bodies, that result," asking, "How can we continue the absolutely necessary task of challenging toxic pollution and its effects without perpetuating cultural assumptions about the unmitigated tragedy of disability?"[8] Similarly, Eli Clare analyzes an advertisement by the Sierra Club against coal mining that includes the words "Asthma. Birth defects. Cancer. Enough." over an image of a power plant billowing smoke. Clare argues that the ad appears to ask viewers "to act in alliance with the people most impacted by the burning of coal. But digging down a bit, the Sierra Club twists away from solidarity, focusing instead on particular kinds of body-mind conditions—asthma, birth defects, cancer, learning disabilities—transforming them into symbols for environmental damage. This strategy works because it taps into ableism. It assumes that viewers will automatically understand disability and chronic illness as tragedies in need of prevention and eradication, and in turn that these tragedies will persuade us to join the struggle."[9] Kafer, Clare, and other disability studies scholars have critiqued how social justice activists, nonprofit organizations, and public health campaigns often employ ableism in their fight against other forms of oppression. My arguments here build on this existing work and are intended to make clear why activist rhetorical approaches matter so much. Black feminists have a long history of insisting on activism and scholarship that attend to *all* of the intersecting oppressions that impact our lives, and Black feminist theorizing has consistently provided new frameworks and approaches for making sure no one gets left behind or is told to wait their turn in liberation movements. I ground my work here solidly in this legacy.

In the case of the Panthers, the BPP articles use the specter of the "human vegetable" to emphasize the potential danger and harm of psychosurgery and forced pharmaceutical treatments for Black, poor, and incarcerated people, especially in regard to nondisabled activists whom the BPP believed were targeted for such treatment by being labeled violent, insane, or delusional. As mentioned in the previous chapter, historical evidence from scholars like Jenell M. Johnson and Jonathan Metzl highlights how people of color were targeted for psychiatric abuse under the auspices of reducing biologically innate violent tendencies.[10] The Panthers' rhetorical reliance on the specter of disability, however, represents disablement as the ultimate harm and the most dangerous effect of white supremacist control. It suggests that disabled lives are lost lives, unable to continue any form of social protest or activism, completely defeated by larger oppressive forces. In other words, this rhetoric implies that one cannot be a disabled "human vegetable" and also be an activist. The use of the word *vegetable*, especially in direct reference to Byers, a disabled Black man who had undergone psychosurgery, relies on ableist fears of disablement, incapacitation, and loss of autonomy for its rhetorical effect on readers. This approach contrasts with the rest of the rhetorical tactics of the *Black Panther* in protesting psychiatric abuse, which generally sought alliances with disability activism by consistently emphasizing the connections between mental hospitals and prison spaces. My goal here, however, is not merely to identify and critique the ableism embedded in the *Black Panther*'s figurative use of the word *vegetable* but rather to think through what other options they may have had—in the hope that theorizing alternative approaches may be useful to current and future Black activism that seeks to include disability justice.

What, then, is the alternative to this use of disability as symbolic of oppression in social justice organizing and awareness-raising efforts? Should disability be removed from these efforts entirely, distanced from any suggestion of trauma or negativity? Nirmala Erevelles contends that a purely celebratory and pride-based approach to disability and disabled identity cannot be the solution to this issue when disability is so "inextricably linked to the violence of social/economic conditions of capitalism" for so many people, especially for people of color.[11] Erasure of the fact of disability from activist approaches to resisting violence and oppression that can and do result in disablement for marginalized people would avoid rather than solve this dilemma. Instead of critiquing rhetorical approaches alone, we must also imagine and offer alternatives.

Clare does this reimagining in his analysis of the Sierra Club ads, envisioning "a slightly different series of billboards and commercials, integrating a broad-based, multi-issue politics of chronic illness and disability. They would locate injustice in many places all at once; in coal burning; in extracting fossil fuels from the ground; in poisoning the planet and the many beings that make home here, including humans; in the racism and classism that force poor people and people of color to live and work near environmental destruction. Cancer and asthma would become not symbols, but lived realities amidst injustice."[12] Clare's imagined alternative here implicitly suggests two possible approaches that I would like to make explicit. First, this imagined new series of ads identifies the various forms of violence and neglect that unnecessarily produce disability as the problem to be solved, not disability itself. Second, Clare's alternative ads emphasize the multiple, complicated, and intersecting social justice issues at play, refusing the notion that one can fix one area of social injustice, such as the environmental effects of coal mining, without addressing the other concerns with which it is deeply intertwined, such as racism and capitalism. In addition to these two approaches drawn from Clare's imagined replacement Sierra Club ads, I suggest a third way for social justice and nonprofit groups to protest injustice and violence without making disability a symbolic specter of oppression: fighting for concrete efforts to support those already disabled by this violence with their financial, medical, emotional, and community needs. These three tactics collectively form an alternative approach for social justice movements to protest and raise awareness about specific forms of violence and oppression that can result in disablement without making disability the symbolic specter of injustice to evoke ableist emotional responses from the audience. To reiterate, these tactics are (1) focusing on violence as the problem, not disability; (2) emphasizing the intertwined nature of multiple social justice issues; and (3) supporting people disabled by social injustice and violence. One contemporary example of where this alternative approach applies is the story of Jacob Blake.

On August 23, 2020, Jacob Blake, a twenty-nine-year-old Black man, was celebrating his son's birthday in Kenosha, Wisconsin, when a fight broke out between the mother of Blake's children and a neighbor. Blake broke up the fight and then tried to leave with two of his children, but their mother called the police to prevent Blake from leaving with her vehicle. Blake had an outstanding warrant, so when the police arrived, they immediately attempted to arrest him without explaining why or reading him his rights, according to Blake. The police officers grabbed Blake, and he pulled away. They wrestled with him before tasering him twice, as nearly twenty people outside yelled at them that they had the wrong person, according to a witness.[13] Blake, who had been beaten by police as a teenager when he was sneaking into his house after curfew, stated in an interview that he "resisted to being beat on" because he "didn't want to be the next George Floyd ... didn't want to die."[14] Blake removed the taser prongs, picked up his pocket knife that he had dropped, and walked around to the driver's door of the vehicle to put the knife away and check on his children.[15] The police officers followed, and Officer Rusten Sheskey grabbed the back of Blake's shirt and shot him seven times in the back in front of Blake's children, who were still in the car.[16] Blake, believing he would die, counted his breaths and said to his sons, "Daddy loves you no matter what."[17]

> Shot. Seven times. In the back. In front of his children.
> Sit with that. Don't rush past it. Feel for Blake. Feel for his children.
> He was shot seven times in the back by a police officer in front of his children.
> Shot. Seven times. In the back. In front of his children.
> "Daddy loves you no matter what."
> Sit with it. Don't rush past it. Feel.

The entire incident was filmed by a neighbor and quickly went viral, resulting in mass protests in Kenosha.[18] Sheskey claimed the shooting was in self-defense, and no charges were filed against him.[19] Blake miraculously survived the shooting, but two of the bullets severed his spinal cord, resulting in paralysis from the waist down and neuropathy, a condition that causes sharp nerve pain. Blake's colon, small intestine, kidney, and liver were also damaged.[20] While in the hospital, Blake, a newly disabled Black man recovering from massive gunshot wounds and unable to walk, was initially handcuffed to the hospital bed with deputies constantly watching him until Blake's father brought the issue to the public, causing enough outcry, including condemnation from Disability Rights Wisconsin, that police removed the handcuffs and deputy presence.[21]

Take a moment to sit with the layers of trauma here.
Handcuffed to a bed and denied privacy to process after being shot and paralyzed.
Handcuffed to a bed and denied privacy after being shot and paralyzed.
Handcuffed. Denied privacy. Shot. Paralyzed.
Sit with that. Don't rush past it. Feel.

There is much to say about the disabling police violence that Blake experienced and about how Blake's personal history and behavior at the scene were used by right-wing and mainstream media, as well as by the public, to excuse this violence. For the purposes of discussing how to enact Black disability politics here, however, I focus specifically on how to apply the three tactics for fighting disabling violence in this contemporary case. I chose to include this contemporary example because when the news broke that Blake had survived but could no longer walk, I saw multiple news outlets such as CNN use phrases like "suffering from paralysis" and read several social media posts where people called Blake's injuries horrific, a tragedy, and a fate akin to death.[22] The emphasis on pain in public discussions of Blake stems partially from Blake's social media message (via his lawyer's Twitter account) on September 5 in which he mentions being in constant pain.[23] Most news and social media reactions failed to acknowledge, however, that anyone, with or without a spinal cord injury, would be in pain thirteen days after being shot in the back seven times. The physical pain Blake was experiencing, and continues to experience with the neuropathy, is not synonymous with paralysis, spinal cord injury, or disability, but these things frequently get conflated in an ableist world that believes most or all disabled people are constantly suffering because of their disabilities. When it comes to Black disability politics, however, we must work to acknowledge and empathize with the reality of Blake's pain without making pain and disability the entire focus. The first tactic in approaching Blake's story as a Black disability political issue is to focus on the excessive violence by the police—two instances of tasering and seven gunshots to the back—as the problem, the source of the harm.

One way to retain the focus on police violence as the problem is to acknowledge that Blake's physical injuries are not the only harm caused by Officer Sheskey's unconscionable violence. Blake, his children, and the nearly twenty eyewitnesses to the shooting (not to mention the millions who watched the shooting video online) will have experienced psychological harm and potential psychiatric disability as a result. This emotional and psychological harm is rarely recognized in media coverage, even though in a news conference, Blake's attorney, Ben Crump, explicitly stated that Blake's sons "are going to have psychological problems for the rest of their lives," while Blake's father described the children as "stuck right now," repeatedly asking him, "Why did police shoot my daddy in the back?"[24] In one of the few pieces to attend to this issue, Rhea Boyd details some of the short- and long-term effects on children's physical and mental health when they witness or experience violence, framing the continual exposure of Black, Latinx, and Indigenous children to police violence as a public health issue.[25] Boyd carefully attends to how children of color and disabled children are more likely to witness and directly experience police harassment and violence. In doing so, Boyd articulates a form of Black disability politics that acknowledges how disability can be both the impetus for and the result of police violence, keeping the focus on the violence that causes harm rather than the potential disability resulting from harm.

To enact the second tactic for fighting disabling violence without being ableist, we must also attend to the multiple oppressions at play in the Blake shooting, namely, anti-Black racism and classism. Blake's race and class were signaled in news coverage and opinion pieces through images and frequent references to his previous encounters with police, his children outside of marriage, and other details of Blake's life that have nothing to do with the fact that he was shot. Identifying how anti-Black racism and classism shaped not only how officers responded to Blake but also how the public responded to the shooting is an essential part of enacting Black disability politics. Calling out and naming the multiple intersecting oppressions at play forces us to reckon with the mutually constitutive nature of oppression and in particular how certain populations are more likely to be subjected to disabling and debilitating violence. We must be vocal and clear that no one deserves to be shot seven times in the back, no matter what they have done previously. No one.

Finally, the third tactic is to provide material and social support for the people disabled by violence. This would include Blake, his children, and the other witnesses. Material support in this case could include fundraisers for Blake and his family, the provision of free medical and mental health care, or pro bono legal support for Blake's federal civil rights lawsuit against Officer Sheskey. Social support might include engaging in public vocal support for Blake, his family, and the lawsuit; continuing to call for Sheskey to be removed from the police force; and connecting Blake and his family with people with similar experiences: other survivors of police violence, other Black disabled men, other people with spinal cord injuries, and so on. This latter form of social support is particularly important for newly disabled people to help them see a future for themselves and encourage them to ask questions of those with similar lived experiences. If, collectively, Blake's immediate community and the larger movement for Black lives could enact such anti-ableist tactics for addressing and fighting back against disabling police violence, we could continue the work of abolishing prisons and police in a way that aligns with disability justice. This is simply one brief contemporary example to help illustrate my arguments; these tactics can also be used to understand how the BPP could have done better in their fight against psychiatric abuse.

In the case of the *Black Panther* articles, I argue that their figurative use of *vegetable* is quite unnecessary to their overall arguments. In each of the seven uses of the word, *vegetable* can easily be replaced by more specific, less hyperbolic and figurative language. For instance, in "New Vacaville Drug Control Program Makes Vegetables out of Inmates," the author could have replaced "makes vegetables out of inmates" (used in both the title and the body of the article) with "seeks chemical control of inmates," in order to focus on the oppressive control of an already disempowered group via forced pharmaceutical treatment as the problem to be addressed.[26] In the other articles using the word *vegetable* to describe the effects of psychosurgery, more specific, less figurative language would reduce or eliminate the use of ableism for emotional effect. Instead of describing inmates subjected to psychosurgery as "vegetables" and Lou Byers as "nearly a human vegetable," these articles could have described the effects of psychosurgery more neutrally and accurately as brain damage, cognitive impairment, or mental disability while also arguing more directly about the intersection of incarceration, medical control, and violence toward racialized populations.[27] I use *accurately* here not because there is a standard effect of psychosurgery but because, when one is discussing specific cases, the language could be more precise. For instance, although Byers is described twice as "nearly a human vegetable," the articles also state that he speaks, moves, and interacts with people, even as his memory, language, and cognitive functions are less strong than before the psychosurgery.[28] This is representative of how the hyperbolic use of *vegetable* as an ableist term departs widely from the specifics of the vegetative state as a particular medical condition.

As a whole, the term *vegetable* is used infrequently across the body of work on psychiatric abuse published in the *Black Panther*, but its use is unnecessary. While the articles use the ableist emotional responses to disability that *vegetable* evokes, the articles don't actually rely on or require these ableist emotions to further their arguments. In many ways the articles collectively tend to partially enact the anti-ableist approaches outlined above. They generally focus on the medical and prison industrial complexes as the problem, consistently highlighting the intertwined nature of these systems and their relationship to race and class, as well as to the military industrial complex in the case of Byers. These arguments, in lieu of using the word *vegetable*, could have been strengthened with increased focus on the impossibility of noncoerced consent to medical procedures and research among inmates and mental hospital patients who are involuntarily confined, or with more attention to the vague parameters for psychiatric diagnosis and treatment. In fact, these arguments are already performed more obliquely in the articles via the scare quotes around words like *incorrigibles, psychotic, violence control, treatment*, and *volunteer*.[29] Last, while most of the articles are predictive, suggesting what *could* happen should certain laws and programs be approved and implemented, in the case of Byers, there was an actual Black disabled person living with a disability resulting from psychosurgery. In the two articles on Byers original to the *Black Panther*, the BPP briefly, yet importantly, enacts the third anti-ableist approach to protesting disabling violence: insisting on and providing concrete support for those disabled by social injustice, oppression, and violence. One article states that "the Black Panther Party's Free Legal Aid and Educational Program is looking into various resources so as to assist Lou Byers," and the final article adds that Byers's mother, "with the aid of the Black Panther Party, is seeking legal and medical help for her son. The law offices of BPP chief counsel Charles Garry are investigating young Byers' case."[30] It is clear that the BPP was invested in not only protesting and stopping the disabling violence of forced pharmaceutical and psychosurgical treatments but also highlighting the interconnected nature of multiple oppressions and social systems that permit such violence, and seeking justice, care, and support for people disabled by this violence.

The BPP's work was neither perfect nor without ableist missteps. One of the challenges of studying Black disability politics is acknowledging the good—what worked and how it worked—while also being clear about where the efforts faltered, could have been better, or engaged in ableist tactics. This is why scholars of Black studies and disability studies need to be conversant in each other's theories, methods, and lexicons and why antiracist and anti-ableist activists must do the same with one another. Of course, even disability rights organizations have been accused of ableist behavior by engaging in a disability hierarchy, so identifying these issues does not mean wholesale rejection or condemnation; rather, it entails being realistic about liberation movements and the people within them, who each have their own internalized and unrecognized biases. It means learning from these mistakes and moving forward together. We can learn from the Panthers' missteps and aim to engage in less ableist rhetoric in our own work, and we can remain aware and staunchly critical of such ableist rhetoric when we witness it in our academic and activist communities. Contemporary social justice movements can increase engagement with disability justice by taking up these anti-ableist approaches to fighting disabling violence and oppression, as the Panthers imperfectly model in their fight against psychiatric abuse. For Black activist movements and organizations in particular, the Black disability politics of the BPP explored throughout the first two chapters and this praxis interlude provide models for how antiracism and anti-ableism can be combined and also give examples of ableist pitfalls to avoid.

For instance, scholars and activists today, building on existing work in disability studies, can use and adapt the approaches of the BPP when identifying, raising awareness about, critiquing, and fighting various forms of disabling violence in our world without making disability the symbolic specter of injustice. That is, rather than using the image of disability to represent the wrongness of social ills, such as environmental destruction, medical discrimination, or war, thereby relying on ableist emotional responses to disability, we must instead take a different approach that balances the lived realities of disabled people with attention to how the intersections of larger social systems of oppression produce additional disablement and make living with a disability increasingly difficult. This change in activist argumentative, representational, and rhetorical approaches includes three tactics I've articulated by building on the work of Kafer and Clare. First, focus on violence as the issue/problem to be solved, not disability. Second, emphasize the interconnected nature of social justice concerns. Third, incorporate material support for people disabled by the violence of injustice and oppression.

These alternative tactics for fighting disabling violence apply beyond Black activism alone but are especially important for antiracist work since so much racial violence, from police brutality to racism within medical care to environmental hazards situated in poor and nonwhite neighborhoods, debilitates and disables people of color. These tactics need to be implemented now in Black liberation work because, as the example of how police violence disabled, debilitated, and harmed Jacob Blake, his children, and the community members who witnessed Officer Sheskey shoot him seven times in the back shows, disabling violence is viciously ongoing for Black people in

the United States. We must resist these injustices, but if we fight back by relying on emotional responses to disability as pure tragedy or lost life, we reify
ableist oppression in the name of fighting racial, class, and other oppression.
This common approach also erases the reality of disabled lives and the possibility of a happy and fulfilling life with a disability instead of envisioning
an oppression-free world that is fundamentally free of disabled people. We
owe this to Jacob Blake and his children, who can live full lives with their
disabilities with the right support, medically, financially, and socially. We
owe it to all Black people who have been physically and mentally disabled
by police violence, lead poisoning in the water, medical neglect, and more.
We can and must do better because this all-too-common approach of using
disability as an ableist rhetorical device within our fight against disabling
violence fundamentally cannot lead to the collective liberation we need.

In the next two chapters, I continue my exploration of how Black cultural
workers have articulated and enacted Black disability politics by analyzing
the work of the National Black Women's Health Project, a Black feminist
health activist organization started in the early 1980s. This continued analysis of disability politics within Black activism historically provides further
evidence that Black people have long engaged with disability as a social and
political concern but have used approaches that diverge from the white
mainstream disability rights movement. The work of the National Black
Women's Health Project is similar that of the BPP in ways that further support my identification of the four central aspects of Black disability politics.

3

EMPOWERMENT THROUGH WELLNESS

Black Disability Politics
in the National Black
Women's Health Project

Politics do not stand in polar opposition to our lives. Whether we desire it or not, they permeate our existence, insinuating themselves into the most private spaces of our lives.
—ANGELA Y. DAVIS, "Sick and Tired of Being Sick and Tired: The Politics of Black Women's Health"

On June 24, 1983, the National Black Women's Health Project (NBWHP), at the time a new program under the auspices of the National Women's Health Network, hosted the First National Conference on Black Women's Health Issues at Spelman College, a historically Black college for women. The conference organizers expected a few hundred Black women to register and attend. In the end, nearly two thousand attendees showed up from across the country. The conference focused broadly on Black women's health, from stress management, diabetes, mental health, and self-esteem to domestic violence, sexual health, aging, and cancer. In addition to more traditional plenary sessions, keynote lectures, and academic presentations, the conference also included health screenings, group exercise opportunities, a concert by Sweet Honey in the Rock, and interactive workshops, several of which directly engaged with disability, such as "The Mask of Lupus," "Dispelling the Myths of Mental Illness," "Health Concerns of the Physically Disabled," and "Diabetes."[1] The conference's most popular workshop, however, was Lillie Allen's "Black and Female: What Is the Reality?," which was reserved exclusively for Black women only to discuss what being a Black woman has meant for them, to discuss the impact of history on Black women, and to begin to face and deconstruct internalized oppression. As Allen writes in a reflection on the workshop, "We have internalized too long the lies and myths which taught and preached to black women self-invalidation, self-doubt, isolation, fear, feelings of powerlessness and despair that led us to say 'I don't think I'm good enough.' … *Internalized oppression exists anytime you feel intolerant or, irritated by, impatient with, embarrassed by, ashamed of, not as black as, blacker than, better than, not as good as, fearful of, not cared about by, unable to show support or not support by another black woman.*"[2] The workshop encouraged Black women to tell their stories and to truly listen to other Black women in order to bear witness to both the similarities and differences between their lived experiences.[3] The workshop was such an incredible success that it became an early cornerstone of the NBWHP's self-help philosophy and practice.

As this brief overview of the organization's first conference suggests, the NBWHP engaged in a multifaceted, comprehensive, intersectional, and explicitly political approach to health that built on the legacies of previous health activism in feminist, civil rights, and other progressive movements.[4] The NBWHP, however, enacted a specifically Black feminist form of health activism that focused on improving the health of Black women holistically in order to gain, in NBWHP founder Byllye Avery's words, "empowerment through wellness."[5]

Black women have long been central in health activist movements although the term *feminist* has not always been applied to this work. Black women served Black communities as midwives and later, when medicine became a more formalized profession, as nurses, fundraisers, and volunteers in Black hospitals. More recently, Black women were the majority of the "health cadre" members who ran the Black Panther Party's free clinics, and many Black women, such as Byllye Avery, played major roles in feminist health organizations like the National Women's Health Network.[6] Women, however, are not automatically feminists, and feminists are not exclusively women. I use the term *Black feminist health activism*, therefore, to refer to health activism by Black people that is critically attuned to intersectional gender, race, and class politics, whether or not the word *feminist* was used by the organizations or activists involved. Although in the case of the NBWHP, the vast majority of members and all of its leaders were Black women, it is certainly possible to call work by other, more mixed-gender Black organizations Black feminist health activism.

The NBWHP was the first organization to focus exclusively on the health of Black women and the first of many women-of-color-specific health organizations that eventually emerged within the feminist health movement.[7] The many women involved in the NBWHP, from doctors, nurses, therapists, and social workers to academics, politicians, writers, mothers, and teens, did not all necessarily identify as feminists, but their advocacy, writing, and organizing on Black women's health was undoubtedly grounded in the legacies of Black feminist theorizing and activism. This is particularly evident in the fact that several major Black feminist scholars such as Angela Davis, Beverly Guy-Sheftall, and Dorothy Roberts each at one point served on the NBWHP board.[8]

The NBWHP was a grassroots Black feminist activist organization that sought to reduce health disparities and instances of preventable diseases/conditions while simultaneously insisting on the political nature of health and disability. In this chapter, the first of two on the organization, I analyze the NBWHP's Black feminist health activism as another prime example of Black disability politics. More specifically, I assess how disability was explicitly and implicitly included within its organizational mission, self-help philosophy, and holistic, cultural, and political approaches to health and wellness. Importantly, this chapter explores how spirituality was incorporated into this public health work, providing a needed intervention and invitation to further explore the intersections of race, disability, and spirituality, faith, or religion in both Black studies and disability studies. Overall, I argue that the NBWHP consistently addressed disability and took anti-ableist stances but did so within a Black feminist health activist framework rather than under the banner of disability rights. Although explicit engagement with *disability* as a term, let alone *disability rights*, is rare within the NBWHP's publications and archival documents, the politics expressed are nonetheless anti-ableist and critical to advancing our understanding of the common qualities of Black disability politics. In what follows, I first provide an overview of the organization's history, including its primary mission and central self-help philosophy, before delving into a more detailed analysis of disability politics within the NBWHP's holistic, cultural, and political approaches to health. This chapter argues that the NBWHP's general Black feminist health activism was Black disability politics in order to then perform a close analysis of the organization's disability-specific work on HIV/AIDS in the next chapter.

A Brief History of the NBWHP

The NBWHP was started in 1981 as a project within the National Women's Health Network to focus on the specific health needs of Black women. Following the success of and excitement from its first conference, the NBWHP was incorporated into an independent nonprofit organization in 1984 with its base in Atlanta, Georgia. Early organizational documents define the NBWHP as

> a health education, advocacy and empowerment project designed and directed by Black women to critically examine the health care concerns and issues pertinent to the lives of all Black women and their families.... The Project sees its mission as empowering Black women to take an active part in the decisions that govern our lives—and teaches us to seek affirmation, validation and support within ourself first, and then within the network of our "sisters." Only through an analysis of the forces that have shaped our lives as Black women, through the telling of our life stories, does the NBWHP believe that we can regain and control the quality of our lives, and future generations.[9]

From its inception the NBWHP promoted an intersectional and specifically Black feminist approach to addressing health disparities and health crises for Black women with the aim of improving health across Black communities in general.

The NBWHP was founded by Byllye Avery. Although many Black women health activists, particularly Lillie Allen, were involved in shaping the organization from the start, Avery was the consistent face of the organization. She served as executive director from 1981 to 1989 and as president from 1990 to 1995 before shifting into a more honorary role as "founder," writing pieces for annual publications and speaking at events but no longer involved in the day-to-day workings of the NBWHP. As a result of Avery's importance in the organization, a brief discussion of her personal history, especially in relationship to disability, is pertinent to my analysis of disability politics within the NBWHP.

Before working in health activism, Avery had personal and professional experience with people with disabilities that may have influenced the NBWHP's approach to disability politics. On a personal level, Avery's brother had multiple sclerosis, and according to her, "he suffered with it for a long time, a long time before it was ever diagnosed."[10] Avery also lost her husband to a heart attack when he was thirty-three years old. In an oral history interview, she states, "He was hypertensive. We didn't know it. He had had a couple of exams earlier that should have let us know.... [T]he doctor told him that his pressure was high and that he needed him to exercise and to diet to bring his pressure down. But that was all that was told to him. It wasn't put into a way that he would have known that it had the dangers that it carried." Avery describes the death of her husband as "truly a radicalizing experience," which, combined with the lack of diagnosis and intervention for her brother and the effects of heart disease and diabetes on multiple members of her extended family, made her realize that "it doesn't really matter how much formal education you have. If you don't know how to take care of yourself, you're still basically in a state of ignorance."[11] These personal experiences with loved ones with disabilities and disabling diseases were foundational to Avery's activism and her emphasis on self-help, education, and empowerment around health issues in Black communities.

On a professional level, Avery earned a degree in psychology from Talladega College in 1959 and then worked for six years at the North Florida State Mental Hospital. After her first child was born, she worked for a few years at "a school program for emotionally disturbed children" before going on to get a master's degree in special education. In October 1970 she took a new job at a "university-based children's mental health unit."[12] These educational and professional experiences inside of programs and institutions for people with disabilities, particularly people with mental disabilities, likely influenced Avery's consistent emphasis within the NBWHP on the importance of mental and emotional health and well-being. Avery eventually moved from practitioner to organizer and activist via the women's health movement and her work with multiple women's health and birthing centers in Florida and Georgia.[13] This work led her to become an active member of the National Women's Health Network, within which she initiated the NBWHP after discovering the dearth of health research specific to Black women and the dire nature of the findings of the limited existing research at the time.

Under Avery's leadership, the NBWHP undertook a wide variety of programs to address and improve the health and wellness of Black women. The NBWHP's activities ranged from national conferences and leadership institutes to the Walking for Wellness program to encourage more physical activity and the Plain Talk program for creating dialogue between Black mothers and daughters about sex and sexuality. Additionally, the NBWHP produced policy briefs, sponsored and published research, and developed programming on HIV/AIDS, diabetes, hypertension, and substance abuse in Black communities. From 1988 to 1996, the NBWHP operated the Center for

Black Women's Wellness in Atlanta, a wellness center and clinic in a public-housing neighborhood that provided free health screenings, vocational training, self-help support groups, and more. The NBWHP also published *Vital Signs*, the organization's official newsletter, which grew and changed over time from a quarterly eight-page newsletter to an annual sixty-page color magazine with advertisements.

While the Black Panther Party's work described in the previous two chapters was intersectional but centered on race, the NBWHP's work was intersectional but centered on race and gender, as a specifically Black feminist health activist organization. Publications and internal documents from the NBWHP always name racism and sexism as major factors in Black women's health with fairly consistent mention of classism and frequent mention of homophobia. Other forms of oppression, such as the oppression of elders, people with disabilities, and fat people, are only occasionally mentioned in some documents and publications.[14] The NBWHP was not a disability rights organization but a health organization that frequently acted in solidarity with disabled people in much of its work and included disabled people in leadership positions, such as Deborah Williams-Muhammed, a Black woman with multiple sclerosis and sarcoidosis who served on the NBWHP board. Williams-Muhammed claims that the self-help skills, knowledge, and support network she obtained through the NBWHP helped her get out of a nursing home where she was overmedicated and under-cared-for, stating, "If it were not for my sisters at NBWHP, I might still be in the nursing home or I might not be alive."[15] The NBWHP's self-help philosophy and practices, which Williams-Muhammed credits for her wellness, were the foundation of the organization's central programming and the context in which the NBWHP's disability politics become more apparent.

Self-help, as a philosophy and a practice, was for many years the core program of the NBWHP. The organization fostered the development of self-help support groups across the country, which were intended to provide sustained supportive environments for Black women, teens, and girls in which to tell their stories, address their health concerns, learn about and combat internalized oppression, and connect with other Black women. This self-help philosophy combined Lillie Allen's expertise in reevaluation counseling and the legacies of self-help and consciousness-raising groups in the women's liberation movement while also prioritizing the cultural and social contexts of Black women's lives.[16]

The NBWHP self-help groups ranged from three to ten women who would meet on a regular, typically weekly, basis for two to three hours. Self-help groups sometimes formed around specific health issues but more often were based on existing social networks, meeting in women's homes, community centers, or churches. Groups were led and organized by codevelopers who received training and leadership development three times a year from the organization. The importance of self-help to the NBWHP is illustrated not only by how much of the organization's time and resources went into developing and supporting self-help groups nationwide but also by the fact that leaders and employees of the organization were encouraged or even required to participate in the self-help process.[17] While the exact numbers of women who attended these groups are difficult to ascertain—an issue that eventually became a problem for the organization when seeking funding—in 1989 the organization estimated that two thousand women were participating in a NBWHP self-help group each month, and in 2000 they estimated that over thirty thousand women had participated since the organization's founding.[18]

While self-help groups may not seem like the most radical grassroots activity, the philosophy undergirding the creation and maintenance of these groups was explicitly political and praxis focused. A 1989 annual report explains the political potential envisioned for these groups: "NBWHP self-help group development is predicated on the realization that an increased health consciousness and personal commitment to wellness for Black women require an environment of understanding and support. Through sharing collective experiences and a validation of our individual efforts in the unique struggles to overcome racism, sexism and class elitism, our members learn that our health problems are part of a larger picture. We learn that physical health, emotional health and spiritual health are all linked and that the empowerment of individuals can transform a distressed community."[19] The NBWHP's self-help groups combined political education with public health education in a nonmedical, explicitly Black- and woman-centered setting. In groups, Black women gained self-empowerment through telling their stories and connecting with others with similar experiences in a free, nonjudgmental space. This self-empowerment was then intended to help women to take action regarding their health and the health of others in their communities. As one self-help meeting guide explains, "The goal is to develop a sense of empowerment and activism to take actions.... The Self-Help Group is not the action or organizing group, but is the place where women develop a greater sense of capacity to be able to make change."[20] The NBWHP therefore envisioned self-help groups as a means to impact Black women's and Black communities' health at the micro (individual and family) and macro (community and nation) levels.

The self-help philosophy of the NBWHP, which undergirded most of its work for over a decade, can be interpreted within a Black disability political framework. For instance, while self-help groups occasionally formed around specific disabilities or diseases, such as diabetes, the groups were neither based in disability identity nor segregated by disability or health status, and they strongly encouraged women with and without disabilities and diseases to participate and understand their bodyminds as impacted by the histories and politics of race, gender, class, and sexuality. As a Center for Black Women's Wellness funding proposal to the Kellogg Foundation states, "Self-help groups do not stigmatize their members because of health or social conditions; they may therefore have as members women who are single parents, chronic disease sufferers, homeless persons, and so forth, as well as career and professional women, and women of varied educational backgrounds, health challenges, and ages."[21] This is an example of Black disability politics because it is explicitly inclusive of Black disabled women without being dependent on a disability identity.

The NBWHP self-help groups also moved away from a strictly medical model of disability, health, and disease by emphasizing the need to address internalized oppression and to have a broad network of emotional and material support. Organizational materials repeatedly make clear that self-help groups were not therapy—not because therapy was bad or to be avoided but because therapy typically involves an expert and a recipient of expertise, along with payment. As one self-help manual for codevelopers states, "No one person is the expert. It is a relationship between peers/equals. All the members of the group use the expertise gained from their lives to help self and each other.... No one pays or gets paid. No medical tools are used.... The goal is wellness—not elimination of symptoms! Professional therapy may be used in conjunction with self-help to augment and accelerate the healing process."[22] This quote suggests that the NBWHP fully embraced the need for quality medical care, including psychotherapy, while simultaneously believing that providing access to and improving the quality of medical care alone was not enough to fully address the legacies of racism and sexism that shape Black women's experiences of disability and disease. In this way, the NBWHP remained vigilantly focused on contextualizing and historicizing Black women's health, broadly construed, in a fashion that I argue constitutes Black disability politics.

As the NBWHP grew, becoming increasingly reliant on major federal and foundation funding and putting more efforts into policy briefs, lobbying, and research—emphasizing macro- more than microlevel change—self-help became far less central to its work. In an organizational brief in 2000, the

NBWHP states, "Although self-help provides a philosophical richness and is the 'brick' in our foundation, NBWHP has been unable to measure its effectiveness nor have we been able to replicate the model for use by larger groups of women.... It was acknowledged that self-help is no longer the cutting edge technology that it was in the 1980s and now there is a proliferation of self-help models."[23] By the turn of the century, self-help groups were mentioned less and less in organizational materials, before disappearing entirely. In 2002 the organization officially changed its name to the National Black Women's Health *Imperative*. This name change was long overdue, marking not only the organization's move away from the self-help philosophy and practices on which it was founded but also other major organizational shifts that had been slowly occurring since 1996, when the organization relocated its headquarters to Washington, DC, and ceased its operation of the Center for Black Women's Wellness (which continues to operate independently today). As a result of these major shifts between 1996 and 2002, for the purposes of this and the next chapter, I focus on the disability politics of the NBWHP's work in the 1980s and 1990s.

In the next section, I demonstrate how the NBWHP's holistic, political, and cultural approaches to health and wellness are emblematic of Black disability politics. This section's discussion of how the NBWHP articulated Black disability politics provides the framework for analyzing how the organization actually enacted these politics in its work regarding HIV/AIDS in the next chapter.

Holistic, Cultural, and Political Approaches to Health and Wellness

The NBWHP's approach to defining and addressing health was very different from that of typical public health organizations. The NBWHP's materials typically define health as "not merely the absence of illness, but the active promotion of physical, spiritual, mental, and emotional wellness of this and future generations."[24] This definition draws largely from the definition of health by the World Health Organization (WHO), first published in 1948, which "defines health positively, as complete physical, mental and social well-being, not merely negatively as the absence of disease or infirmity."[25] There are, however, a few key differences. First, the NBWHP's definition drops mention of infirmity, which suggests the inclusion of the elderly and/or the disabled within states of health. Second, the NBWHP's definition of health includes spiritual and emotional wellness in an attempt to account for the role of spirituality in the lives of Black women as well as the need to tend to emotional well-being, particularly stress and relationship dynamics. The terms *emotional* and *mental* are used in different ways over the course of the organization's history; sometimes both appear in the same document, and sometimes one or the other, but at least one of these terms (*emotional* or *mental*) always appears along with physical and spiritual well-being. Last, the NBWHP's definition of health emphasizes action in "the active promotion of" wellness and the need to think communally and long term in the phrase "this and future generations." These differences between the NBWHP and the WHO definitions of health begin to show how the NBWHP's work as an explicitly Black feminist public health organization differed ideologically from that of more general public health organizations.

The related terms *wellness* and *well-being* appear in both the NBWHP and the WHO definitions of health and therefore warrant additional comment. Although both terms are used often in NBWHP publications, they are never explicitly defined. However, one undated pamphlet in the organization's archive, titled *Black Women Helping Ourselves*, provides some insight. It states, "Our Self-Help Groups are a model for Black women to create the space and take the time to define wellness for ourselves in the context of the larger social forces that impact our lives." The suggestion here is that wellness can be self-defined in the context of one's wider social and political world. This sentiment, though not explicitly stated elsewhere, is reflected in the holistic, cultural, and political approaches to health undertaken by the NBWHP. Wellness includes things not directly of the bodymind, such as finances and housing, which nonetheless have a real impact on physical, mental, and emotional health. Wellness must be self-defined, therefore, because it is about one's own needs, desires, capabilities, and norms. What is necessary for one person's wellness may be unnecessary for another. Furthermore, in both the NBWHP and WHO definitions of health, wellness and well-being are understood as foundational to health, as part of its definition. As a result, health within the NBWHP can also be understood as deeply personal and contextual rather than merely medical and objective, as health is dependent on wellness, which is self-defined. This personalized and contextualized approach to health and wellness is evident, for instance, in the introduction to the NBWHP's self-help health book, *Body and Soul: The Black Women's Guide to Physical Health and Emotional Well-Being*, which states, "Good health is about intuition. That means being in tune with everything and everyone around us. In this scientific world, we don't give credence to the idea that our intuition can lead us to the right place. When faced with health challenges, we must collect all the information, talk to all the doctors, and then go inside ourselves and take direction from our inner voices. We have to believe in ourselves and believe in our ability to make the decision that will lead to healing."[26] Here it is clear that rather than understanding health and well-being as self-evident, medically determined, objective states of being, the NBWHP understood these terms to be deeply personal and contextual.[27]

These broad, individualized, and overlapping understandings of health and wellness are important not only for understanding the Black disability politics of the NBWHP specifically but also for understanding Black disability politics in general. Expressions of a desire for wellness or healing by Black and other racialized groups are sometimes construed within disability studies and disability rights circles as (internalized) ableist expressions of desire for able-bodiedness and able-mindedness when that is not inherently the case. As the discussions of language and ableism in chapter 2 and praxis interlude 1 make clear, a major task for disability studies scholars as well as for disability activists working among racialized populations is to resist impulsive knee-jerk reactions to language that is often, but not always, used in ableist ways. To analyze and explore how Black activists have engaged with disability means understanding the purpose and intention with which people use certain words, such as *wellness* and *healing*, assessing how such discourses do or do not reflect solidarity with disabled people in general.

In this case, the NBWHP was a Black feminist public health organization that was not simply interested in improving physical health or reducing instances of preventable disease among Black people. Instead, the NBWHP was invested in a holistic, cultural, and political approach to health and wellness that would ensure long-lasting positive effects on generations of Black people. The NBWHP definitions of health and wellness do not exclude disabled people nor fixate on cure; rather, the organization sought wellness, broadly and individually defined, for all people regardless of health or (dis)ability status. As the next chapter details more specifically in relationship to HIV/AIDS, throughout its work, the NBWHP sought to reduce instances of preventable disabling diseases and conditions among Black people while also advocating for improved personal, social, and material supports for existing disabled or chronically ill Black women, including the right to intangible aspects of wellness such as dignity and joy. Interpreting the Black disability politics of the NBWHP's work means holding this latter solidarity with disabled people in tension with the former desire to reduce the number of Black disabled people overall through disease prevention and treatment.

As discussed in praxis interlude 1, it is possible to fight disabling violence and oppression without using disability as a pathetic or terrifying symbol of such harm by instead emphasizing the mutual constitution of oppressions and supporting people disabled by social injustice and violence. The NBWHP, I contend, did just that. In its work the NBWHP articulated and enacted Black disability politics, refusing to stigmatize or shame Black women for their health and promoting wellness for all. In the following sections, I further detail how the NBWHP approached health and wellness in holistic, culturally attuned, and politicized ways. In each of these three overlapping approaches, we can further understand the Black disability politics of the organization.

Holistic Approaches to Health

As the above-discussed definition of health suggests, the NBWHP took a holistic approach to health that included physical, mental/emotional, and spiritual well-being. The NBWHP believed that one could not address physical symptoms or concerns alone without addressing and caring for the mental/ emotional and spiritual elements of a person, which would equip them with the knowledge, support, skills, and confidence to attend to their physical health. This holistic approach meant that although the NBWHP often created disease/condition-focused programming around common health concerns among Black women, such as HIV/AIDS, diabetes, and hypertension, its work addressed a wide variety of health and wellness topics. This is most apparent in its major publications in the 1980s and 1990s: *Vital Signs*, the organizational newsletter/magazine, and *Body and Soul: The Black Women's Guide to Physical Health and Emotional Well-Being*, a self-help health book published by the NBWHP in 1994 and edited by Linda Villarosa.

In each of these two major publications, there is consistent recognition of and attention to all of the NBWHP's major aspects of health and wellness. Issues of *Vital Signs* consistently include articles attending to physical, spiritual, and mental/emotional health. In particular, from 1993 to 1995, when the publication briefly changed from a simple eight-to-twenty-page photocopied or newsprint quarterly newsletter to a forty-to-sixty-page quarterly magazine before shifting to an annual publication, *Vital Signs* contained a regular section called "Well Woman," which included the tagline "Empowerment through Wellness: Mental, Physical and Spiritual," with typically thematically related columns addressing each part of holistic health in the section in every issue. An example of this section is shown in figure 3.1. Similarly, the NBWHP's self-help health book, *Body and Soul*, while heavily focused on physical (especially reproductive) health in its first seventeen chapters, also

FIGURE 3.1
Example of a "Well
Woman" page
from *Vital Signs*.

contains in its second half chapters on emotional health, self-help, spiritual health, self-love, relationships and sex, domestic violence, incest and child abuse, HIV/AIDS, and workplace and environmental health hazards. These latter chapters in more and less explicit ways address both mental/emotional and spiritual health.

The NBWHP understood the physical, mental/emotional, and spiritual aspects of health to be overlapping and mutually dependent. That is, one's mental/emotional well-being could impact one's physical and spiritual well-being and vice versa. This is evident, for example, in a 1986 *Vital Signs* article titled "Emotional Aspects of Chronic Illness," which begins with the statement "Emotional aspects of chronic illnesses are real and often long-lasting" and then provides examples of how chronic illness emotionally impacts people, such as grief or shame produced by loss of the ability to work or maintain levels of productivity, changes in self-esteem as a result of changes in physical appearance, and feelings of being objectified and denied privacy within the medical industrial complex.[28] Here and in other articles and publications, it is clear that the NBWHP understood and promoted a holistic version of health that was dynamic and interconnected. Importantly, unlike many holistic approaches, which tend to understand whole bodyminds as including the physical and mental/emotional, the NBWHP explicitly included the spiritual in its conceptualization of holistic health. The inclusion of spirituality, faith, and religion in the NBWHP's work is an example of its cultural approach to health, which I address further below.

By taking such a holistic approach to defining and understanding health, the NBWHP's publications and activities, like the work of the Panthers in the previous two chapters, regularly addressed a broad range of health topics and concerns, which vary in their proximity to disability as typically defined medically or legally. For instance, *Vital Signs* issues include articles on the following conditions, diseases, disabilities, and health concerns: lupus, HIV/AIDS, kidney disease, fibroids, diabetes, rheumatoid arthritis, depression, chronic illness, cancer (especially breast and ovarian), sickle cell anemia, hypertension, stress, toxic shock syndrome, suicidal ideation, and sexually transmitted diseases. *Body and Soul* similarly addresses addiction, heart disease, cancer, diabetes, lupus, sarcoidosis, sickle cell anemia, asthma, chronic fatigue syndrome, Alzheimer's disease, arthritis, osteoporosis, anxiety disorders (phobias, panic disorder, post-traumatic stress syndrome, and obsessive-compulsive disorder), depression, bipolar disorder, and schizophrenia. The wide variety of illnesses, diseases, conditions, and disabilities on these two lists is typical of much Black health activism, which tends to be inclusive of disability but not primarily focused on it. This broadness in particular reflects the reality that Black people are more likely to be disabled by secondary health effects of otherwise nondisabling and/or preventable illnesses as a result of a lack of educational, social, and financial access to preventative care and early treatment as well as of environmental racism, medical racism, and racist violence.[29]

Historically, the relationship of and differences between disability on the one hand and illness, disease, and other health concerns on the other has been contentious within disability studies and the disability rights movement, demonstrating that the boundaries of what constitutes disability have been challenged even within white and mainstream disability communities. The disability rights movement, for example, has been criticized for developing platforms and activist concepts like the social model of disability based primarily on the bodyminds and experiences of white, heterosexual, wheelchair-using disabled men.[30] Disability rights activists have also identified intracommunity hierarchies of disability in which those with chronic illnesses, mental disabilities, and intellectual and developmental disabilities are devalued, marginalized, and even excluded from activist work.[31] Relatedly, the field of disability studies has been critiqued for focusing heavily on physical and sensory disabilities as the basis for theorizing disability generally.[32] More recently, the term *disability/disabled* itself has been critiqued as being overdetermined by whiteness, wealth, and rights-based political platforms. Jasbir Puar in particular argues for using the term *debility* to discuss those whose bodyminds are purposefully, slowly, worn down by the violence of capitalism, racism, colonialism, and other forms of oppression but who are denied access to the label of disability and the small amount of resources begrudgingly provided to those legally and medically recognized as disabled.[33] All these critiques and arguments demonstrate that even within existing disability studies and disability activism, there are disputes about the appropriate boundaries of the word *disability* and its related academic and activist discourses. What becomes apparent in studying Black disability politics historically, however, is a frequent lack of investment in disability as a clearly defined and politicized identity and instead an investment in an umbrella approach to health activism that is inclusive of disability broadly defined. This has increasingly changed over time, and I say more about the role of disability identity in contemporary Black disability politics in praxis interlude 2.

For the NBWHP, a holistic approach to health meant addressing physical, mental/emotional, and spiritual well-being and engaging with a wide variety of disabilities as well as potentially disabling illnesses, diseases, and health conditions. As will become further evident in my discussion of the cultural and political aspects of the NBWHP's approaches to health, the organization's engagement with disability was consistently grounded in the real experiences of Black women. The NBWHP's holistic approach was less invested in legal and medical definitions of disability and more concerned with the material impact of oppressions on the health and well-being of Black women and their communities. Nonetheless, the NBWHP's approach was inclusive and supportive of Black disabled women, as is further reflected in the cultural and political aspects of its philosophical approach to health and health activism.

Cultural Approaches to Health

The NBWHP's approach to health and wellness was influenced by African diasporic cultures and rooted in the lived experiences of Black women. This cultural aspect of the NBWHP's approach to health is emblematic of the contextualized and historicized approach to disability typical of Black disability politics. At its core, the NBWHP believed in the need for health initiatives created for us, by us. This culturally contextualized approach to health is primarily represented in, first, its inclusion of spirituality; second, its emphasis on the importance of telling and listening to Black women's health stories; and, third, its promotion of culturally informed public health initiatives.

The NBWHP recognized the need to value and include spiritual health within Black feminist health activism in order to reach their intended audience. The NBWHP did this, importantly, without promoting any particular religious and spiritual beliefs, even as individual members discussed their specific faith practices and experiences—both good and bad—in articles for *Vital Signs*.[34] The chapter on spirituality in *Body and Soul* asserts that "the spirit" can mean God, Allah, ancestors, or one's own spirit. The book further explains that "spirituality has been a part of African tradition since long before the birth of Christianity" and is especially present in Black resistance traditions, such as using spirituals to send messages during slavery and singing spirituals during civil rights marches, largely because of the religious roots of leaders like Dr. Martin Luther King Jr., Malcolm X, and Fannie Lou Hamer.[35] The chapter then includes stories of "how three Black women find sustenance through spirituality," including the narrative of a woman who used Yoruba traditions to help her with depression after a suicide attempt.[36] Spirituality within the NBWHP therefore encompassed a wide range of practices and beliefs that allow individuals to attend to their inner life and feel connected to a larger system or purpose in ways that shape their behaviors in the world. For example, in a *Vital Signs* article about her experience with dialysis, Berlinda Hawkins writes, "I had kidney failure, and my only survival depended upon being hooked to a machine three times a week. I learned to cope by praying to God for the strength to adjust to my sickness. With the help of God and my family, I made up my mind that I wanted to live."[37] This is one example of how Black women members of the NBWHP incorporated spirituality into their understandings and experiences of disability, illness, and disease. The NBWHP understood, therefore, that including spirituality in its Black feminist health activism was essential to reaching and empowering Black women, though this did not, importantly, prevent critique of the oppressive role religion and the church have played in the lives of many Black women as well.[38]

Spirituality is not a common element of disability studies or public health work, and yet spirituality, faith, and religion are major parts of Black culture and are therefore critical to interpreting Black disability politics. Disability studies scholars have engaged with religion primarily through discussions of ableism in Christian churches, critiques of faith or prayer healing, and challenges to notions that disability is either a gift or curse from God.[39] There is limited work on the relationship of disabled people to spirituality and religion, much of which focuses on families of disabled people and on Christian churches specifically.[40] While many Black people identify as Christian and the NBWHP often partnered with Black Christian churches as locations for programming, the organization's cultural approach to health conceived of spirituality much more expansively, often explicitly discussing non-Christian African and Caribbean spiritual practices.

The issue of religion and spirituality for disabled people came up multiple times in my interviews with contemporary Black disabled cultural workers. Several participants mentioned the tendency in Black communities to believe that (some) disabilities and illnesses can be treated with faith and prayer alone—potentially because of Black people's negative experiences with the medical and psychiatric industrial complexes. This emphasis on religion over medicine sometimes leads to blaming and shaming of Black disabled people, particularly those who reject faith healing and laying on of hands as well as those who openly prioritize treatments and medication, especially for psychiatric disabilities. As Tinu Abayomi-Paul explains, "People seem to try to, you know, throw God at it ... [but] it's not, you know, something that I'm praying away. I'm treating it. God made the doctors, and the doctors are treating me ... you have people [who] feel like you haven't prayed hard enough ... [who want to] lay hands on you without your permission ... to basically erase part of your identity and swap it out for whatever identity they think that you should have.... [They accuse the disabled person] of being a faker or being not religious or not being strong enough."[41] T. S. Banks echoes this sentiment, stating that when he told loved ones about needing help for mental disabilities, he was told that "you should pray things away or that more church ... more scripture" would help, but Banks explains that as a Black disabled person of faith, he believes in "Jesus *and* medication, Jesus *and* therapy."[42] While religion did not come up in every interview, the insights provided by those who did discuss religion, faith, or spirituality within Black communities make clear that there is still much work to be done to better integrate disability justice into Black faith communities. Our communities, especially our Black liberation movement communities, need to be holistically supportive of wellness and healing without overemphasizing cure or shaming Black disabled people for the choices they make to care for their bodyminds in a racist and ableist world. The NBWHP modeled some of the ways this work could occur.

The NBWHP's inclusion of spiritual practices also intersects with its engagement with alternative and non-Western healing practices. Julie Avril Minich discusses the importance of cultural healing practices, such as the botánica in Latinx communities, which supplement or provide alternatives to medical and social systems that have failed, excluded, or harmed marginalized communities.[43] The botánica is typically a small store that sells herbal medicines, oils, and teas as well as religious candles, crystals, incense, and other products for spiritual, magical, or ancestral practices. Similar types of alternative healing practices, many with spiritual or ancestral roots, are represented in *Vital Signs* articles and advertisements as well as within *Body and Soul*, often with discussion of the history of these practices in Black diasporic cultures.[44] Versions of these practices appear contemporarily among antiracist, feminist activist organizations, such as Harriet's Apothecary, Kindred Southern Healing Justice Collective, and BadAss Visionary Healers, who use the concept of healing justice as a revolutionary practice that does not equate healing with cure or able-bodiedness and able-mindedness.[45] Minich argues that a disability studies perspective can help us interpret representations of and engagement with alternative healing practices among low-income and racialized communities as both evidence of the need for an improved health-care system and an indication of how "bodily difference can have diverse social and cultural meanings."[46] Although the ableism of some religious, spiritual, and alternative healing communities is undeniable and worthy of critique, critical race and disability studies scholars must balance such critique with attention to the racism and classism that shape interpretations of what spiritual and healing practices are deemed acceptable and explore what such practices bring to the lives of disabled people of color. The NBWHP's cultural approach to health provides a model for leaving space for spiritual and alternative healing practices within Black feminist health activism and Black disability politics.

A second aspect of the NBWHP's cultural approach to health is the valuing of personal stories from members of the organization. A major and regularly asserted goal of the NBWHP was to fight against "the conspiracy of silence" among Black women and Black communities regarding health, especially sexual and reproductive health.[47] In an article for the organization's publication *Sister Ink*, JoAnne Banks-Wallace draws from a number of Black feminist writers to explore "the power of storytelling as a tool for health and healing from whatever ails us," as well as "the value of storytelling as a tool for self-definition and self-determination."[48] The NBWHP's self-help groups and "Black and Female: What Is the Reality?" workshops were the primary venues in which the NBWHP facilitated the sharing of stories among Black women. Additionally, however, organization publications regularly included personal narratives submitted by members about their health concerns, struggles, and victories alongside more traditional health information and education.

The value of storytelling within the NBWHP reflects its emphasis on the importance of cultural context in understanding Black women's experiences of disability, illness, and disease. This is evident, for example, in *Vital Signs* articles on lupus. In one article A. D. Moreau-Morgan describes seeing a public health awareness poster for lupus featuring a white woman's face and then details some of the medical research that shows Black women are actually three times more likely to have lupus than white women and that flare-ups are often stress induced.[49] In another article Angela Ducker Richardson discusses how the particular stresses of her life, such as planning a wedding and trying to find a job after college, led to lupus symptoms, which were consistently misdiagnosed and therefore mistreated by doctors as nerves and allergies. For a long time, Richardson simply lived with pain, itchiness, and swelling throughout her body, explaining, "I didn't immediately go to the doctor because I thought I would once again be told that it was all my nerves, and treated like some first-class hypochondriac."[50] In multiple issues of *Vital Signs* over the years Black women with and without lupus discuss how various factors—including lack of research into the racial and gendered aspects of lupus, the high stress of many Black women's lives, and the sexism and racism of medical professionals which facilitate misdiagnosis—all impact Black women's specific racialized and gendered experiences of the disease. These and other stories published by the NBWHP illustrate its attempt as a Black feminist health activist organization to promote prevention and/or awareness of specific illnesses and diseases for those not yet affected while also providing advice to and from women already impacted by disability, illness, and disease in order to help them care for themselves, be self-advocates, and manage their health as well as possible. The stories shared in NBWHP publications are immensely valuable in that they collectively help articulate some of the cultural norms and expectations of Black women that impact their physical, mental/emotional, and spiritual health. By reading about and sharing these themes, individual women could feel less alone and more empowered with knowledge and resources, while public health workers and researchers partnering with and learning from the NBWHP were better able to develop programs drawing from the actual experiences, desires, and needs of Black women. These culturally based initiatives are the third aspect of the NBWHP's cultural approach to health.

In addition to attending to spirituality and valuing personal narratives, another way the NBWHP took a cultural approach to health is through the promotion and creation of culturally based public health initiatives. The NBWHP was explicitly critical of public health programs developed for communities by people outside of those communities. NBWHP members instead promoted and created programming that met people where they were, understood their life situations intersectionally and holistically, and took a community's own desires and needs into account. This aspect of the NBWHP's cultural approach to health, like the inclusion of spiritual and alternative healing practices, reflects how organization leaders adapted their Black disability politics to the specific needs of communities of Black women.

The NBWHP was explicit and insistent about the need for public health officials and researchers to learn about, honor, and incorporate cultural perspectives and values into the development and implementation of programming because public health initiatives that do not account for the lived realities, priorities, and desires of the targeted population are destined to fail. This explicit insistence is evident, for example, in a funding proposal for the NBWHP's Center for Black Women's Wellness, which states:

> We respect the opinions and recognize the dignity and the personal resources of persons in this population [of Black women living in public housing in Atlanta]. We recognize that the people most affected by a problem and who live with it daily often carry the solutions within themselves. Health educators, medical providers, and service program planners can benefit greatly from the involvement of people as active participants in their own health care rather than as passive recipients of services. Indeed, the success of these services depends on the acceptance and active involvement of the people expected to benefit from them.[51]

Here the organization makes clear, even in a request for funding, that its work will center the recipients of health education and health-care programs. The NBWHP's tactic for culturally based public health initiatives involved asking Black women what they wanted and needed to attend to their health rather than telling them what to do or developing programs without regard to how such programs would be interpreted and experienced by the populations supposedly being helped.

When I refer to these programs as *culturally based* or *culturally informed* here, I am not equating culture with race. The NBWHP's public health initiatives understood culture broadly as encompassing a variety of social factors such as race, class, gender, religion, and geography. There is not, therefore, one Black culture to which the NBWHP adjusted its goals but rather a variety of Black cultures that influence individual Black women in various ways. This is why, for example, in addition to partnering with subsidized-housing projects and churches, the NBWHP also developed programming that targeted students at historically Black colleges and universities. Each of these communities required an adaptation of tactics as more information was obtained through programmatic successes and failures. Gwen Braxton, a leader of the New York City chapter of the NBWHP, addresses the possibility of failures, in multiple senses, within the organization's culturally based public health work. She writes:

> For you and I to assist others in reclaiming their power means we do whatever is necessary for them to make the best decisions that they can make for themselves with the resources that they have or have the ability to develop. This means that you and I have to accept that they might not make the decision that we want. They will make mistakes despite our advice and learn from their mistakes. I haven't met anyone who wanted to get AIDS, but because their priorities are different, their decisions will be different than our decisions for them. The program may not achieve its measurable objective, and may lose its funding.[52]

Braxton acknowledges that part of a culturally based initiative means trusting and empowering people to make their own decisions about their health and bodyminds based on their individual priorities, needs, and abilities, with the recognition that such an approach also allows individuals to make mistakes. Importantly, Braxton also highlights that this approach challenges traditional models of public health program funding from private foundation and government grants because the impact may not be immediate, obvious, or easily measured in a fashion that can be exhibited for funders.

Overall, the NBWHP's cultural approach to health, which includes recognition of spirituality, valuing of personal narratives, and development of culturally based public health initiatives, is an example of how Black cultural workers articulate Black disability politics in very contextualized ways that account for the way race, gender, class, and culture intersect with experiences of disability, health, and disease. This cultural approach to health, which builds on the holistic approach, also necessitated engagement with the broader politics and history of Black women's health. Above all, the NBWHP emphasized that health is inherently political, and the organization sought to draw attention to and change the conditions that damage Black women's health.

Political Approaches to Health

The NBWHP tackled a wide variety of health issues from an explicitly political, antiracist, and feminist perspective. In a meeting guide for self-help groups, the organization asserts:

> Our commitment to our health includes understanding the umbrella of oppression that hovers over us and the reality for all Black women of the pervasiveness of oppressive conditions in our lives. These oppressions are interlocking and affect us in all areas of our lives, even when we believe ourselves to be surviving and thriving in our personal and occupational lives. By better understanding the ways in which these interlocking oppressions affect health status we can look at our wellness within the broader social/political/economic context that is our reality. In this way, our efforts to promote our health are clearly political in nature as we take control of our lives and support each other to do the same.[53]

Politics were consistently at the center of the NBWHP's work at all levels, as is likely already evident from my discussion of its holistic and cultural approaches. However, in this section I aim to highlight not only how the NBWHP positioned health as a political issue—that is, as something that is both experienced within larger contexts of oppression and directly impacted by political policy—but also how it sought to raise political consciousness and political engagement among its membership. There are two aspects of the NBWHP's political approach to health that I highlight here: historicizing and contextualizing Black women's health and providing political education, empowerment, and training for Black women. These aspects of the NBWHP's political approach to health are examples of two trends in Black disability politics: taking a contextualized and historicized approach to disability in Black communities and simultaneously seeking both micro- and macrolevel change.

The first way the NBWHP took a political approach to health is by historicizing and contextualizing Black women's health within the legacies of racism, sexism, and classism in the United States. In a *Vital Signs* article titled "Slavery Still in Effect: Lamentables of a Women's Health Advocates [*sic*]," Marlene Braxton Fisher confronts the strong Black woman stereotype and its impact on Black women's physical, mental/emotional, and spiritual health.[54] She begins, "I always believed that African American women were physically, emotionally, and spiritually the strongest women in the world who could endure any hardship without lamentation. We are often encouraged to persevere [through] sickness and social ills by recanting the mythical stories of Amazon women of African descent."[55] Fisher details how the strong Black woman myth negatively impacted her own health and then returns to slavery, stating, "I learned a few facts about my mythical ancestors. Instead of being the inherently healthy, physically capable women I thought they were, female slaves were never even half as healthy as white women. How could they be healthy as malnourished and battered as they were?"[56] She follows this rhetorical question with details about the life span and health trends of enslaved Black women before making direct connections to health-care systems in the present, including the lack of inclusion of Black women in pharmaceutical trials. She concludes, "Medicine practiced to heal the masses does not take into account the tremendous pressure imposed on African Americans by poverty, racism and environmental stress.... We need attention that is real, constant and understands our culture."[57] This article is particularly emblematic of all three of the NBWHP's approaches to health—holistic, cultural, and political—in that Fisher includes her personal narrative, historical information, contemporary health statistics, pharmaceutical research information, and calls for political change all in one piece.

The historicizing of Black women's health continues in other articles and publications, which address how slavery, medical abuse, forced sterilization, and environmental racism have negatively impacted Black health for generations.[58] The NBWHP worked to trace and highlight these impacts in order to position health as always already a political issue for Black women. The organization, through publications, self-help groups, and workshops, sought to link histories of racialized and gendered violence to contemporary health concerns, including the impact of internalized oppression on individual Black women's health.

Importantly, although the primary focus of the NBWHP was addressing racial and gender oppression, in *Body and Soul* there is also brief engagement with the impact of ableist oppression on disabled Black women, though the term *ableism* is not used. The text contains five paragraphs on physical disability generally (mental disability is addressed separately later), including the story of a Black disabled woman named Janice Jackson. These paragraphs conclude the chapter on diseases most common among Black women, in which specific disabilities and potentially disabling diseases and conditions, including hypertension, cancer, diabetes, lupus, sickle cell disease, asthma, and chronic fatigue syndrome, are each provided lengthier and more focused discussion than physical disability as a whole. This general physical disability section places disabled people within the context of oppression, stating, "Having a disability of any kind can be difficult, especially in a world that generally ignores the physically and mentally challenged.... Ignorance of the differently abled extends beyond personal interactions. The rights of the blind, deaf, those who use wheelchairs, who speak different or are mentally challenged are too often disregarded." The text then emphasizes intersectionality, stating, "And the situation is worse for Blacks who are physically challenged: A recent congressional study reported that for the past thirty years African-Americans have been much more likely than whites to be rejected for benefits under Social Security disability programs. But many folks like Janice are forming support groups and fighting back against the insensitivity and discrimination so common in the 'abled' world."[59] The section concludes with a list of relevant books and organizations, ranging from national advocacy groups like the American Council of the Blind to more charity-oriented groups like the National Easter Seal Society and smaller support groups like the Black Women with Disabilities Alliance.[60] The engagement with physical disability in this section of the book reflects a clearly political understanding of disability and an acknowledgment of ableism. The language, however, runs the gamut from "confined to a wheelchair" and "physically and mentally challenged" to "differently abled" and "handicapped," which suggests that the leaders of the organization and the book editor were not well connected to or inclusive of disability rights activists in the 1990s, who had by that time moved to predominantly using *disability* over all of these other terms.[61] I provide further critique of the NBWHP's lack of engagement with contemporaneous disability rights movement work in praxis interlude 2.

The language used in the *Body and Soul* section on physical disability is another example of how Black disability politics have often emerged independently from mainstream disability rights even as the intent may be anti-ableist solidarity with disabled people. Scholars researching disability politics among Black and other marginalized groups typically excluded from the priorities and activities of the mainstream movement must not allow the use of outdated or ableist language alone to be the barometer of disability politics. As this chapter has already shown, the NBWHP was clearly invested in a social and political model of health that included disability.

Its political model of health has much in common with the social, political, and relational models of disability common in disability studies and disability activism today, but it is grounded in holistic and cultural approaches that strongly differentiate their approach from mainstream disability rights at that time. Part of my work here is not to claim that the NBWHP was perfect in its articulations and enactments of disability politics but rather to demonstrate that the organization is part of a legacy of Black disability politics that has been overlooked, ignored, misunderstood, and dismissed because of how it presents itself as race centered and not based in disability identity, thereby utilizing frameworks and language that sometimes conflict with standard practices in the white mainstream movement and "white disability studies."[62]

The second aspect of the NBWHP's political approach to health and well-being was its investment in political education, empowerment, and training, which included patient rights education, policy briefs, and training for political engagement through leadership institutes. In the organization's own words, "NBWHP works at the primary prevention level, with individuals and groups; at the community action level, where groups influence local health policies which affect them; and at the national policy level, where the perspectives of African American women influence policy makers and the public."[63] This part of the NBWHP's political approach to health demonstrates a commitment to both micro- and macrolevel change and an understanding of how progress at one level necessitates and encourages continued progress at the other. The NBWHP believed the adage that knowledge is power, but it also asserted that knowledge without the empowerment, means, and skills to use it is of little value to Black women. This sentiment is reflected in founder Byllye Avery's often shared experience early in her health activism of running a support group for fat Black women in which she realized that the women all understood what diet and exercise regimes were considered healthy, but the material circumstances of their lives made perfectly executing such regimes impossible.[64] In the end, Avery realized "that it's not just about giving information; people need something else," and this need for "something else" helped launch her vision for the NBWHP.[65] Throughout their work the NBWHP's political approach aimed to connect individual health education to individual and collective empowerment with the goal of widespread political and social change.

One way the NBWHP sought to empower Black women with knowledge and skills was via patient rights education. The organization believed in the need to be knowledgeable about one's own bodymind as well as about one's rights within the medical industrial complex. *Body and Soul*'s chapter 19, "Dealing with Doctors and Hospitals," enacts this combination of patient rights education and empowerment. The chapter provides questions to ask when choosing a new doctor; advice on how to prepare for a doctor's appointment; information on what to ask, expect, and do during a doctor visit; a descriptive list of medical specialists one might encounter in a hospital; and an example of a patient bill of rights from a Brooklyn hospital. Similarly, the NBWHP published *Vital Signs* articles in 1993 and 1994 that detailed how Black women with HIV/AIDS could qualify for Social Security disability benefits and gave instructions on how to apply.[66] By including such detailed information, the NBWHP taught Black women how to advocate for themselves and their loved ones within the medical-industrial complex. This information is particularly invaluable for Black disabled women and nondisabled Black women serving as caretakers for loved ones, as they are likely to have above-average amounts of interaction with medical professionals and are more likely to experience combinations of racism, sexism, ableism, and classism within medical interactions, which necessitates knowing one's rights. Patient rights education occurs similarly within disability activism and communities of people with similar disabilities, such as the contemporary chronic illness "spoonie" digital community, in which people share life hacks and tips on how to navigate complicated, bureaucratic, and oppressive health-care systems.[67]

In addition to the more individual, microlevel political education and empowerment of patient rights education, the NBWHP also sought to use a political approach to health to enact more macrolevel change via policy briefs and updates and training for political engagement. By encouraging Black women to be aware of planned policies that would impact their health and well-being and by teaching them how to respond to and impact local and national politics, the NBWHP not only supported Black women's politicized awareness of health but also provided training and support for them to take action. The majority of this more formal legislative and lobbying work occurred in the 1990s after the establishment of the NBWHP's Public Policy and Public Education Office in Washington, DC, which worked to disseminate "information, data and perspectives of Black women and the NBWHP Self-Help Network ... to broaden the national Reproductive Health/Rights Agenda; and to promote public policies for the improved health status of Black women, their children and communities."[68]

From 1991 to 1999, the NBWHP regularly published a featured section called "Public Education and Policy" in *Vital Signs*. This section contained position statements, policy briefs, and legislative updates on topics such as health-care reform, abortion, birth control, welfare reform, family and medical leave, and sexual and domestic violence. This was part of the organization's new policy committee, which, according to a *Vital Signs* update on organizational governance, aimed to "bring to the membership major policy statements about positions affecting ourselves, our families and our communities" while also "testifying in Congress, allied with other women's organizations in the struggle for change, and empowering our membership through education and information exchange."[69] The NBWHP did not, however, simply provide this information to the membership. As this quote suggests, the NBWHP aimed to empower members to do something in response to local, state, and federal policies impacting their health by publicizing political-action events such as marches, demonstrations, and days of solidarity as well as by creating institutes and trainings to develop individual Black women's health activist skills and engagement.

Early in the organization's history, the NBWHP established ways for members, particularly self-help group leaders, to come together for community and education. This occurred through the Self-Help Developers Task Force meetings, annual conferences, retreats, and leadership institutes. The meetings and institutes for self-help group developers and local NBWHP chapter leaders were intended "to increase skills; identify problems; share information regarding the status of the self-help group process; identify emerging health trends and developments among the membership; discuss and evaluate the effectiveness of various program models that are being used and tested in the field; discuss national public policy issues; and develop strategies for more effective utilization of social service and preventive health resources at the local and national levels."[70] Additionally, Black women not yet established as leaders of self-help groups or local chapters could develop their own leadership skills through workshops at annual conferences. For example, the 1993 conference included one workshop on public policy that aimed to teach attendees "how to become an active participant in health advocacy at the local, national, and global level"; and another workshop for general leadership training sought to show participants "how to become an effective leader in your community through 'grassroots' organizing, networking, and coalition building."[71] These multiple leadership development opportunities, combined with the patient rights and policy education provided through NBWHP publications, sought to ensure that Black women had the information, confidence, skills, and support to enact change in their local communities as well as at the state and national levels if they so desired.

The two major aspects of the NBWHP's political approach to health, historicizing Black women's health in the context of oppression and providing political education, empowerment, and training, are perhaps best summarized by the organization's health information booklet *Our Bodies, Our Voices, Our Choices*. The booklet states that the NBWHP operates on the "fundamental belief" that "every woman—whether heterosexual, bisexual, or lesbian—may substantially increase her chances of achieving overall health and well-being if: She is knowledgeable about her body; she is aware of her rights and empowered to ask necessary questions; and she knows that she is entitled to information and services that are delivered with dignity and respect. We also believe that when women appreciate how history and contemporary events combine to impact our ability to make decisions and to have choices, they will want to get politically involved on matters close to home, across the nation, or around the world."[72] Here it is clear how the multiple tactics within the NBWHP's political approach to health and wellness come together into a single Black feminist health activist mission that sought radical and revolutionary change. Although the organization became less grassroots oriented over time, focusing more on policy, lobbying, and research funding, this eventual organizational transformation does not negate the important intersectional, multimodal work it performed in the 1980s and 1990s to improve health outcomes for Black women and their communities.[73]

Conclusion

Together, holistic, cultural, and political approaches to health shape the way the NBWHP articulated and enacted its particular form of Black disability politics. The individual aspects of each of these three approaches illustrate all of the common qualities of Black disability politics generally. The NBWHP's approaches to health were intersectional but race centered, not based in disability identity, historicized and contextualized, and holistic. Understanding the history and mission of the organization and its holistic, cultural, and political approaches to health allows us to trace how the NBWHP engaged with disability in politicized ways.

There are several important lessons to be drawn from the Black disability politics of the NBWHP. First, the organization's work clearly demonstrates how health activism can be inclusive of disability politics even as the work may emphasize concepts of health, wellness, and healing typically considered antithetical to disability inclusion and acceptance. Indeed, it is critical that scholars take culturally contextualized approaches to analyzing health activism and engagement with alternative healing practices, especially spiritual ones, within racialized, poor, and otherwise marginalized communities in order to understand the place of disability and disabled people within such work. I want to emphasize again here that the role of spirituality in the NBWHP's health triad is important, and yet disability studies has few to no frameworks for discussing the spiritual beliefs and practices of disabled people, particularly disabled people of color. This is work that needs to be taken up by Black studies and Black theology scholars in conversation with existing work in disability studies.

This chapter has provided an overview of the history of the NBWHP, followed by a detailed analysis of how the organization engaged with disability and included disabled Black women within its holistic, cultural, and political approaches to health. My aim here has been to highlight the varied ways disability is included, engaged with, and politicized within the NBWHP's publications, programming, and overall Black feminist health activist philosophy in order to frame the organization's work as engaged in Black disability politics. This broader overview of the NBWHP's engagement with disability lays the foundation for the next chapter, which takes a more focused look at the organization's work regarding HIV/AIDS specifically. This second chapter on the NBWHP allows for a deeper understanding of how the holistic, cultural, and political approaches to health discussed here played out in programming and publications aimed at supporting Black women with disabilities and chronic diseases. In particular, I build on the framework-oriented work of this chapter to specifically engage with how health activist work that promotes prevention or reduction of potentially disabling diseases and conditions can still be anti-ableist when it is combined with work to support existing disabled people.

4

MORE THAN JUST PREVENTION

The NBWHP and the Black
Disability Politics of HIV/AIDS

In an informational packet for potential new members, the New York chapter of the National Black Women's Health Project (NBWHP) asserts, "The complexity and diversity of health problems experienced by Black women requires a comprehensive plan of action with strategies designed to identify and eliminate root causes, promote prevention and wellness by creating new healthy ways of living and relating, early diagnosis, treatment and follow-up, and maintenance of life with as much comfort, independence, dignity and joy for everyone, including those who have severe disabilities, or are chronically or terminally ill."[1] This statement reflects how the organization's holistic, political, and cultural approach to health was not focused on prevention alone; rather, the NBWHP's Black feminist health activism also sought to support people with disabilities.

There are three main parts of the "comprehensive plan of action" articulated by the New York chapter's informational packet. First, "to identify and eliminate root causes" of health problems, as the previous chapter discussed, meant dealing with all of the larger social and political issues that shape and limit life choices for Black women.[2] Second, "to promote prevention and wellness" through "*new* healthy ways of living *and relating*" included regular engagement with the medical industrial complex to receive early diagnoses and treatment if necessary.[3] Here I emphasize *new* and *relating* because although the NBWHP promoted typical public health agendas, such as receiving regular checkups and understanding basic health practices regarding eating and exercise, the organization also addressed mental, emotional, and spiritual wellness in a politicized fashion that changed the way Black women related to themselves and to other Black women, particularly via understanding the role of oppression in their lives. Third, and most important for the purposes of this chapter, the New York chapter of the NBWHP argues here that the final part of a comprehensive health activist action plan is to help people, including disabled and chronically ill people, maintain their lives with "as much comfort, independence, dignity and joy" as possible.[4] The explicit inclusion of disabled and chronically or terminally ill people in this action plan is indicative of how the organization understood health activism to be about not only prevention and awareness but also material support for people with disabilities, illnesses, diseases, and other health concerns. This chapter explores how the NBWHP balanced prevention and public health education with support for disabled people, specifically in its Black feminist health activism on HIV/AIDS.

In addition to the ways Black disability politics were articulated generally in the philosophy and mission of the NBWHP, as discussed in the previous chapter, the organization also enacted Black disability politics in its work on HIV/AIDS. The NBWHP addressed HIV/AIDS in a dual-pronged fashion that aimed simultaneously to reduce the number of new HIV infections and provide material and social support for Black women living with HIV/AIDS. I use the NBWHP's HIV/AIDS work to demonstrate how health activism that attempts to reduce the incidence or severity of disability, illness, and disease can nonetheless participate in disability politics by aligning with and supporting those already disabled, sick, or ill. The NBWHP illustrates how public health initiatives can work in antiracist, feminist, and anti-ableist ways when grounded in the experience and expertise of multiply marginalized people. Further, the approaches the NBWHP used in this work model central qualities of Black disability politics by connecting the racial disparities of the AIDS epidemic at the time to racism, sexism, classism, and ableism within public health and medicine in the United States. This politicized prevention work emphasized how the racism, sexism, and classism undergirding mainstream American understandings of and approaches to sexual health actually exacerbated the prevalence and severity of sexually transmitted infections and diseases in Black communities. The NBWHP argued for, and at times created, culturally specific approaches to education, prevention, and support in regard to HIV/AIDS. As a result, the NBWHP's HIV/AIDS work is another example of how Black disability politics often operate differently from white mainstream disability rights work by necessity.

In what follows, I first provide a historical and theoretical overview of the AIDS crisis in the 1980s and 1990s, with an emphasis on the role of race, gender, and disability within the medical, cultural, and activist discourses at that time. I then provide analysis of the NBWHP's work on HIV/AIDS, demonstrating how its Black feminist health activism balanced prevention with support. This work was intersectional but centered on race and gender, contextualized, and holistic. More specifically, the NBWHP's Black feminist health activism on HIV/AIDS models how Black disability politics can fight the ways racism and ableism intersect and collude in the lives of Black people without distancing them from disabled people or using disability as a static symbol of violence, trauma, or neglect.

HIV/AIDS: Historical and Theoretical Overview

There are numerous useful and important histories of the AIDS epidemic from various social, political, medical, activist, and identity perspectives.[5] For the purposes of my arguments here, I want to briefly cover the specific racial, gendered, and disability history of the epidemic to provide the cultural backdrop against which the NBWHP was performing its work regarding HIV/AIDS among Black women. This section therefore provides a historical and theoretical overview of the relationship of HIV/AIDS to disability, womanhood, and Blackness in the United States in the 1980s and 1990s, the period of the NBWHP's work on HIV/AIDS under discussion in this chapter.

In 1981 AIDS first became a medical epidemiological concern when hundreds of predominantly white gay men had documented cases of severe immune deficiency.[6] Initially, medical professionals and laypeople alike assumed that the disease occurred primarily or even exclusively among gay men, who were also at the forefront of early activism around the disease. In addition to gay men, in the first few years of the US epidemic, HIV infection was also associated with intravenous drug users. In fact, the first documented cases of HIV in women occurred in 1982, primarily among intravenous drug users and sexual partners of intravenous drug users.[7] Despite these early cases, it was not until 1995 that women were more fully recognized as part of the epidemic and that symptoms more common among women with HIV, such as chronic yeast infections, were added to the list of AIDS symptoms.[8] In a similar fashion, although there are early documented cases of AIDS among people of color, particularly among Haitians and gay men of color, it wasn't until 1986 that Black and Latino populations were identified as disproportionately impacted by HIV/AIDS and therefore in need of targeted preventive care and testing.[9] By 1990 Black people represented 28 percent of AIDS cases, despite making up only 12 percent of the total US population at that time. These numbers continued to increase, with Black people representing 40 percent of AIDS cases in 1995 and 57 percent in 1998.[10] In short, although the AIDS epidemic has been most firmly associated with white gay men in medicine, in the media, and among the general lay population, HIV/AIDS cases have never been exclusively among this population, and, in fact, by the 1990s the epidemic was increasingly impacting Black people and women.

The cultural association of HIV/AIDS with white gay men stems in part from the incredible activism that emerged in the wake of the epidemic. White gay men, many of whom had access to not only medicine and wealth but also media and arts outlets, organized quickly and loudly, demanding medical services, research, social services, and real concern for those sick and dying in their communities. As Nancy E. Stoller documents, many women, the majority of whom were white and/or lesbian, were also directly involved in the earliest stages of activism even though most were not HIV positive. In contrast, for numerous reasons, including the association of the disease with gay men and drug users, Black communities were slower to respond collectively to HIV/AIDS, but eventually this activism did emerge. The work of the NBWHP on HIV/AIDS in the 1980s and 1990s therefore was on the cutting edge in many ways. It was one of the earliest Black organizations to mobilize around the disease and the first to focus on Black women's experience with HIV/AIDS specifically. The NBWHP's activism in this area has not been discussed in other histories of the disease in part because the organization was not exclusively focused on HIV/AIDS activism but also because the NBWHP was based in Atlanta and Washington, DC, whereas most major HIV/AIDS activist efforts in this period were based in either New York or San Francisco due to the size of these cities and their statistically larger population of gay men.

In terms of disability, as early as 1985 AIDS activists, such as those involved with the National Association of People with AIDS, were using rhetoric similar to that of disability activists, resisting their positioning as passive patients or dying victims and explicitly linking their fight to the civil rights, feminist, and disability rights movements.[11] In the late 1980s, as disability rights activists worked to get the Americans with Disabilities Act (ADA) passed, the inclusion of people with HIV/AIDS was a sticking point for many conservative politicians, who associated the virus and disease with homosexuality and drug use and wanted HIV/AIDS to be removed from the legislation as a condition covered by the ADA.[12] In fact, in her history of the ADA, Ruth Colker writes that "the primary source of controversy under the ADA was an exemption for restaurants so that they could fail to employ individuals who were HIV-positive."[13] Despite this controversy and the unabashedly homophobic resistance to the protection of people with HIV/AIDS, disabled activists and Democratic politicians who were authoring the legislation refused to change their position, and HIV/AIDS remained a disability condition under the ADA.[14]

Notwithstanding this political alliance and recourse to related activist discourses, as Robert McRuer writes, "people with other disabilities have at times, over the course of the epidemic, distanced themselves from the concerns of people with AIDS."[15] This distancing has occurred not only within disability activism and community work but also within disability studies. Despite the continued cultural impact of HIV on multiple marginalized communities, including queer men, Black people, Latinx people, sex workers, and people living with drug addictions, disability studies as a field has had limited engagement with HIV/AIDS.[16] Generally this exclusion aligns with the lack of engagement with chronic illnesses and diseases in the field, especially those like HIV/AIDS and diabetes that are stigmatized via association with personal failure (to use a condom, to maintain a certain weight or diet, etc.). Further, as feminist disability scholars Alison Kafer and Julie Avril Minich have each noted, the disabling conditions most often left out of conversations and theorizations within disability studies are also primarily those associated with people in poverty and people of color.[17] Disability studies scholars studying and analyzing HIV/AIDS as a medical, political, and social concern, however, make clear that "the cultural management of AIDS is of a piece with the cultural management of disability."[18] Disability studies theories and frameworks therefore strongly inform my interpretation of the NBWHP's HIV/AIDS Black feminist health activism as Black disability politics. I draw more heavily in this chapter, however, on work in the fields of Black studies, queer studies, and gender studies, which each have longer and more robust histories of scholarly engagement with HIV/AIDS, even though this engagement has not tended to take a disability studies approach or even to conceptualize HIV/AIDS as disability.[19]

Balancing Prevention and Support: A Black Feminist Health Activist Approach to the AIDS Crisis

In line with its overarching political, cultural, and holistic approach to health and wellness, the NBWHP understood the AIDS epidemic in the Black community, particularly among Black women, as a political and social concern rooted in health-care access, racism and sexism among medical and public health practitioners, and patriarchal sexual norms. The NBWHP's approach to HIV/AIDS was intersectional but centered on race and gender, not based on disability identity, contextualized and historicized, and holistic. As stated in a 1988 "AIDS Education Project Proposal," the NBWHP aimed to "promote individual and collective behavioral changes that will lessen the risk and potential deaths of Black women and children from AIDS."[20] Concretely, this promotion of individual and societal/collective change manifested through coverage in its organizational newsletter/magazine, *Vital Signs* (including special issues focused on HIV/AIDS in 1994 and 1995; the former of which is shown in figure 4.1); a chapter on HIV/AIDS in its health self-help book *Body and Soul: The Black Women's Guide to Physical Health and Emotional Well-Being*; panels, speeches, and workshops at NBWHP annual conferences; a special conference focused entirely on HIV/AIDS and Black women; and the development of culturally specific HIV/AIDS programming. According to the organization's AIDS program report in 1989, between July 1988 and January 1989, 2,410 people participated in NBWHP AIDS Program presentations, workshops, and self-help groups, and 73.8 percent of participants were Black women.[21] These numbers underscore the significance and impact of the NBWHP's work in this area. In addressing the AIDS epidemic, the NBWHP balanced attempts to prevent the spread of HIV/AIDS with work to socially and materially support Black women already living with HIV/AIDS. This combined approach represents an enactment of Black disability politics because the NBWHP approached the AIDS epidemic as a political concern inextricably tied to racial and gender identities, experiences, and norms and did so in a fashion that refused to stigmatize or abandon disabled Black people.

Generally, prevention of illness and disease is taken as an inherent, unquestionable good in American culture. And yet the medical research and public health practices that have undertaken the prevention of illness and disease have historically entailed abuses of power that subject marginalized populations, especially the disabled, people of color, and the poor, to isolation, incarceration, medical experimentation, and nonconsensual or nontherapeutic medical treatment in the name of the common good.[22] Part of the challenge of contemporary work in disability studies, especially work at the intersections of disability and race, gender, sexuality, or class, is to offer historicized and contextualized analyses of specific medical and public health practices. This includes critical interrogation of prevention practices as political because the idea of prevention as an inherent good relies on larger cultural conceptions of cure.

FIGURE 4.1
Cover of the 1994
Vital Signs special
issue on HIV.

Cure has long been the object of critique in disability studies as an able-ist trope that assumes that all disabled people desire to be nondisabled and that nondisabled lives are inherently better, easier, more productive, or more valuable than disabled lives. Eli Clare argues that the ideology of cure in American culture includes not only cure strictly defined as the complete elimination of disability, disease, illness, or infirmity but also diagnosis, treatment, management, rehabilitation, and prevention. Clare writes that cure as ideology is "an inflexible set of values" that requires identifying and locating bodymind damage or harm and seeking an original, supposedly superior state of no harm, but cure as practice is "multifaceted and con-tradictory ... [with] thousands of different technologies and processes. Each variation comes with its own cluster of risks and possibilities."[23] In other words, engagement with the many practices that fall under the um-brella of cure, such as prevention, means dealing with the messy dangers and potentials of each individual practice. Further, I would add that we must perform this engagement with sustained attention to the sociohistorical context, power dynamics, and people involved in the use of these practices.

My engagement with prevention in this chapter therefore bears in mind prevention's relationship to ableist discourses of cure while recognizing that, as scholars of chronic illness have explored, there cannot be a singular approach to cure and prevention practices when the bodymind effects of different disabilities vary so widely and can include pain and other effects that disabled individuals may seek to lessen or be rid of entirely.[24]

In this portion of the chapter, I first explore how the NBWHP took a Black feminist approach to the prevention of HIV through culturally based education initiatives that included work to destigmatize HIV. I then discuss how this destigmatization work served as the bridge to other work the NBWHP performed to materially and socially support Black women with HIV/AIDS. While many organizations undertook similar combined prevention-support approaches to the AIDS crisis during this period, the attention to race, gender, and disability as mutually constitutive categories within the NBWHP's Black feminist health activism represents a little-discussed and intellectually instructive example of enacting Black disability politics.[25]

Prevention

The NBWHP recognized that to reduce the devastating mental, emotional, and financial toll the AIDS crisis was taking on Black communities, especially urban poor ones, efforts to prevent the spread of HIV had to take into account cultural norms within these communities in regard to sex/sexuality, gender, drug use, and engagement with medical professionals. The NBWHP critiqued existing prevention models formulated with or based on white communities, stating in a 1988 AIDS Education Project Proposal:

> The messages designed to make a difference appear to be geared to the white population, are developed primarily among white professionals with little input from or representation by minority group members, and do not reflect the thinking or mores of the ethnic communities most at risk.... Further, these messages are inconsiderate of family planning beliefs, sexual behaviors, and religious attitudes of many of the people they profess to be interested in serving. Thus, there is a very real gap in the intent of the messages and their overall effectiveness in reaching and modifying or changing behaviors in order to save lives.[26]

The NBWHP aimed to fill this gap by creating educational publications and programming aimed at HIV prevention that took "into consideration many of the cultural and religious beliefs which form the norm for behaviors within our community" with an "increased focus on the psychological/sociological issues that operate in the lives of the majority of Black women, whether adolescent or mature, which impact on their relationships, reproductive rights, and sexuality decisions."[27] These quotes demonstrate the overarching politics and ethics of the NBWHP's HIV/AIDS work, which sought to understand and promote the particular needs of Black communities, especially Black women, to reduce the severity of the epidemic among Black people. Importantly, the NBWHP aimed to do this work in a way that understood HIV/AIDS not as an exclusively personal, medical concern but rather as a political issue inextricably tied to race and gender in its transmission and in its representation in medical literature and mainstream media.

The NBWHP's prevention work operated primarily in the realm of education with an emphasis on educating Black women. The NBWHP created HIV/AIDS education materials and workshops that were attuned to the norms and needs of their primary audience. These materials first aimed to debunk myths about who is infected by the disease, how the disease is spread, and how the disease can be detected, making clear that Black people, straight people, and lesbians can all contract HIV.[28] The debunking of myths was essential because of the widespread misinformation in Black communities about HIV/AIDS due to its association with white gay men. The NBWHP's first goal in its HIV/AIDS prevention work was to make Black women aware that anyone could contract HIV. The organization then aimed to create safer-sex education materials that addressed specific concerns about and barriers to safer sex for Black women. This included non-HIV/AIDS-specific materials like the NBWHP's Plain Talk program, which facilitated discussions between Black teenage girls and their mothers about sex, and the NBWHP's fight to break "the conspiracy of silence" in Black communities regarding intercommunal sexual and domestic violence.[29] These other programs and initiatives not focused exclusively on HIV/AIDS complemented and supported the NBWHP's HIV/AIDS-specific programs and publications targeted at Black women because one cannot understand a social problem outside of its social context. The NBWHP made clear that understanding and addressing how sexuality is discussed and experienced in Black communities is essential to any public sexual health initiative that wants to reach Black people.

For example, in one of her multiple *Vital Signs* articles on HIV/AIDS, Dazon Dixon reflects on her experience hosting safer-sex parties for Black women, which taught her the complexities of sexual choice and freedom. She writes, "We facilitators learned quickly that there were many things on these women's agendas that came way ahead of AIDS or condoms or even sex. 'What about my man who beats on me? I'd rather f__ him than fight him' one stated. 'How you expect me to deal with finding some condoms when I can't even find a job or a man with a job?' another queried."[30] In a later article, Dixon elaborates for *Vital Signs* readers how simply telling Black women to make men use condoms is pointless if organizations do not address the general lack of sexual freedom for Black women, which may prevent them from safely advocating for their sexual health needs. She asks:

> What about the women who fear getting beat if they change the dinner plans, much less their sex lives? What about the women who just don't have the equal power in their heterosexual relationships to say what they want, when they want and how they want? Who supports and talks openly with the women who have had sexual violence or abuse in their histories and can't even relate to their sexual selves yet, much less someone else's hang-ups? Do we honestly expect that the messages around the connections between all sexually transmitted diseases including HIV/AIDS are going to suddenly galvanize struggling women into doing things differently than from what we've been taught and socialized to do for generations?[31]

In each of these articles, Dixon makes clear that educational materials and prevention programs that do not understand or address the reality of Black women's sexual lives will be simply ignored or forgotten as the suggestions will seem impossible to implement. Further, the NBWHP argued that presenting strategies like "use a condom" and "get tested regularly" as simple, easy, and straightforward things one can and should do to protect against HIV infection creates distance, distrust, or lack of faith in public health officials and organizations because such things are not simple and straightforward for many Black women and other multiply marginalized people. Such ignorance of the realities of Black women's lives on the part of public health researchers and practitioners results in Black communities being more severely impacted by sexual and other public health crises, increasing the likelihood of Black disablement, debilitation, or death. To counter the failures and ignorance of existing public health approaches to HIV/AIDS in Black communities, the NBWHP created educational prevention materials and programs that acknowledged and attended to the lived realities of their target audience.

To address the needs of Black women, the NBWHP disseminated and/or presented its own tailored prevention and education materials and workshops in spaces with the widest impact and reach in Black communities.

The NBWHP ran workshops and self-help groups in community centers and neighborhood churches, where Black women were more likely to show up and feel comfortable talking about intimate issues like sex. Also in line with bringing the work to the communities one intends to impact, the NBWHP also organized educational workshops for Black beauticians because of the central role and influence of the Black beauty shop in Black women's lives and communities.[32] All of these place-based initiatives allowed the NBWHP to do HIV/AIDS prevention and education work in Black-women-exclusive or Black-women-dominant groups where speaking and asking questions about sex and sexuality would likely feel safer. The choice of culturally specific locations in which to disseminate HIV/AIDS prevention education is also important because it moves public health education out of the space of clinics and schools and into places that feel more comfortable for many Black women, places they already frequent on a regular basis.

In addition to debunking myths, addressing barriers to safer sex for Black women, and disseminating information in key locations in Black communities, all of the NBWHP's culturally specific prevention education also consistently politicized HIV/AIDS by connecting the disease to larger sociopolitical issues central to Black communities and Black empowerment. This broad, intersectional, contextualized approach to HIV/AIDS is a major reason I argue that the NBWHP's HIV/AIDS prevention work enacts Black disability politics. In *Vital Signs*, Dixon writes, "If AIDS has done nothing else, it has magnified all the social, political, health and economic problems that have plagued people of color, especially African-Americans.... Many educators and activists in the Black community feel AIDS is a part of the bigger picture for survival, and not an isolated, number-one priority."[33] This quote demonstrates how the NBWHP's HIV/AIDS work was disability inclusive rather than disability centered because HIV/AIDS was and is one of many health and wellness issues facing Black communities—issues that require Black disability political approaches. This perspective is further emphasized in the conference report "From Cries and Whispers to Action: African-American Women Respond to AIDS," in which the NBWHP specifically names medical racism, health-care access, reproductive justice, and the prison industrial complex as political issues for Black people that intersect with the spread of HIV/AIDS in Black communities.[34] By placing HIV/AIDS into a larger social and political context, the NBWHP emphasized that all Black people should be aware of and care about the spread of HIV/AIDS.

Part of the NBWHP's goal in this broader politicization of HIV/AIDS for HIV-negative Black people was to destigmatize the disease. Destigmatization for the NBWHP involved reducing blame or moralizing around HIV/AIDS, including addressing the role of homophobia in the Black community and discussing the complexities of drug use and sex work among Black people.[35] By moving away from the individualized, moralized approach to HIV/AIDS that blamed people for their own disease or disablement, the NBWHP promoted a clearly politicized understanding of this disabling disease. By destigmatizing the disease and positioning it as a Black community political concern, the organization encouraged HIV-negative Black people to move into an ally role for people with HIV/AIDS. Destigmatization and politicization therefore serve as bridges between the NBWHP's prevention education work and its work to directly support Black women with HIV/AIDS. While debunking myths and destigmatizing the disease in its prevention work, the NBWHP actively encouraged social support of people with HIV/AIDS on individual and collective, micro and macro, levels. For example, "From Cries and Whispers to Action" states: "Just as critical as individual support from family, sisters and lovers, is for that support to be multiplied into strong organizational advocacy for better care and treatment of African-American women with AIDS. In other words, sisterhood means not only the demonstration of individual kindness, but a willingness to speak openly within the organizations in our lives to call for a change in the health care system's AIDS policies."[36] This statement is followed by a discussion of the role of the church and the ways Black women can help churches move forward in responding to the AIDS crisis. Here it becomes clear how the NBWHP not only aimed to prevent the spread of HIV/AIDS in Black communities through culturally specific educational materials and workshops disseminated in culturally relevant locations in Black communities but also sought to destigmatize and politicize HIV/AIDS. In doing so, the NBWHP laid the groundwork for increased social, political, and material support of Black women living with HIV/AIDS.

Support

What makes the NBWHP's Black feminist health activism on HIV/AIDS truly an enactment of Black disability politics is the way its prevention work bridged into work to support people already living with HIV/AIDS. As discussed in praxis interlude 1, prevention alone, no matter how politicized or culturally attuned, can easily veer into ableist tendencies to use disability as a scare tactic if that prevention work is not grounded in support of disabled people as well. The NBWHP's support work occurred in part through its above-discussed work to destigmatize the disease. In addition, however, the NBWHP also advocated for and sometimes actively provided social and material support for Black women with HIV/AIDS.

One way the NBWHP provided support to Black women with HIV/AIDS was by publishing numerous stories in *Vital Signs* that aimed to build a community among Black women with HIV/AIDS where they could share knowledge and fight internalized oppression or shame.[37] Articles were written by Black women living with HIV/AIDS as well as by HIV-negative Black women involved with HIV/AIDS activism in Black communities. As a whole, however, the NBWHP tried to center the voices and experiences of Black women with HIV/AIDS, including Black lesbians with HIV, who were almost nonexistent in most literature on the epidemic at the time.[38] This centering of the voices of those most impacted by the epidemic and the need to provide broad forms of support for people with HIV/AIDS are most clearly articulated in the proceedings of and publications resulting from a conference on Black women and AIDS organized by the NBWHP in 1988—important archival material that I discuss at length here.

According to the conference report, "FROM CRIES AND WHISPERS TO ACTION: BLACK WOMEN TALKING ABOUT AIDS was a strategy development conference for Black women leaders sponsored by the National Black Women's Health Project (NBWHP) on October 17–18, 1988 in Washington, D.C. This 'think-tank' conference was a first-time opportunity for Black women, who are most severely affected by the AIDS crisis, to meet on a national level. We were women living with HIV/AIDS (PWAs), advocates, caregivers, health and social service providers, educators, and government representatives."[39] As this description indicates, the conference aimed to bring together a variety of Black women leaders invested in addressing the AIDS epidemic. The conference was organized into three panels of speakers, one made up of women with AIDS speaking about their experiences and needs, a second made up of government representatives, and a third made up of service/advocacy representatives. Each panel was followed by a small-group discussion session in the model of the NBWHP's self-help groups, with preassigned groups of Black women with and without HIV/AIDS. The conference report transcribes the panel discussions and features the stories of the individual women with HIV/AIDS who spoke about their experiences. The report also offers strategies collectively created by the conference attendees. These strategies highlight not only how the NBWHP framed HIV/AIDS as a social and political issue for Black communities, as already addressed, but also how the organization explicitly centered and politicized the need to provide better social and material support for people with HIV/AIDS.

Before offering solutions and strategies, however, the conference report first acknowledges the way stigma impacts people with HIV/AIDS above and beyond any physical symptoms of the disease. The report asserts: "The AIDS stigma, combined with existing racist, sexist and homophobic prejudices, produces discrimination against PWAs, and others who are associated with AIDS in any way. People with AIDS often face abandonment by families and friends, loss of their jobs and health insurance, and eviction from their homes. Many are denied needed services such as ambulance transportation or emergency medical and emotional care. PWAs especially at risk of discrimination are those who have been stigmatized as a class—IV drug users, homosexuals, prostitutes, and (until recently) Haitians—who have been beaten up, bankrupted, evicted, and now disproportionately infected."[40] Here the NBWHP indicates that although people with HIV/AIDS unquestionably need quality medical care, a significant barrier to living well with HIV/AIDS is social stigma and discrimination. As a result, the conference report (and the subsequent HIV/AIDS programs and educational materials developed from the ideas generated at the conference) emphasized the need to support people with HIV/AIDS and their family members and caretakers physically, emotionally, socially, and financially. In doing so, the conference report also situates HIV/AIDS for Black women in political relationship to health-care reform, welfare reform, reproductive justice, and housing rights to build coalitions. These larger political arguments are an example of how the NBWHP, while deeply focused on microlevel (individual) changes, also pushed for macrolevel (national) policy changes, viewing these arenas as interconnected and inextricable from one another in the effort to minimize or eliminate the AIDS epidemic.

Following the conference and its resulting publications, the NBWHP used the knowledge and momentum gained there to create programming that would more immediately support individuals with HIV/AIDS. First, the NBWHP created self-help groups for Black women with HIV/AIDS. As one informational publication explains, "Self-help is one mechanism for demonstrating what many African-American women with AIDS frequently ask for—a sense of sisterhood. They note that counselors and service providers who visit them in hospitals and shelters are often people who cannot empathize with and understand their concerns. Most of these people are white and demonstrate a limited appreciation of the impact of racism on African-American

AIDS sufferers' lives."[41] By creating self-help groups specifically for Black women with HIV/AIDS, the NBWHP created spaces for these women to form communities, share information, and provide hope to one another in ways that drew on their particular gendered and racialized experiences of the disease. These groups addressed a need for specific kinds of connection and support for Black disabled women, a need examined just a few years earlier in Audre Lorde's *Cancer Journals*, published in 1980. In this text, one often discussed in feminist disability studies, Lorde reflects on how the white, straight woman who brought her a pink lambswool temporary prosthetic breast could not understand or talk with her about what a mastectomy or breast augmentation might mean for her as a Black lesbian.[42] Instead, Lorde seeks advice and conversation from other lesbian breast cancer survivors and discusses the need for breast cancer survivors generally to be able to publicly identify and connect with one another.[43] In a related fashion, the NBWHP responded to the frustration of Black women with HIV/AIDS with white counselors and health-care providers who did not understand their experiences, concerns, and needs by creating self-help groups specifically for Black women with HIV/AIDS.

In addition to this more direct form of support for Black women with HIV/AIDS, the NBWHP also created programming for people without HIV/AIDS that ultimately aimed to improve support for people with HIV/AIDS as well. For instance, the NBWHP proposed creating "self-help/support groups for 'first line' health care workers: orderlies, nurses' aides, licensed practical nurses who, due to their often-invalidated role within the system, may allow unexpressed fears, prejudices and attitudes to influence their interactions with potential AIDS/HIV-infected patients."[44] Although it is unclear based on archival records if funding was secured to create these groups, the idea itself is incredibly important. Using the information gathered from talking directly with Black women with HIV/AIDS about their primary needs and concerns, the NBWHP sought to educate and support the first-line health-care workers who have the most contact with people with HIV/AIDS in medical settings. The NBWHP also recognized that these first-line workers, unlike doctors, are often working-class people who, despite spending the most time with patients, are generally provided less professional develop-ment and support in addressing their own biases and areas of ignorance. As the education proposal explains, "Our support group development will provide a safe, trusting atmoshpere [*sic*] in which these workers can consider and confront the myths and misinformation that may prevail among them, and be supported and appreciated for their pivotal role in the dispensing of care and attention to AIDS patients and their families."[45] Similar to the conference report's assertion that the family members of people with HIV/AIDS need financial, social, and emotional support, here the NBWHP sought to provide and improve support for people with HIV/AIDS by also addressing the educational and support needs of those who directly provide their health care.

Overall, the NBWHP took a holistic approach to providing support for Black women with HIV/AIDS, including publications prioritizing their voices and stories, self-help groups specifically for Black women with HIV/AIDS, and efforts to educate and support the individuals with the most direct contact with people with HIV/AIDS, such as family members, caretakers, and first-line health-care workers. The NBWHP's efforts to create material and social support for Black women with HIV/AIDS, whom I consider Black disabled women, occurred alongside its prevention work within Black communities, demonstrating a careful, balanced enactment of Black disability politics.

Conclusion

The NBWHP's balance of prevention and support in its HIV/AIDS Black feminist health activism reflected the organization's political, cultural, and holistic understanding of health and wellness, discussed in the previous chapter, and also enacted Black disability politics. The organization unquestionably approached HIV/AIDS as a Black disability political concern that required an intersectional, contextual approach that attended to change on micro and macro levels in order to be effective. The way the NBWHP balanced prevention and education targeted at nondisabled people with education, support, and resources targeted at disabled people is also reflected in other disease/impairment-specific activism, such as the NBWHP's work on mental health, depression, and suicide. This balance of prevention and support therefore reflects the Black disability politics of the organization overall, not just in regard to HIV/AIDS. Throughout its Black feminist health activism, the NBWHP never acted as if the mythical norm of total able-bodiedness or able-mindedness was achievable; rather, the organization sought a future in which people could make informed choices about their bodyminds and be supported, not shamed, in their health and disability statuses.

In this regard, the NBWHP's Black feminist health activism explored here and in the previous chapter provides a potential model for bridging disability studies/disability justice and public health research and programming. There is limited engagement with disability studies in public health scholarship.

As Elena M. Andresen acknowledges, there are conflicts between public health and disability studies methodologies, particularly when it comes to perspectives on prevention work. Andresen writes, "For many people in disability studies, and certainly for disability advocates, talking about prevention of disability suggests prevention of people with disabilities," whereas in public health it refers to "prevention of incidence and severity of injury, impairments, diagnoses, and conditions" via education and laws, such as seatbelt laws to reduce incidence of spinal cord and head injuries or prenatal nutrition education to reduce the likelihood and severity of certain congenital disabilities. Public health does not, Andresen notes, consider eugenic methods like abortion and euthanasia part of prevention work.[46] However, as Katharine Hayward argues, "Past public health campaigns have played upon emotions of fear generated by possible disability to advocate desired health practices," thus alienating and further marginalizing people with disabilities as "bad outcomes" to be avoided and even potentially blamed for their own disability status, such as in antismoking ads that depict sad, isolated individuals with oxygen tanks or drunk-driving-prevention commercials that depict sad, isolated people in wheelchairs. Hayward acknowledges that public health work uses both medical and social models of disability, with some campaigns, research, and programs leaning more heavily toward one model than the other. The variability of public health campaigns across time, space, and communities further necessitates close interrogation of specific initiatives and interventions, from their undergirding ideological assumptions to their potential impacts, materially and socially, on target populations.[47] In other words, when bringing together public health and disability studies scholarship, we ought to ask, How does this specific public health program, campaign, or research help certain communities and ignore or even harm others? In the case of the NBWHP, the balance of prevention with destigmatization, education, and material and social support of Black women with HIV/AIDS made the organization's work a useful model for better engaging disability studies and anti-ableism in public health work.

This chapter demonstrates how the NBWHP's Black feminist health activism, although not exclusively about disability, clearly incorporated disability as a political concern. While the organization valued health and wellness, it did so in a way that was also anti-ableist and inclusive of Black disabled people. The Black disability politics of the NBWHP are therefore apparent not only in its general holistic, political, and cultural approaches to health and wellness, which shaped the organization's mission and tactics, but also in the programming and publications the NBWHP produced in regard to HIV/AIDS and other disabilities and health conditions like depression, hypertension, and diabetes. The NBWHP's work simultaneously attempted to reduce instances of disability in Black communities and support Black disabled people in living well—whatever that meant for an individual's bodymind. The NBWHP did not succumb to the common ableist move used in some public health work in which disability is represented as purely frightening, tragic, or pitiful. Disability is not used symbolically as a warning, but rather the severity and quantity of disablement in Black communities are understood in the NBWHP's work as a consequence of racism, classism, and sexism that demands larger, intersectional approaches to health and politics, especially within the fields of public health and medicine. The NBWHP understood that only holistic, politicized, and culturally attuned prevention and care work would lead to improving health and wellness among all Black people, including disabled Black people. Importantly, the NBWHP didn't just care about existing disabled people as part of prevention (i.e., take care of people with HIV so they don't spread HIV further) but rather identified supporting Black people of all abilities and health statuses as integral to the organization's Black feminist health activism. The organization did not, therefore, seek a disability-free world but a world in which people can make educated, supported choices about their health, well-being, and engagement with the medical industrial complex. From the Black disability political perspective of the NBWHP's Black feminist health activism, life is not over or ruined once you become disabled or sick; the battle for health and wellness merely continues.

This chapter concludes the historical portion of this book with its focus on disability politics in Black activism in the late twentieth century. These four chapters have established, via analysis of the Black Panther Party and the NBWHP, that there is a history of Black activist engagement with disability as a social and political concern in the post–civil rights era that holds important lessons and information for us as scholars and activists in the twenty-first century. This historical portion of the book accomplishes two main tasks. First, it supports my claim that Black people have long engaged with disability politics but have done so in ways that diverge from the approaches in the white mainstream disability rights movement, resulting in this work often going unrecognized as disability activism. Second, these historical chapters also concretely demonstrate the four main aspects of Black disability political approaches that I have identified: that Black disability politics are intersectional but race centered, not (necessarily) based in disability identity, contextualized and historicized, and holistic.

Next, in praxis interlude 2, I provide a critique of how rarely the NBWHP engaged disability identity in order to then discuss how Black disability politics in the present might better critically engage with disability identity. This second praxis interlude engages more heavily with my interviews with contemporary Black disabled cultural workers, whose work and ideas are the focus of the final chapter.

Approaches to Disability Identity in Black Disability Politics

In this book thus far, I have argued that a central quality of Black disability politics is that it is not necessarily based in disability identity. However, the lack of explicit engagement with disability as a social and political identity becomes more deserving of critique when we look at work closer to and within the twenty-first century. The National Black Women's Health Project (NBWHP) did excellent work in including disabled people without stigma in their Black feminist health activism, but the lack of explicit engagement with disability rights warrants some critique. In this praxis interlude, I first discuss how the NBWHP failed to engage sufficiently with disability rights and disability identity. Second, I draw on my interviews with contemporary Black disabled cultural workers to discuss how to approach disability identity within Black disability politics. Finally, I envision how a Black disability political approach to disability identity could have been used by the NBWHP to benefit its Black disabled members.

The NBWHP's work began in the 1980s and continued into the twenty-first century. Despite establishing the Public Education and Policy Office in Washington, DC, in 1990, the NBWHP does not appear to have had any active involvement with the passage of the Americans with Disabilities Act (ADA) that same year, nor did the organization cover it in *Vital Signs*.[1] *Vital Signs* also does not contain any coverage in the following four years of ADA regulations going into effect.[2] The ADA is a landmark piece of civil rights legislation that prohibits discrimination against people with disabilities in public sectors including employment, education, transportation, and government services.

This law is relevant to the NBWHP because many of their members had disabilities and could have received protections under the ADA. The NBWHP failed to inform all Black disabled members about the ADA and the ways it would impact them, even though the organization's health book, *Body and Soul: The Black Women's Guide to Physical Health and Emotional Well-Being*, explicitly mentions that "African-Americans have been much more likely than whites to be rejected for benefits under Social Security disability programs."[3] It is clear the organization understood in some regard that Black disabled people might need more education on what the ADA covers and how to advocate for one's access needs under the new law. However, even in a *Vital Signs* article on how people with HIV/AIDS can apply for Social Security disability benefits, the author avoids referring to HIV/AIDS as a disability or to people with HIV/AIDS as disabled, even putting *disabled* in scare quotes once.[4] In a similar, more detailed article a year later, the unnamed author also uses passive language when referring to people with HIV/AIDS and the Social Security disability benefits application process, such as "common HIV-related conditions that may result in a finding of a disability" and "he or she will be found disabled" by the evaluators.[5] This avoidance of disability identity language in favor of disability medical language and passive voice is largely shaped by the authors' focus on disability benefits rather than disability justice, community, or identity. This particular lack of engagement with the ADA and disability politics beyond medical and legal frameworks on the part of the NBWHP reflects a disconnect between the inclusion of Black disabled women in the organization's work and the NBWHP's understanding of the value of disability rights and identity for its membership beyond the receipt of Social Security disability benefits. Even as the NBWHP published articles detailing the social and emotional effects of chronic illness, HIV/AIDS, and other disabilities, the leap to a politicized disability identity beyond one's specific disability or diagnosis remained absent.[6] The NBWHP did not make connections between Black women with chronic illness, diabetes, and HIV/AIDS in ways that could have encouraged and built Black disability identity in the 1980s and 1990s.

I want to explicitly state here that being critical of the NBWHP's lack of engagement with disability identity does not discount the value of its work with Black disabled women. When studying Black disability politics, we must hold the successes and the failures together in the light to understand what was useful and what was not, what we want to hold on to and what we want to change. I argue that contemporary Black disability politics must have a more explicit engagement with disability identity, but our approaches cannot be the same as those of the predominantly white mainstream disability rights movements and organizations. To begin theorizing some Black disability political approaches to disability identity, I draw on the expertise of the contemporary Black disabled cultural workers I interviewed for this book.

One of the most significant differences between the Black disability politics of the Black Panthers or the NBWHP and those of contemporary Black disabled activists and cultural workers is the place of disability identity. Every interview participant I spoke with identifies as D/disabled. As T. S. Banks puts it: "I am proud to say that I'm a disabled person within the Black community. I think that I deserve all the rights and protections and love and community like anyone else."[7] This widespread open identification with the words D/disabled and disability is different from what I have analyzed in the work of earlier Black activist engagement with disability even as Black people with disabilities were involved in the work. Contemporary Black disabled cultural workers understand the complexity and the value of Black disability identity to liberation work. They express clear historicized and contextualized understandings of why Black people may avoid identifying as disabled while simultaneously developing tactics that would bring more Black people with disabilities into a politicized Black disability identity. These tactics, which I discuss in more detail below, include (1) boldly claiming one's own Black disability identity (including encouraging such claiming among Black public leaders); (2) offering new language and spaces for Black disabled people to develop their own distinct relationship to disability as an identity, experience, and community; and (3) not demanding that individuals claim the word disability in order to participate in or receive support from disability cultural work. But first I want to highlight how the Black disabled cultural workers I interviewed historicized and contextualized what TL Lewis refers to as the "Black disability consciousness gap" and the complex nature of Black disability identity.[8]

Multiple interview participants theorized why Black communities generally or Black activists specifically have "avoided" disability as a political concern and/or identity. I put avoided in quotes here because while almost every interviewee acknowledged that disability has been avoided in certain ways within Black communities, the majority also provided important historical and cultural reasons for that avoidance. Cultural and historical reasons for this gap identified by interview participants include historical events like enslavement, segregation, medical experimentation, standardized tests, and literacy tests as well as more generally the avoidance of further stigmatization due to the historical association of Black people with inferiority or laziness—a concern Tinu Abayomi-Paul identifies as stemming from internalized racism.[9] As Patrick Cokley further explains: "One of the reasons why, you know, the Black community has always been hesitant even to have discussions about disability is because disability has consistently been used as a bit of a hammer—the concepts of institutionalization or determining that a group of people is unfit to participate in society or even to procreate. Those aren't new issues that were just brought up, you know, from the institutional period of disability, those were left over from our old slavery periods."[10] Dustin Gibson similarly states that for Black and other racialized people, "when disability comes to you in those [violent] ways and it's responded to in those [violent] ways, whether it be through policy [or] individual treatment, all of those different things factor into how we think about it, how we view it, if we're proud of it, if we're ashamed of it." Gibson continues, "The narrative is that people that are not white don't discuss these things and haven't discussed them. And I think that that is a false narrative. I think it is one that erases the ways in which, quite frankly, folks have survived, and it doesn't acknowledge how disability lives in the bodyminds of different people."[11] TL Lewis agrees, explaining, "Our communities just don't talk about disability in the same way as white-led organizations and [white] people do, and that doesn't invalidate the fact that we do experience disability ... literally at higher rates than non-Black peoples ... with the exception possibly of non-Black indigenous peoples." As these quotes make clear, these Black disabled cultural workers are aware and critical of the ableism and disability consciousness gap that exist in Black communities, but they refuse to address these issues as separate from the effects of racism and ableism generally and the white insularity, racism, and ableism of many disability and Deaf rights groups and organizations specifically.

TL Lewis discusses the role of white supremacy in creating and maintaining the Black disability consciousness gap in a way that demands extensive quoting. Lewis argues:

> People shame Black disabled people for not identifying as disabled, and it is really important to push back on that. Somewhere I have written that often our survival depends on *not* identifying as disabled; and in the historical context, for example, identifying as disabled meant forced familial separation.... [W]hat white supremacy does is it removes the context for why things are happening and why people are behaving in particular ways ... when you remove that context, you end up with these

shallow and incomplete narratives, but when you actually provide that context, we find that the source of the trauma, the pain, the violence, and the wrongdoing is usually the people who are accusing people of wrongdoing. In this case, white disabled people say, *Why aren't the Black people doing this, that [and] the other?* It's like, why didn't you all make it safe for us to identify as disabled in the first instance? Why did you all maintain a monopoly on this narrative for all these years? Why when we say we're disabled, do you say, *You need a piece of paper to prove that.* Those are the kinds of questions that should be asked in response ... to offer analyses for and perspective around these so-called shortcomings or lack within Black Deaf/Disabled communities.... It must be said that white people are the culprit of this. The reason that Black folks are *arguably* not understanding [disability and disability politics] is because white people have had a monopoly on the manufacturing and distribution of what disability is, whose disabilities are valid, and what laws should be applied to remedy what they have determined are unacceptable disability-based injustices.... So it is important to put the onus on the people who are responsible.

Lewis makes immensely clear that white people, disabled and nondisabled alike, have socially, medically, and legally defined disability in a way that frequently leaves Black, racialized, poor, and other multiply marginalized experiences of disability unaccounted for and excluded from disability rights political work. This exclusion endangers Black disabled people and makes identification with disability more difficult. This exclusion is similarly reflected in the work of (white) disability studies, which has historically prioritized and theorized from white experiences of disability and lacked substantive engagement with the chronic illnesses and disabilities more common in racialized and poor communities, such as diabetes, HIV/AIDS, and asthma. For Black disabled cultural workers today, it is clear that historicizing and contextualizing Black experiences of and engagement with disability is a necessary practice for understanding how we got to where we are so that we may move forward toward collective liberation in ways that attend to existing failures and harms rather than ignore or exacerbate them. This historicizing and contextualizing of the Black disability consciousness gap also allows us to develop a more robust approach to disability identity in Black communities now and into the future.

Most interview participants for this project made clear that in an ideal world, Black and other marginalized people with disabilities would identify as disabled. Participants named several benefits for individuals and for society that would result from more Black people with disabilities openly and publicly identifying as disabled. Vilissa Thompson, for instance, states that is it important "particularly [for] Black leaders and activists to understand disability, to self-identify [as] disabled, to create that visibility and ... help erase that stigma and shame that can accompany certain disabilities."[12] Thompson's sentiments here echo the work of the NBWHP to reduce stigma and shame around HIV/AIDS for Black women even as the organization did this work without encouraging connections between Black women with HIV/AIDS and a larger disability identity or community. Candace Coleman elaborates on the value of disability identity, arguing that, politically speaking, if a person doesn't identify as disabled, then it is harder for them to be counted and have their particular concerns incorporated into disability policies that impact them. Further, Coleman explains that embracing a disability identity can be "freeing" for people because they feel less alone, "have a sense of community to know some things that they were dealing with ... [were not] just their own experience," and consequently get less "stuck and tripped up on these various systems that oppress us the most." Coleman asserts that "when you really are a powerful being who recognizes your disability identity and your cultural identity and [are] able to just be yourself ... that's very empowering to me, and I feel like you could take over any role, any anything you want to do."[13] TL Lewis similarly embraces "being bold about the fact that we identify as disabled—and no, we might not have a formal diagnosis, but guess what, we out here ... you can still identify as politically disabled [without a diagnosis], and you'll be more powerful for it.... So I feel like [disability identity,] it's a way of just saying, I see you and being seen, having needs met, and then moving forward together ... it's literally in our marrow. It's in our bones. It's what has held and kept my ancestors. We couldn't have gotten through all that we've gotten through without disability." For Black disability political work today, there is clear value in disability identity for being "able to find our people" and "have some type of common language," as Dustin Gibson puts it. At the same time, Gibson and others insist that claiming disability identity is not the most important thing in Black disability politics for two reasons: first, the way disability has typically been used and defined does not align with the experiences and needs of Black people; and, second, the goal is ultimately to provide bodymind liberation, safety, and care for everyone regardless of identity.

While all the interview participants identify as D/disabled themselves and the majority spoke to the political and social value of disability identity, many were quick to contextualize their comments and explain why Black people with disabilities and chronic illnesses may be less likely to openly identify as disabled. These reasons often spoke deeply to my own experiences and helped me in my process of identifying as disabled, as discussed in the introduction. In short, Black disabled activists and cultural workers are critically aware of how white (disabled) people have homogenized our understanding of what counts as disability in ways that exclude and even deny the experiences of Black disabled people. I provide numerous and at times lengthy direct quotes here because this issue is incredibly important for contemporary Black disability politics.

First, Kayla Smith argues that white autistic people "dominate the conversation" about autism, often with no awareness of their privilege, thus violating or denying the experiences of nonwhite autistic people so that "Black autistics don't feel safe" speaking about their particular racialized experiences of disability.[14] Dustin Gibson similarly contends "that white supremacy has done a good job at allowing certain folks to be able to identify as disabled and helping to shape a disabled identity" that does not resonate with Black people. He elaborates by saying, "I think the process of disablement is so different for people that are marginalized that the language also has to be different … [because] disability lives differently in the bodies of Black folks." Vilissa Thompson echoes this sentiment, stating:

> I just really feel that [the] disabled community is not doing enough to address racism, is not doing enough to address race…. Your disability does not nullify your white privilege, you know, and, honestly, this is why, when it comes to certain disabilities, white folks get diagnosed more often than people of color. This is why, when it comes to treatment, white folks get things, get better quality of care…. We live in a very white supremacist society. Race plays a very big role in disability [with] who could get support and services, who doesn't and why, who gets mistreated and why. And for the [disability rights] community to not be willing to just understand that on a basic level, it's asinine … and it's harmful because it helps to perpetuate the white supremacy that exists.

Finally, TL Lewis contends that "you don't have to call it disability for it to be considered disability. And I think that is important because a lot of white disabled folks are out here demanding that everyone 'Say the word *disability*!'[15] Shouting at people. It's like, yo, relax. Everybody doesn't have to speak how you speak, identify how you identify, or invoke the things that you invoke. You still need to give us credence and respect and our just due because we out here and we've been holding disability down since before a word existed for it."

This issue of how Black people have lived and continue to live with disabilities despite erasure of our experiences was particularly evident in interview mentions of self-diagnosis in the face of financial exclusion and racism within the medical and psychiatric industrial complexes. T. S. Banks, for example, argues that the medical and legal systems that define disability and control who has access to accommodations and support were not made for—and in fact actively exclude and oppress—Black people so that "even with winning a class like disability ... that is only a privilege" for those with racial and class privilege.[16] Across the interviews these Black disabled activists and cultural workers were clear on how the racism of white disabled people and white-dominated disability rights organizations as well as the racism and classism of medical, psychiatric, and legal systems in the United States have made identifying with disability difficult to impossible for many Black people.

This awareness of the limiting, exclusionary, and white supremacist ways that disability has been socially, medically, legally, and politically defined was often paired with discussion of the need to have experience-informed strategies to combat this exclusion, particularly among participants who work within white-dominated disability rights and policy organizations, and who seek to create change from within. Patrick Cokley explains that "the disability community has done a poor job of moving the engagement into spaces ... where there's more majority people of color, and up until recently we have not done the best work at creating the language." What he finds "disconcerting is that when you do things like that, when you leave out certain parts of your culture and certain aspects of your community, it then becomes harder and harder to bring them back into the fold. It takes a substantial effort to say we are going to address this differently ... [but] we cannot afford to do this this way anymore. There has to be a change." To provide an example of how he has attempted to do this sort of integration of disability political work in Black communities, Cokley shared the story of speaking about disability identity to a group of Black parents of students with disabilities as part of a White House initiative on historically Black colleges and universities. He states:

> I was really trying to get them to understand some of these concepts with disability pride ... and there was a lot of hesitancy.... So I said, "Okay. Tell me how you talk to your children about race," and you know, all the

hands went up and they said, *Look, it's an aspect of who you are. It's not a defining thing, but it is something important. You should be knowledgeable of it. You should know your history, should take pride in your personal identity and make sure that no one tells you that you're less than because of it. You represent who you are, and you represent all of us.* And I said, "Okay, fine. Now, what do you tell them about disability?" They said, *Well, it's nobody's business. You know, you only say something if asked. You keep it to yourself . . . it's not a big deal. You don't have to think about it.* I was like, "Okay, now let's unpack what we've just learned there. We take pride in our cultural and racial heritage. We are told not to hide it but to use it as a sword and shield, and we gain strength from that. . . . You guys are in here talking about how you are having problems managing disability with your kids. It's like you're taking the power away from them. We can't advocate for . . . self-realization on one hand and then at the same time turn around and say, *Well, this one aspect, don't talk about it all.*" . . . Everything we've learned about the positive aspects of having strong Black identity in this country we have to use to apply to ourselves in the disability space, and it tends to make us a little stronger for it.

In this useful anecdote, Cokley's own relationship to and knowledge of Black communities allowed him to present ideas about disability identity in ways that were more understandable and relatable to these Black parents. Candace Coleman similarly discussed her work with a campaign to address the "complexities of people within our [Black] culture in not being okay with the word *disability* and only looking at the stigma." The campaign aimed "to center and have community conversations with folks who don't identify with disability and folks who do" because, as Coleman explains, "you just have to meet people where they're at. I think the more folks say it out loud and say it proud, the more we're able to shatter myths and misconceptions and live life to the fullest. Some people are just not there, and that's fine." In each of these instances, Black disabled people have worked to shape and create disability identity within Black communities in ways that attend to issues of race and that center the experiences and needs of Black people.

What is apparent across the interviews is that Black disabled activists and cultural workers find value in disability identity yet fully recognize the reasons that Black people may be resistant to the word. Ultimately, interviewees did not want the word *disability* to be a barrier to participating in disability political work or to receiving protections and support for disability-related needs. These contemporary Black disability political approaches to disability identity differ both from the Black disability politics of the Black Panther Party and the NBWHP, which mostly avoided engagement with disability as an identity, and from the bulk of mainstream, white-dominated disability rights work, which can be so focused on identification that other issues get lost. Dustin Gibson states that "it feels like [the] disability rights movement is largely concerned with people identifying as disabled in order to have the benefits that come along with that; to say, *we're the largest minority group*, to say that *we have this major voting bloc*, to say that *we represent this amount of people*," and that the movement is "less concerned with actually being able to respond to the needs of people like me. I don't care if somebody says, *I'm disabled*, but if they have diabetes, I care that they have access to insulin.... [W]hether or not we call it disabled or disability doesn't necessarily matter as much as creating systems that hold all of us." T. S. Banks echoes this emphasis on ensuring people are supported, explaining that even if someone doesn't identify as disabled or is self-diagnosed, they "still should have access to everything that folks who identify as disabled and have documented access to those things" receive as well. Ultimately, therefore, contemporary Black disability politics values disability identity but is not fixated on it as a requirement for entry into the work.

To recap, approaches to disability identity in Black disability politics include encouraging people to publicly claim Black disability identity, developing new language and spaces for Black disabled people to develop their relationship to disability identity, and not demanding that individuals claim disability in order to participate in disability cultural work or receive support. If we apply these approaches to the NBWHP, it is clear that the organization engaged in the third tactic of not limiting access to the work and the support if one did not identify as disabled, but the organization could have done more to encourage and develop Black disability identity among its membership. For example, the NBWHP could have included articles in its newsletter and other publications that more explicitly encouraged members, especially those with HIV/AIDS, chronic illnesses, and psychiatric disabilities, to understand themselves as disabled by featuring Black women discussing why they identify as disabled and how being part of a disability community benefits them. While the NBWHP's health book, *Body and Soul*, did include sections on psychiatric disability and physical disability, each of which included a profile on one Black disabled woman, the lack of extended engagement with disability identity and the inclusion of charity-oriented organizations are notable. The most interesting aspect of these sections was the mention of a group called the Black Women with

Disabilities Alliance, but there were no further details on what the group did or who was involved.[17] I retroactively long for the NBWHP to have done a feature article in *Vital Signs* on the Black Women with Disabilities Alliance for our Black disability politics historical record.

Finally, the NBWHP could have used the spaces of its self-help groups, conferences, and workshops to explore and develop members' understanding of what a Black disabled woman identity entails. As chapters 3 and 4 indicate, the organization did have some disability-specific self-help groups for Black women with HIV/AIDS and diabetes and some condition-specific workshops at conferences. Since what happened within those groups remained confidential and as each group's activities and discussions varied by the wants and needs of the group members, it is not impossible that this work did occur, but it remains mostly undocumented—like so much Black disability history. For instance, one woman with a psychiatric disability writes in the newsletter for the New York chapter of the NBWHP that she did not feel accepted or welcomed in other spaces. She explains that she thought she was "losing [her] mind" due to "blackouts, intense fears, and hallucinations," but "it felt like sensationalism" whenever she would speak in other spaces about her experiences. She writes that her NBWHP self-help group "has been a Godsend" because it emphasizes, recognizes, and validates "the common stressors in black lives—racism, classism," so she feels that she is "no longer an other with a special problem."[18] The feeling of no longer being Other as a Black disabled woman seems to suggest a level of disability consciousness and acceptance within the group, but that consciousness and acceptance do not appear explicitly in the national-level organization's archive or publication.

Black cultural workers today can learn from the missteps and oversights of the NBWHP and from the approaches to Black disability identity articulated by my interview participants in order to improve and increase engagement with disability justice at the personal and organizational levels. In the next chapter, I return to the present and take a deeper dive into Black disability politics now, as articulated and enacted by the Black disabled activists and cultural workers I interviewed for this project.

BLACK DISABILITY POLITICS NOW

We are not an afterthought.
We are here.
We are fighting for all of our lives.
We are Black. We are Disabled. We are Deaf.
We are Black.
Our Black Disabled Lives Matter.
Our Black Deaf Lives Matter.
—THE HARRIET TUBMAN COLLECTIVE, "Disability Solidarity:
Completing the 'Vision for Black Lives'"

On August 1, 2016, the Movement for Black Lives, a coalition of over fifty Black organizations, released "A Vision for Black Lives: Policy Demands for Black Power, Freedom, and Justice." The ambitious vision statement and policy platform sought to center "the experiences and leadership of the most marginalized Black people" by demanding an end to the war on Black people via a broad set of issues including reparations, economic justice, prison abolition, education, health care, political power, legislation, and an end to state violence. The vision statement explicitly named women, queer people, trans people, gender nonconforming people, femmes, Muslims, formerly and currently incarcerated people, poor and working-class people, undocumented people, and immigrants as the most marginalized Black people and incorporated issues specific to these groups into the descriptions of the movement's demands. Disabled people, however, were relegated to a single reference as "differently-abled" in the third paragraph listing populations of most marginalized Black people. In many ways, "A Vision for Black Lives" has strong similarities to the Black Panther Party's ten-point platform, particularly in its call for "community control" and its recognition that "we are a collective that centers and is rooted in Black communities, but we recognize we have a shared struggle with *all oppressed people*."[1] While the Movement for Black Lives' vision statement, in the Black radical tradition, extended into a wide array of social justice issues, the document was constructed with extremely limited input from Black disabled activists.[2]

Following numerous conversations and exchanges, and in response to the failure of the drafters of "A Vision for Black Lives" to adequately incorporate Black disability politics into their statement, Black disabled activists from the United States and Canada organized the Harriet Tubman Collective (HTC). The collective released a response statement entitled "Disability Solidarity: Completing the 'Vision for Black Lives'" via Tumblr and Medium on September 7, 2016.[3]

In the statement the HTC questions the erasure of disability, "especially considering the critical role ableism and audism play in *every* institution named by the Movement as a purveyor of violence against Black bodies and communities," including police violence, poverty, the prison industrial complex, and the educational system.[4] The HTC continues: "Many Black Deaf/ Disabled leaders—especially those who have given their time and talent to the Movement for Black Lives—have noticed this deficit and believe that it reflects much larger problems with ableism and audism in the Movement. We, the undersigned, united under the coalitional name the Harriet Tubman Collective, are here to remind the Movement that liberation will never come without the intentional centering of Black Disabled/Deaf narratives and leadership. We know this because it never has."[5] This powerful statement engages the ethic of centering those most impacted by oppressive systems in the fight against those systems that is valued in both Black feminism and disability justice. It also, in the final sentence especially, asserts contemporary Black disabled cultural workers' knowledge of and respect for their particular activist genealogy—from the legacies of Black historical figures only recently being recognized as disabled to the participation of Black disabled people within activist movements.

This sense of Black disabled activist legacy is reiterated in the second half of "Disability Solidarity," which calls the erasure of disability "a grave injustice and offense" and argues unequivocally that "this platform and work is wholly incomplete if disability is not present. To be sure, no successful movement has existed without our leadership, and no movement will be successful without us." In the final paragraphs of the statement, the HTC calls "upon organizations that label themselves 'intersectional' to truly embrace that framework" and states that they, as Black Disabled/Deaf leaders, "remain as a resource and network of support to any who seek" collective liberation. "Disability Solidarity" ends with a list of names of "Black Disabled/Deaf victims of police brutality" and with the words from the epigraph to this chapter.[6] The statement was signed by seventeen Black D/disabled and Deaf cultural workers.[7]

After the release of the HTC's statement, the Movement for Black Lives updated their "Vision for Black Lives" statement and policy plan to include disability in a more robust way, with language that aligns with current work in disability justice.[8] The term "differently-abled" was replaced with "disabled" in the introduction to the platform, and people with disabilities are now explicitly named thirteen times across four of the six policy/issue statements.[9] For example, people with disabilities are named as one of several populations who are most likely to be profiled by police, to experience poverty, and to be negatively impacted by failed health-care systems and restrictive voter registration laws.[10] The most detailed engagement with disability appears in the "End the War on Black People" section, which contains a full paragraph about the abuse and harm suffered by incarcerated people with mental disabilities. These changes are substantial and important, and there is no question that the HTC's "Disability Solidarity" response statement was a—if not the—major factor in bringing about this explicit inclusion, asserting disability as a Black political issue essential to any vision for Black lives. This story is one example of how, in the beginning of the twenty-first century, thanks to the work of disability justice activists generally and Black disabled activists specifically, increasing numbers of Black social justice organizations and movements have begun to better incorporate and name disability as part of their liberatory politics.

Since the "Disability Solidarity" statement in 2016, the HTC also released additional statements via various open-access digital platforms in 2017, 2018, and 2019. These other statements address racism from and exploitation by white mainstream disability rights organizations and explicitly engage in an abolitionist stance against the prison industrial complex from a Black disability politics perspective.[11] I cite these statements to recognize that the HTC has not merely critiqued Black activist organizations for their ableism but is also actively engaged with identifying racism within white-majority disability rights organizations. I encourage readers to use the works cited in this book to locate and read the HTC's important and ongoing Black disability political work.

This chapter aims to uplift the voices and work of contemporary Black disabled activists and cultural workers, particularly members of the HTC, by exploring how Black disability politics operate in the present. In what follows, I argue that Black disabled cultural workers are growing Black disability politics in new ways and, as a result, changing how we organize for social change. The eleven people I interviewed are drawing attention to a legacy of Black disabled activism, articulating a robust critical understanding of the relationship of ableism and racism, and developing what it means to engage in Black disability political praxis. Collectively these contemporary modes of Black disability political praxis aim to shape present and future liberation work more broadly. I analyze the contemporary Black disability political work discussed in the interviews and make connections to the qualities of Black disability politics I identified in the historical work of the Black Panther Party and the National Black Women's Health Project. Then, in the conclusion, I briefly discuss three sites of social justice work where disability politics are being articulated and enacted by Black activists and cultural workers not interviewed for this project. These short concluding examples are intended less to provide close analysis and more to demonstrate ways of identifying Black disability politics (for scholars) and incorporating disability politics into Black-focused and Black-led social justice work (for activists and cultural workers). This chapter also allows me to highlight what I believe to be some of the most important work of Black disability politics today, work that I hope more scholars will study and more cultural workers and activists will join.

Contemporary Black Disability Political Praxis

My interviews for this project produced an immense amount of knowledge that I do my best to condense into a few key tactics that these Black disabled cultural workers are further developing in Black disability politics today. First, in addition to claiming Black disability identity and encouraging identification with disability in Black communities, contemporary Black disabled cultural workers are also claiming Black disability history and drawing attention to a legacy of Black disabled organizing and activism. Every single interview participant mentioned that to understand the experiences and political needs of Black disabled people, one must understand our history. Candace Coleman, for example, asserts, "We have some bomb ancestors who have had disabilities, but their story hasn't been told."[12] A similar sentiment was expressed by Tinu Abayomi-Paul, who states, "The disability part of the history of Black people is removed a lot of the time and revealed later."[13] Acknowledging the erasure of Black disabled people's stories,

Heather Watkins explains that it benefits "younger people when we tell them how many of our cultural icons had disabilities like Harriet Tubman, Brad Lomax, Sojourner Truth, Fannie Lou Hamer; all these people had disabilities, and the disability helped govern their lives. It impacted the way they moved politically."[14] This shift to recognize the cultural and political value of the history of Black disabled people, to acknowledge the fact that, as Dustin Gibson puts it, "Black disabled folks have been doing activism for long time," is important to Black disability politics in the twenty-first century.[15] Patrick Cokley states, "What I think is important about Black disability thought is that it requires you to take into account that history and then when you are addressing policy changes or political changes to then use those skill sets as a means of basically creating better activism, better engagement, better policies."[16] The recognition of the history of Black disabled people was clear across the interviews, and several participants even specifically mentioned the work of the Black Panther Party. Most participants also tied this recovery of history to its cultural and political utility today in addressing disability as a political concern within Black communities and social movements. By making our presence in history more visible, we can more effectively lay claim to leadership roles as Black disabled people and help our movements develop strong understandings of the relationship between and manifestations of ableism and racism in order to shape future political praxis.

Black disabled activists and cultural workers in the early twenty-first century tend to recognize that the work must be intersectional in such a way that race does not take primacy over disability because social systems of oppression have to be addressed and fought against as interrelated and mutually constitutive rather than as separable. As a result, they are challenging and changing our understanding of what ableism is and does in our world. This aspect of contemporary Black disability politics echoes, but shifts, the intersectional quality of Black disability politics discussed thus far and also reflects one of the tactics for addressing disabling violence from praxis interlude 1: emphasizing the intertwined nature of multiple social justice issues. Multiple interview participants insisted on an understanding of ableism and racism as inseparable and mutually constitutive, meaning that they help create and inform one another and rely on each other to function. Dustin Gibson argues that "race and disability were pathologized in a way that we can't separate them now.... I think we can't literally talk about ableism without talking about racism"; therefore, he continues, "I don't think that there's such thing as anti-Black ableism ... ableism is inherently anti-Black."

Patrick Cokley similarly explains that in some regards "ableism is very much one and the same with racism because what we're really talking about is who has agency in our culture."

The relationship between racism and ableism (and other systems of oppression) is most expansively articulated by TL Lewis, whom I quote at length in order to make clear not merely how Lewis and other Black disabled activists and cultural workers understand the relationships between these systems conceptually but also how this intersectional understanding shapes political approaches to social change. Lewis states:

> I always chuckle about this because my brain doesn't disconnect them. There is no racism without ableism. There is no ableism without racism ... you quite literally can't have one without the other.... There is a fundamental lack of understanding of the connections between racism and ableism, classism, and other structural and systemic oppressions that is killing us because if we understood those things—how they are connected, how there's an unbroken chain between asylums, plantations, zoos, circuses, and prisons—then we would be able to actually fight all of those things collectively and very differently.... [If we did make those connections,] then we would be able to have a much more holistic understanding of what is going on in our society but also a much stronger framework from which to unearth the histories ... these collective histories and then dismantle the system—all of these systems.... So long as we continue to allow people to think that it is just one or the other, we are going to keep spinning our wheels and not being able to identify the cause of the harm, which is *all* of these systems operating simultaneously. This is what made Fred Hampton so dangerous. This is what made Martin Luther King Jr. toward the end of his life so dangerous in many regards, [and] Malcolm X for the same reason. It's because there was a deep understanding of the need to have an anticapitalist, anti-imperialist, antiracist [approach to change]. It was, is, why the Black Panthers were engaged in and supporting disability justice work. This is why Black folks have been fighting for universal health care since quite literally the 1800s.... These are the things that we have always understood, but if you don't have a historical understanding, if you don't have a lens from which to view these struggles other than race, race, race, race ... [then] we'll end up fighting against or harming one another.[17]

From the perspective of these interview participants, Black disability politics fundamentally understand racism and ableism as mutually constitutive and assert that this understanding of the relationship between systems of oppression is *required* to create systemic change and collective liberation.

This particular aspect of the intersectional quality of Black disability politics today is why Lewis, in conversation and relationship with Gibson and other Black and racialized people, has developed and continues to refine an expansive definition of ableism. The most recent version at the time of writing was released in January 2020 on social media. It defines ableism as "a system that places value on people's bodies and minds based on societally constructed ideas of normalcy, intelligence, excellence and productivity. These constructed ideas are deeply rooted in anti-Blackness, eugenics, colonialism and capitalism. This form of systemic oppression leads to people and society determining who is valuable and worthy based on a person's appearance and/or their ability to satisfactorily [re]produce, excel and 'behave.' You do not have to be disabled to experience ableism."[18] This definition of ableism importantly contains race within it, making clear how racism and ableism not only intersect in the lives of Black disabled people but collude with and uphold one another's functions in ways that impact even nondisabled people. This is a key way intersectionality—with attention to both identity and systems of oppression that operate violently regardless of identity—works in Black disability politics today. As Lewis clarifies in our interview, "What makes ableism so dangerous is its fluidity and ability to morph. It's like a chameleon.... It morphs into whatever the system needs it to be to perpetuate the violence or deprivation that is being produced." This expansive, chameleon nature of ableism and its mutually constitutive relationship to other oppressions further reinforce the need for Black disability politics today to remain holistic as well. As Dustin Gibson explains, he and other multiply marginalized radical activists and cultural workers are "attempting to abolish the systems that inflict violence because we know from history that if an apparatus is built for one people that it'll expand itself and it'll be for more people; that once harm is allowed to take place and it goes unchecked that the goalpost for what is fucked up then moves ... we know that the harm will beget more harm, and the death-making machines will just grow stronger and stronger, and there are people being killed there right now, whether it's happening [today], gonna happen tomorrow, or if it's methodically over a seventy-year period and ... it'll be on us for not resisting now." Indeed, Black disabled cultural workers are resisting multiple systems of oppression and harmful institutions. In the process, they are modeling methods for Black disability political praxis.

In the interviews several participants insisted that one aspect of their praxis is to hold no person or community above critique. This practice is evident in my opening example of the HTC's work holding both the Movement for Black Lives and white-led disability rights organizations accountable for their ableism and racism, respectively. Vilissa Thompson, an HTC member, explains that Black disability politics mean "holding the community we're part of accountable," and that means every community: white-led disability communities, Black communities, and beyond. As Thompson further asserts in regard to Black social movements and organizations, "if your politics doesn't include disability ... [then] you're not for the true inclusion and liberation of Black people, particularly disabled Black people, and we see you. We know who's for us, and we know who's against us ... you are not above being critiqued. If white people are being critiqued, you're gonna be critiqued."[19] While the work of Black disability politics in previous chapters focused on the disabling impact of racism from a race-centered or race-and-gender-centered critique, Black disability politics today hold all communities accountable, with appropriate attention to the history and context that shape how oppression manifests in different communities, as discussed in praxis interlude 2 and in this chapter thus far.

Another aspect of Black disability political praxis today, operating in the tradition of Black feminist politics and theorizing, is centering those most marginalized and most impacted by oppression. In their 1977 statement, the Combahee River Collective, a group of Black feminists often credited as early progenitors of intersectional theory, wrote, "If Black women were free, it would mean that everyone else would have to be free since our freedom would necessitate the destruction of all the systems of oppression."[20] Several interview participants echoed this Black feminist sentiment from a Black disability political perspective. Candace Coleman, for instance, states that if you center "Black and disabled people, then you center everyone else in the world ... look at things through a Black and disability lens [and] you could most definitely serve everyone else." T. S. Banks expresses a similar belief, asserting that "if we can make accessibility [mean] thinking about access to food, health, housing, heart, art, you know, everything that makes us thrive instead of just surviving, you know, human beings, I think if we can do that for Black disabled, trans folks, nonbinary folks, intersex folks, I think, you know, basically the world has won."[21] This particular Black disability political sentiment and activist approach, of course, also draws from the ten principles of disability justice articulated by Patricia Berne and Sins Invalid, a performance collective of disabled queer people and disabled people of color. After the first principle, intersectionality, Sins Invalid names the second principle of disability justice as "Leadership of Those Most Impacted," explaining, "We know ableism exists in the context of other historical systemic oppressions. We know to truly have liberation we must be led by those who know the most about these systems and how they work."[22] The Black disabled cultural workers interviewed for this book are unquestionably leaders in the liberation movement precisely because of their deep knowledge of how multiple systems of oppression operate in their individual lives and communities. They collectively assert that their leadership as Black disabled people is a distinct advantage for Black disability political work.

Digging further into doing the work of Black disability politics, several interview participants discussed the need for a holistic approach to activism, organizing, and other change work that centers care and accessibility, broadly conceived. One aspect of this holistic approach in contemporary Black disability politics is paying attention to and addressing the various ways oppression impacts our bodyminds. TL Lewis, for example, states that systems of oppression are "set up to exhaust people who are actually fighting them ... the mental, physical, emotional, economic, spiritual, political, and any other way in which you can imagine; so in that way they are quite effective." T. S. Banks similarly notes that "there's a lot of people that we lost because they were fighting and unwell at the time"; therefore, there's a need for "care webs within our networks," which Banks believes we need to work on more.[23] The acknowledgment of the toll that living within violent systems takes on the bodyminds of marginalized people, particularly cultural workers actively fighting these systems, is an important part of Black disability politics—the acknowledgment of our full selves and our need for self-care, community care, and state care. Part of this need for care includes calls for increased attention to accessibility within organizations and liberation movements.

Multiple interview participants mentioned the lack of accessibility and at times outright ableism in certain organizations and movement spaces. Lorrell Kilpatrick, a member of the Gary, Indiana, chapter of Black Lives Matter, states:

> There are only two of us [from the HTC] that are still members of more mainstream ... Black radical groups [Black Lives Matter and Black Youth Project 100 specifically]. . . . The rest of these folks are anti- all of these groups because of the rabid ableism ... that they've encountered. I have

had to call another Black Lives Matter planner in another city on behalf of a person in Harriet Tubman Collective to let them know that they are actively excluding Black people with disabilities and got hung up on.... The reason why BLM Gary is not rabidly ableist is because I'm in BLM Gary, that's it. Had I not been, people would have been, you know, very honestly ignorant of accessibility issues, but the other folks who are not part of these two groups used to be, and have vowed they will never be again because of the intense intense ableism, disregard, disrespect, that they got from these activists who are so-called freedom fighters who are treating them in the same way that they say they're being treated by white liberals.[24]

Attention to accessibility not only ensures the participation of disabled people, which, as Kilpatrick notes, can transform the practices of an entire organization, but also ensures that people can participate in movement work in sustainable ways because the multiple needs of their bodyminds are being considered and care, for one's self and each other, is valued. As Dustin Gibson contends, "All of the influx of sustainable practices that we [in disability justice work] center for survival will be key to actually being able to do the work long term." Prioritizing accessibility (physical, sensory, financial, and otherwise), therefore, is an essential part of Black disability political praxis today.

Finally, similar to the work of the Panthers and the National Black Women's Health Project earlier in the book, a major part of contemporary Black disability politics is to attend to and value both the micro and macro levels of change in order to achieve long-term success—that is, remaining holistic in tactics as well as in topics and issues.[25] Lorrell Kilpatrick explains that though many seek to have widespread impact and influence, "that doesn't mean that the impact we have on the individual is small. The impact we have on the individual means the world to the individual. So it means the world to me ... there's levels to the effectiveness that we have." Patrick Cokley echoes that sentiment, stating, "One of the things I think is very important in the disability space and all spaces that are about social justice is to remind us that there are different types of work that are needed to move freedom and justice forward." Black disabled people are increasingly organizing online, including participating in virtual marches and sharing ideas with one another in order to mobilize for change in new, more accessible ways. The ability for Black disabled people to be less isolated and more involved means that Black disability political work must acknowledge and value the varied ways people participate in collective liberation. I will say a bit more about my own experiences with accessible Black disability organizing during the 2020 uprisings in the nonconclusion that follows this chapter.

Recognizing the value of micro- and macrolevel work is further reflected in TL Lewis's metric of success for social justice work, which "is really important when you're battling an entire system because if you don't have your own metrics for success, it can drive you mad." Lewis works, unpaid, with Helping Educate to Advance the Rights of Deaf communities (HEARD), a volunteer-dependent organization that works to end abuse and imprisonment of D/deaf and disabled people. Regarding this work, Lewis states, "I have learned that in this system we have to have a different metric for 'success,' and in this moment, my metric is: *How many people love more deeply? How many communities grew closer? How many families did you keep together in the hundred-year battle to tear apart our families? How many children knew they were loved despite the system—that wires, walls, windows, and bars could not separate them from that which they deserved most . . . ?*" Here Lewis places immense value on the individual and community level of change in the ongoing fight to dismantle systems of oppression at the macro level, viewing the work and impact at each level as necessary and meaningful. Lewis makes clear, in fact, that "usually folks in mainstream disability communities can only see the law as a means of allegedly remedying abuses . . . when often the law is the cause and perpetuation of more inequality."[26] What Lewis notes contemporarily, Kilpatrick reflects on historically in regard to the early disability rights movement, stating, "The way that they got these young scary disabled people out of the streets and out from under those buses [was that] they gave them government jobs and insurance for the first time ever. They legitimized them, and everybody wants legitimization. But with those jobs, with those benefits, with the way to pay for your education, with the way to gain respect as a person, came the sacrifice, of course, of the radicalism." What both Lewis and Kilpatrick indicate is that a primary emphasis or overreliance on working within institutions like the federal government and the law to create radical change will ultimately fail. The range of work performed by the Black disabled activists and cultural workers I interviewed, combined with their emphasis on the importance of multiple kinds and levels of justice work, indicates clearly that Black disability politics today remain holistic in ways very similar to the work of the Black Panther Party and National Black Women's Health Project discussed in previous chapters. This chapter (and praxis interlude 2 before it) also makes clear that contemporary Black disability politics remain intersectional (without centering race above disability), not necessarily based in disability identity (though contemporary work includes and values disability identity much more than the historical work analyzed in this book), and contextualized and historicized. The central qualities I identified in the work of the Black Panther Party and the National Black Women's Health Project therefore appear in similar and sometimes shifted ways in the work of contemporary Black disabled activists and cultural workers. As a result, I argue that that we can use these qualities as one way to locate and assess historical Black disability politics and develop present and future Black disability politics.

Black Disability Politics in Contemporary
Social Justice Movements

The practices that I've identified in Black disability politics today are, of course, based on a small sample population of experienced Black disabled cultural workers. I believe there is immense value in scholars doing more in-depth interviews with Black disabled activists and cultural workers to better understand the methods and perspectives of Black disability politics in the twenty-first century. I have written this chapter, however, to ensure that the lessons of the past are directly connected to the work of the present and to highlight the leaders whose perspectives are being increasingly incorporated into the work of a variety of social justice movements, organizations, and political campaigns but hardly engaged by scholars in Black studies or disability studies.

It is unquestionable that Black disabled activists and cultural workers are at the forefront of developing Black disability political frameworks today, but the work is also being taken up in locations that are neither exclusively focused on disability nor exclusively Black. Black disability politics are, after all, not limited to issues specific to Black disabled people alone. Moreover, if we take a Black feminist and disability justice perspective here, then we understand that a politics that centers those who are most marginalized and most impacted will benefit those less marginalized and less impacted as well. In these first two decades of the twenty-first century, there are several places where Black disability politics are manifesting and impacting the work of Black and Black-led social justice organizations and movements. While analyzing all the ways Black disability politics are circulating in contemporary justice work is beyond the scope of this chapter and book, I would like to briefly provide some examples that might seed ideas and future research topics for readers.

First, the Black Youth Project is "a national research project, launched in 2004, that examined the attitudes, resources, and culture of African American youth ages 15 to 25," and that has now expanded into a "cyber-resource center for black youth" intended "to generate new media information, blogs, art, conversations, webinars, and data that will expand the human and social capital of young African Americans, facilitating their general empowerment through highlighting their voices and experiences."[27] The website regularly includes news stories and essays about Blackness and disability that reflect the qualities of Black disability politics discussed here. A January 2020 search for the terms *disability* and *disabled* located just over sixty hits for essays and articles. Some of these pieces simply mention one of these words briefly, such as in a list of marginalized people, but numerous others—such as "Chills down My Spinal Degeneration: Why We Need Black Queer Disabled Kink," "Black People Aren't Resistant to Mental Health Treatment. We're Resistant to Framing It as a Cure," and "Yup. Non-profit Culture and Performative Activism Perpetuate Ableism and Anti-Blackness"—provide extended engagement with disability and ableism as political concerns for young Black people.[28]

Even outside of Black movements and cultural spaces, Black people, especially Black disabled people, are taking up disability as an explicit political concern tied to other systems of oppression. In 2019 adrienne maree brown published *Pleasure Activism: The Politics of Feeling Good*, a collection of essays and interviews exploring the need to revalue and claim our right to pleasure in a politicized fashion, one that demands that our social systems contain space for rest, healing, joy, and satisfaction, particularly for those who are most impacted by oppression and most likely to have their pleasure policed, denied, and devalued. Brown identifies as a fat Black queer woman with disabilities, and she ensured that the politics of disability were acknowledged in various places throughout the book, not only in the two chapters by Leah Lakshmi Piepzna-Samarasinha and myself, which are most explicitly focused on disability. Pleasure activism is grounded in Black feminism, draws from work in harm reduction and healing justice, and is in conversation with social justice work from a wide variety of cultural arenas, from sex work, aging, and parenting to consent, fashion, and trauma. Pleasure activism is an intersectional, holistic framework that focuses on both micro- and macrolevel change in ways that align strongly with Black disability politics even as that language is not central to the work. The politics of disability, I contend, appear throughout brown's work to encourage us to attend to our bodies, to center the pleasure of those most marginalized, and to work to heal from systems of oppression that deny us pleasure and freedom so that we are better prepared to sustainably fight for the collective liberation of all.

There is a similar kind of integration of Black disability politics in the work of Sonya Renee Taylor, a Black queer woman leader in the body positivity and body empowerment movements. Taylor came up with the phrase "the body is not an apology," the title of her influential media and educational website (founded in 2011) and her book (published in 2018), from a conversation with a disabled woman.[29] The Body Is Not an Apology website contains "Disability" and "Mental Health" as two of a dozen central topics addressed by articles and personal essays on the site, along with things like weight/size, sexuality, gender, race, and aging. While only a portion of the articles and essays on disability are written by Black people, this indicates another site of activist and cultural work where Black people are ensuring the politics of disability are being integrated and made explicit.

This integration of Black disability politics outside of Black activist and cultural spaces and into other social justice movements led by Black and Black disabled people is incredibly important for future studies. I could have included additional examples from the abolitionist movement, the reproductive justice movement, and the health-care reform movement—all areas I hope others can research and develop further using the frameworks and ideas articulated in this book. What's important is not that Black disability politics remain owned by Black disabled people alone; rather, what's important is that these politics influence the work of social justice movements broadly, moving us toward collective liberation and a future where we remember and honor the history of Black disability politics and the legacy of Black disabled people who helped us get free.

I say more on the work that still needs to occur in the nonconclusion, but I want to end this chapter with another expression of gratitude to the eleven Black disabled activists and cultural workers who participated in interviews and provided feedback on this book. Our conversations not only helped me work out the arguments and arc of this project but also helped me decide to use this book to come out as disabled after over a decade of working in disability studies. Thank you for entrusting me with your ideas and knowledge.

(NOT A) CONCLUSION

The Present and Futures of Black Disability Politics

This book is and is not for the academy. It is research based and interdisciplinary, and thus, as a scholar, I anticipate and hope that it has influence and value among my colleagues. At the same time, I want this book to have value and utility outside the academy; for Black people, especially Black disabled people, to understand our history of Black disability politics in order to claim it, learn from it, and take it more explicitly into our multiple kinds of justice work in the world. As a result, this is not a conclusion so much as the final words before a pause in the conversation, a pause where people will read or listen to this work and then pick up the conversation in their own fields, organizations, and cultural spaces. I hope that you will talk, post, tweet, critique, write back, and engage others on these ideas to further research and enact Black disability politics.

To write this brief nonconclusion, I use a framework I first experienced as an undergraduate student in the classes of Dr. Kathy McMahon-Klosterman, the first person to introduce me to disability studies, when I was nineteen. Dr. McMahon-Klosterman always had us write reflections on our final projects by answering the questions *What? So what? Now what?* That is: What did you do? Why does it matter? What needs to happen next to further this work? I am and always will be grateful for what Dr. McMahon-Klosterman taught me about integrating one's teaching, scholarship, and activism.

What?

This book has explored how Black people have engaged with disability as a political issue through exploration and analysis of the work of the Black Panther Party, the National Black Women's Health Project, and twenty-first-century Black disabled cultural workers. I have argued that Black people's engagement with disability politics has been overlooked, ignored, and misrecognized because it doesn't always look like the disability political work of the white-dominated mainstream disability rights movement. However, there is unquestionably a legacy of Black people, disabled and nondisabled, working for the liberation of disabled people in direct relationship to the fights against white supremacy and capitalism. In analyzing the political work of Black cultural workers on disability issues, I identified four common qualities of Black disability politics: they are intersectional but race centered, not necessarily based in disability identity, contextualized and historicized, and holistic. These qualities are useful both in identifying previous or existing Black cultural work that we ought to consider Black disability politics and in creating new Black disability political work in the present and future. These qualities remain relatively consistent across the differing eras and groups I've explored; however, importantly, in twenty-first-century Black disability politics, disability is much more explicitly engaged in intersectional approaches and is far more likely to be claimed as an identity by Black cultural workers, though identity claims are not necessary for doing Black disability political work.

So What?

Why does tracing a history of Black disability politics and articulating common qualities matter? First and foremost, this work matters because Black disabled people matter. Black disabled people have a social and political history that we must understand in order to create collective liberation. For scholars, this work demonstrates that our approach to identifying and studying disability and disability politics needs to be rooted in the way disability is understood within a particular community and historical moment. Current definitions of disability and understandings of what constitutes disability politics are far too narrow and based primarily on white experiences and understandings of disability. Scholars of Black people, Black history, and Black culture must look for how Black communities have addressed issues of disability, health, illness, disease, and wellness without depending on medical or legal frameworks. For activists and other cultural workers, my work here matters because it demonstrates an activist legacy that we can not only claim but learn from as well. Throughout I have not merely recounted this legacy, but I have also critiqued its missteps and failures, presenting ideas as to how we might take up the useful tactics and learn from the errors that often unwittingly perpetuated ableism. If nothing else, researching and writing this book has made clear to me that looking lovingly yet critically at the work of our political ancestors is the only way to ensure that our work in the present is effective and lasting. We get better only if we are willing to admit where we have gone wrong, as individuals and as collectives, and if we then truly integrate the lessons we have learned into future work.

Now What?

What happens next with this work? For scholars, I hope more of us can identify and analyze Black disability politics in a range of Black cultural work from activism and organizing to art and literature, including more archival and oral history work. In doing such scholarship, I also would like to see more academics try harder to create accessible ways (financially and intellectually) for people outside of the academy to read, understand, and use our work. I do not believe in knowledge for the sake of knowledge. We live in an era where information can be rapidly shared. And while the process of research might be slow, the spread of the knowledge gained from that research must occur in many ways outside of ivory tower lecture halls, paywalled journals, and inaccessibly written four-hundred-page books. While these methods for disseminating information have some value, we must all fight to ensure they are not the only places where we share what we have learned.

For activists and other cultural workers, the next step is to take this knowledge about Black disability politics and share it, talk about it, follow the lead of the living activists I interviewed, and incorporate Black disability politics into your work and your life. This means moving toward a political model that fully recognizes the mutually constitutive nature of disability, race, gender, sexuality, and class. This cannot be in name only. It cannot just mean saying the word *disability* sometimes. The work has to transform. We must make activism and politics accessible. We must center those most marginalized and make sure all of our people get free, each and every one of us. We must reject models that move at an unsustainable pace, burn people out, and harm, even traumatize, people. The skill set of accessible organizing is needed in *all* activist work, even in work that is not explicitly about disability or health, because disabled, sick, and chronically ill people are involved in all non-disability-explicit work, because they, too, are Black people, Muslim people, poor people, sexual assault survivors, immigrants, and so on. Disabled people are increasingly leaders, demonstrating how to organize and create political and social change in our present moment. We must claim that, recognize that, and do everything we can to ensure the participation and leadership of multiply marginalized disabled people.

Concluding Thoughts during the Uprisings of 2020

I am writing these concluding thoughts in the midst of a global pandemic and what I've begun to call "the uprisings." Everything is surreal. Everything feels urgent. Nothing makes sense and yet … I still feel compelled to write, to finish this book.

When the pandemic began to shut things down in the United States in March 2020, I watched my disabled friends and colleagues offer immense knowledge to the nondisabled world on how to move events and meetings to virtual platforms, how to find and wear masks, how to keep mental wellness intact during long periods of isolation, how to make one's own hand sanitizer, how to connect with others when one could not touch people or leave one's home. Disabled people led the way in showing folks how to care for their full bodyminds through a global pandemic. Then the uprisings began. And again, knowledge about organizing from a variety of bodyminds and spaces emerged from disability justice communities.

Here in Madison I joined Freedom Inc., a Black and Southeast Asian queer feminist activist and advocacy organization for which I am a board member, for a large march on May 30, 2020. Alix Shabazz, a Black disabled queer woman organizer, asked me to be a "care bear" for the event, someone who distributed food, water, and, at that moment, masks, gloves, and hand sanitizer to protesters to help keep everyone safe. Alix later told me that she learned about care roles in protests from disability justice organizers. Several of us acting as care bears, security, and medics communicated in a group chat all day. That night some community members continued their own protest after the march, and property was damaged downtown. Madison police showed up in riot gear, spraying gas at protesters and bystanders in the way, creating chaos, harm, and trauma. The city issued a curfew, and the uprisings officially arrived in Madison.

Some of us in the original security and care network for the march continued to work together privately, slowly, organically, growing our network to include trusted friends. As local organizations and individuals planned protests and marches day after day, our network of over thirty people worked in the background to ensure as much safety and care as possible at every event. What amazed me about this organically formed network, this organized nonorganization, was the incredible leadership and participation by disabled people, particularly Black disabled people. Some of us could not risk being out in public with large crowds, so instead we stayed up late monitoring livestreams from protesters on social media and using information gathered from the streams to communicate with our people on the ground about where to send medics, where to send supplies, and where to avoid the police and National Guard. Others would listen to police scanners, privately fundraise, or make runs to grocery stores and pharmacies for supplies. For a while, it felt as if the state was explicitly at war with us, and we needed every person, every skill, to help our people stay safe as they expressed their righteous anger and demanded radical change: Defund the police. Abolish prisons. Forgive student loans. Put a moratorium on rent and evictions. Value people over property. All echoes of the demands of the Black Panther Party decades before us.

Days later, the curfew was lifted, and the police and National Guard reduced their visible militarized presence downtown while still leaving snipers on buildings, undercover officers in our marches, and tanks on the edges of town, ready to mobilize at a moment's notice. At that point, some of us chose to be on the ground but in our cars only, participating in caravans that shut down major intersections and highways and at other times serving as physical protection for marches by driving in front of or behind the group. There were so many roles for a variety of bodymind and access needs, and each of these roles was valued among my network. This was my first time doing so much on-the-ground protesting and organizing. I had just finished writing everything for this book except the conclusion, and I found myself constantly identifying Black disability politics in our work even as they were rarely named as such. Now, however, I would like to frame them as disability political practices here and document the crip brilliance that made the uprisings as significant and sustained as they were here in Madison.

As I drove at the front of one march, I thought about how keeping a slow pace with lots of stops for people to rest is not only a safety practice to keep the group together but also a disability justice practice to make marches more accessible and to refuse to leave behind those who move at a different pace than the majority. At multiple protests I distributed free water, food, face masks, sunscreen, and/or bug spray from a collapsible wagon I now just keep in my car at all times.[1] This was in one sense an adaptive access practice for my own bodymind because I knew I couldn't carry very much at once, so the wagon allowed me to be more effective in distributing these items through a large crowd without hurting myself. More largely, though, I often thought about the holistic nature of Black disability politics and the way providing food, water, face masks, and other supplies directly connects to the need to practice holistic care for people at protests, especially when folks are new to such events or were perhaps not informed or aware of how long one action can last. We also had medics on-site, and one member of the group carried essential oils and tinctures to events for folks needing help calming down or grounding when things got hectic or scary. When we care for everyone's bodyminds, more people are able to participate for longer periods of time— with more energy and joy. Finally, in my network of organizers, I witnessed people name their self-care practices and access needs openly to the group, such as "I need to take today off" or "I can come to the march, but I need someone to be my buddy and stay next to me" or "I'm running low on energy, can someone let me ride in a car for a while?" While not everyone openly identified as disabled, I was regularly impressed by not only the naming of and response to these needs but the active celebration and encouragement of these disability justice access practices. Once I was going to be late to an event because I couldn't move my therapy appointment. I said so, and not only did folks adjust around my timing without question, but people also responded in the group text with comments like "Yay therapy!" This kind of atmosphere allowed me to bring my full self in whatever capacity I had at the moment into the work.

I rarely heard people use the word *disability* to help explain or politicize these various practices, which is why I want to frame them in this way here. I believe there is value in us naming these as disability political practices because doing so makes care work (for self and others) political and valuable in a world that often feminizes and thus devalues it. Further, if we create a Black liberation movement that understands Black disability politics to be essential, then these practices would be nonnegotiable for all organizing, activism, and protest work, fighting legacies of burnout/overwork culture that allows ableism to flourish. By explicitly naming practices already occurring in many Black movement spaces as disability politics, we recognize the role and value of disabled people in Black liberation work. It is time for all Black people to claim Black disability politics as one of many tools we need in the fight for our freedom.

Right now, admittedly, it is hard to imagine what the future looks like. The days blend together, and the pandemic rages on, seemingly unabated. Black people are dying at disproportionate rates from COVID-19, and for those who survive, it will be years before we truly understand the long-term disabling impact of the virus on our communities.[2] Black disabled people deserve to exist now and well into the future, and that can occur only if all Black people (and our allies) follow the lead of multiply marginalized disabled people who have watched—from their beds, from their homes, from the bus, from hospital rooms—how nondisabled people operate, pretending that these bodyminds of ours will last forever, that this earth will last forever, as if we do not need to slow down, to support each other, to account for—let alone learn from—those we have historically isolated, ignored, and let die. Disabled people know how to survive this. Our knowledge is part of how we as a collective not only make it to the other side but also build a new world that is more capable of responding with care for all of us, not just some of us. What I see emerging in this moment is a time for Black people to embrace disability politics explicitly and consistently, a moment when following the lead of Black disabled people and other disabled people of color who have survived and organized within hurricanes, days without electricity, wildfires, smoke hazards, tear gassing, pepper spraying, COVID-19, and more is our best hope. When this ends—and I do hope this particular crisis ends soon—we cannot go back to things as they were. Based on both my research and my lived experience during these uprisings, I believe the future of the Black liberation movement and its longevity depend on its ability to incorporate Black disability politics. This cannot be a politics only held and enacted by disabled people or when disabled people are visible at a protest. It must always be a part of planning and executing this work. Always. I hope that in some ways this book can contribute to such changes. Thank you for the gift of your time and attention. Thank you for caring enough to make it to the end. May you take something away to help make a better world.

—June 2020, Madison, WI

NOTES

Introduction

1   Black.Seed, "Black Queer Liberation Collective Black.Seed Shuts Down Bay Bridge," *Anti-Police Terror Project* (blog), accessed September 29, 2016, http://www.antipoliceterrorproject.org/new-blog-1/2016/1/18/black-queer-liberation-collective-blackseed-shuts-down-bay-bridge.

2   Yerba Buena Center for the Arts, "How Black.Seed Shut Down the Bay Bridge on Mlk," YouTube.com, accessed May 10, 2020, https://www.youtube.com/watch?v=4G76v_ilDzM.

3   I use *(dis)ability* to designate the overarching social system of bodymind norms that creates categories of disability, impairment, able-bodiedness, and able-mindedness, producing privilege for some and oppression for others in dynamic, intersectional, and context-based ways. I use the terms *disability* and *ability* to designate the specific marginalized and privileged positions within the (dis)ability system as a whole. For more on the rationale behind this language choice, see Schalk, "Critical Disability Studies as Methodology"; and Schalk, *Bodyminds Reimagined*, 6.

4   In addition to the individuals named thus far, additional examples of important Black disability studies scholarship include Samuels, "Examining Millie and Christine McKoy"; Samuels, *Fantasies of Identification*; Bailey, "Race and Disability in the Academy"; Boster, *African American Slavery and Disability*; Barclay, "'The Greatest Degree of Perfection'"; Barclay, "Mothering the 'Useless'"; Knadler, "Dis-Abled Citizenship"; Jarman, "Dismembering the Lynch Mob"; Jarman, "Coming Up from Underground"; and Jarman, "Cultural Consumption and Rejection of Precious Jones."

5   See Waggoner, "'My Most Humiliating Jim Crow Experience'"; Schalk, "Experience, Research, and Writing"; and Tyler, "Jim Crow's Disabilities."

6   Berne, "Disability Justice."

7   Berne, "Disability Justice."

8   Mingus, "Reflection toward Practice," 108.

9   See McRuer, *Crip Theory*; and M. Johnson and McRuer, "Cripistemologies."

10 Mingus, "Reflection toward Practice," 108.

11 Kafer, *Feminist, Queer, Crip*, 10.

12 Kafer, *Feminist, Queer, Crip*, 12.

13 See Schalk, "Interpreting Disability Metaphor and Race."

14 For more on the history of the disability rights movement, see Charlton, *Nothing about Us without Us*; Fleischer and Zames, *Disability Rights Movement*; and Shapiro, *No Pity*.

15 For the historical evidence of Black disability politics prior to the 1970s, see, for example, Tyler, "Jim Crow's Disabilities"; Waggoner, "'My Most Humiliating Jim Crow Experience'"; Knadler, "Dis-Abled Citizenship"; Knadler, *Vitality Politics*; and Barclay, *Mark of Slavery*.

16 Minich, "Enabling Whom?"; Schalk, "Critical Disability Studies as Methodology"; and J. Kim, "Toward a Crip-of-Color Critique."

17 Kafer, *Feminist, Queer, Crip*, 153.

18 Given the limited scholarly work on the specific approaches to disability politics within particular racialized communities thus far, I cannot say how much Black disability politics overlaps with Indigenous and Native disability politics, Asian/American disability politics, or Latinx disability politics, but I am certain future research will trace the connections among these approaches as each group further develops and articulates their specific disability politics.

19 An important example of this work occurring among other racialized groups is the 2013 special issue of *Amerasia Journal* 39, no. 1, titled "The State of Illness and Disability in Asian America," and the *Asian American Literary Review*'s 2016 special issue "Open in Emergency: A Special Issue on Asian American Mental Health."

20 I acknowledge the scholarly debates around the term *intersectionality*, but following the lead of Jennifer Nash, I aim to disrupt Black feminist defensiveness and protectiveness of the term by simply defining and using an intersectional framework rather than spending extensive time defending it. The term works for me and may not work for others, and that is okay. See Nash, *Black Feminism Reimagined*.

21 For scholarship on the complicated relationships of people of color to disability identity, see Day, "Resisting Disability, Claiming HIV"; Nishida, "Understanding Political Development through an Intersectionality Framework"; Erevelles, *Disability and Difference in Global Contexts*; Erevelles, "Crippin' Jim Crow"; and Puar, *Right to Maim*.

22 See Erevelles, "Crippin' Jim Crow"; Dolmage, "Disabled upon Arrival"; and A. Taylor, "Discourse of Pathology."

23 See J. Kim, "Cripping East Los Angeles"; Schalk, *Bodyminds Reimagined*, 33–58; and Puar, *Right to Maim*, 95–155.

24 See J. Livingston, *Debility and the Moral Imagination in Botswana*.

25 Puar, *Right to Maim*, xiii.

26 Puar, *Right to Maim*, xv.

27 Price, "Bodymind Problem and the Possibilities of Pain"; and Schalk, *Body-minds Reimagined*.

28 See Springer, *Living for the Revolution*.

29 For examples of the range of issues addressed by Black feminists, see Hull, Bell-Scott, and Smith, *All the Women Are White*; Combahee River Collective, "The Combahee River Collective Statement"; B. Smith, *Home Girls*; or Guy-Sheftall, *Words of Fire*. For a scholarly analysis of this broad range of Black feminist issues, see Springer, *Living for the Revolution*, 91–93.

30 All participants were paid for their time, and interviews ranged from thirty minutes to just under two hours. I asked participants the same series of eight questions but informed them that they were allowed to skip any questions or come back to them later. I asked:

1 How do you identify or describe yourself?

2 How did you become politicized in your identities or become an activist?

3 What activist work have you done? What are you most proud of in that work?

4 How do you think Black activists and Black communities have addressed or avoided disability as a political concern?

5 How do you think the mainstream disability rights movement has addressed or avoided race as a political concern?

6 How do you see race and disability (or racism and ableism) interacting in the lives of Black people historically and/or in the present?

7 How would you describe Black disability politics or Black disability activism? What are important qualities or aspects of Black disability political work?

8 Is there anything else I should know about you, your work, or Black disability politics?

After the interviews, I sent transcripts to participants to allow them to review them and edit or change anything they wanted. Later I sent the first draft of chapter 5 to the participants to again get their approval and feedback on how I am representing them and their ideas.

31 Talila "TL" Lewis, interview by Sami Schalk, December 6, 2019.

Chapter One: "We Have a Right to Rebel"

1 The original image caption misidentified Dennis Phillips as Dennis Billips, but he is mentioned and quoted in other articles under his proper name.

2 Huggins and LeBlanc-Ernest, "Revolutionary Women, Revolutionary Education," 165. Ericka Huggins and Angela D. LeBlanc-Ernest argue that Panther women are represented less in the literature in part because they wrote less and worked more than leading men in the BPP. They write, "BPP women did

not have time to reflect and write while they were active in the Party. Most Party members worked twenty hours per day, seven days per week. Women's activism was central to Party success. Indeed, women's work in the Party was not separate work. It was seamlessly intertwined with the Party's leadership and activities. Due to the daily trauma women in the BPP experienced from external oppressive forces such as harassment from local law enforcement, shootings, assassinations, arrests, and imprisonment, all of which often caused women to be separated from their children, many privately processed the complexities of being women and mothers, Black critical thinkers, and revolutionary activists." Huggins and LeBlanc-Ernest, "Revolutionary Women, Revolutionary Education," 166.

3 Bloom and Martin, *Black against Empire*, 2.

4 Quoted in "Black Panther Greatest Threat to U.S. Security," *Desert Sun*, July 16, 1969, 17.

5 Rhodes, *Framing the Black Panthers*, 292–93.

6 For more extended histories of the BPP, see Bloom and Martin, *Black against Empire*; and Spencer, *Revolution Has Come*.

7 Austin, *Up against the Wall*, xviii.

8 O. Johnson, "Explaining the Demise of the Black Panther Party."

9 See A. Nelson, *Body and Soul*; and R. Spencer, *The Revolution Has Come*.

10 Hilliard, *Black Panther Party*, 3; see also Austin, *Up against the Wall*.

11 "History of the Black Panther Party: Black Panther Party Platform and Program," the Black Panther Party Research Project, accessed May 20, 2017, https://web.stanford.edu/group/blackpanthers/history.shtml.

12 "History of the Black Panther Party"; emphasis added.

13 "History of the Black Panther Party."

14 Bloom and Martin, *Black against Empire*, 56.

15 Spencer, *Revolution Has Come*, 192–94.

16 "Innerparty Memorandum #24," series 2, box 4, folder 10, Dr. Huey P. Newton Foundation Inc. Collection, M0864, Department of Special Collections, Stanford University Libraries, Stanford, CA.

17 Rhodes, *Framing the Black Panthers*, 308–9.

18 For example, see Fleischer and Zames, *Disability Rights Movement*, 54; Shaw, *Activist's Handbook*, 240; Shapiro, *No Pity*, 67; Longmore, *Why I Burned My Book*, 107; Meade and Serlin, "Editors' Introduction," 2; and Scotch, *From Good Will to Civil Rights*, 115.

19 See D'Lil, *Becoming Real in 24 Days*; O'Toole, *Fading Scars*; Leroy Moore, "Black History of 504 Sit-In for Disability Rights: More Than Serving Food— When Will the Healing Begin?," *San Francisco Bay View*, February 11, 2014, http://sfbayview.com/2014/02/black-history-of-504-sit-in-for-disability-rights -more-than-serving-food-when-will-the-healing-begin/; and Vilissa Thompson, "Black History Month 2017: Brad Lomax, Disabled Black Panther," Ramp

Your Voice!, February 17, 2017, http://www.rampyourvoice.com/black-history
-month-2017-brad-lomax-disabled-black-panther/.

20 Groups who provided support for the 504 protesters "included the Butterfly
Brigade, 'a group of gay men who patrolled city streets on the lookout for
gay violence,' who smuggled walkie-talkies into the occupied building; Glide
Church; local and national labor organizations; members of Delancey Street,
the famous grassroots rehab program for substance abusers and former felons,
who brought breakfast into the building each day; the Chicano group Mission
Rebels, who also provided food; and the Black Panthers." Schweik, "Lomax's
Matrix."

21 D'Lil, *Becoming Real in 24 Days*, 19, 57.

22 D'Lil, *Becoming Real in 24 Days*, 56. Based on the location of this quote in the
book, it's unclear if the quote comes from White's rally speech on April 5 or
from later, most likely on April 8, the fourth day of the protest, which is the
chapter in which this quote and White's photo (captioned as an image from his
rally speech) both appear.

23 Spencer, *Revolution Has Come*, 7–34, 98–99, 154, 203; Bloom and Martin, *Black against Empire*, 97–98, 306–7; and Alameen-Shavers, "Woman
Question."

24 In a footnote Schweik includes informal communication with Fultz in which
he recalls organizing the Panthers' delivery of food and giving an "extempora-
neous" speech at the protest because Elaine Brown, leader of the BPP at that
time, was unable to attend. I have been unable to locate any transcript or date
of Fultz's speech. D'Lil lists Brown as "outside support." D'Lil, *Becoming Real
in 24 Days*, 58.

25 Quoted in D'Lil, *Becoming Real in 24 Days*, 58.

26 "BPP Members Interviewed on Handicapped Protest for Civil and Human
Rights: Disabled Movement Born: 'We Have a Right to Rebel,'" *Black Panther*,
May 14, 1977, 5, 8.

27 K. Rosenthal, "The Intersections and Divergences of Disability and Race."

28 Elaine Brown, "Leader of the Black Panther Party Elaine Brown Talks about
the Party's Involvement and Support of the 1977 Section 504 Occupation," oral
history, Paul K. Longmore Institute on Disability, 2014, DIVA, San Francisco
State University, https://diva.sfsu.edu/collections/longmoreinstitute/bundles
/230640.

29 E. Brown, "Leader of the Black Panther Party."

30 Report by Brad Lomax, September 3, 1977, series 2, box 5, folder 8, Dr. Huey P.
Newton Foundation Inc. Collection, M0864, Department of Special Collections, Stanford University Libraries.

31 The second half of the report briefly discusses conflict with "Chuck," likely
Chuck Jackson from the previously discussed cover-story image. Lomax states,
"I have criticized Chuck constantly on the house condition: floor waxing,
kitchen cleaning, washing the dishes, and washing my clothes. These criticisms

seem to have no effect." Lomax then notes that he told Jackson that if the issues continued, he would "take it too [*sic*] a higher level." Lomax concludes by stating that he would like to go swimming in an indoor pool because "it would help my speech, organize my thoughts etc." Archival records by and about Lomax are extremely limited, and at least one document from or about Lomax and Jackson has been removed from the Dr. Huey P. Newton Foundation Inc. Collection for "confidential" reasons. However, given this report and the fact that Jackson accompanied Lomax throughout the protest events, including the trip to DC, it seems reasonable to infer that Jackson acted as Lomax's roommate in shared BPP housing and as his personal care assistant as part of his duties as a Panther. It's hard to say much more about their relationship without further evidence, but Lomax's report suggests that care work for disabled members (in addition to the care work provided by the clinics and the children's programs) was part of the labor Panther members were expected to take on to sustain the work of the collective. Report by Lomax, September 3, 1977.

32 Robnett, "African-American Women in the Civil Rights Movement."

33 Phillips, "Feminist Leadership of Ericka Huggins," 207.

34 "Rights for Disabled at Issue, B.P.P. Lends Support: Powerful Protest by Handicapped at H.E.W.," *Black Panther*, April 16, 1977, 4, 20.

35 E. Brown, "Leader of the Black Panther Party."

36 "Rights for Disabled at Issue," 4.

37 O'Toole, *Fading Scars*, 60.

38 Quoted in Pelka, *What We Have Done*, 273; emphasis added.

39 The *Black Panther* articles and announcements about the sit-in are as follows: "Rights for Disabled at Issue, B.P.P. Lends Support: Powerful Protest by Handicapped at H.E.W.," April 16, 1977, 4, 20; "Comment: The Harder You Look into the Light, the Brighter You Become," April 23, 1977, 2, 12; "Bulletin," April 23, 1977, 2; "Delegation to Go to Washington, Demand H.E.W. Sign 504: Hearings, Support Rally Highlight Handicapped Protest," April 23, 1977, 4, 12; "Carter, HEW Secretary Califano Snub Disabled Delegation: Handicapped Rally—Sign 504 Now," April 30, 1977, 4, 10; "Pressure Forces Califano to Sign 504 Regulations: Handicapped Win Demands—End H.E.W. Occupation," May 7, 1977, 1, 6; "Editorial: What Price Freedom," May 7, 1977, 2; "504: Civil Rights for the Disabled," May 7, 1977, 5; "BPP Members Interviewed on Handicapped: Protest for Civil and Human Rights Disabled Movement Born: 'We Have a Right to Rebel,'" May 14, 1977, 5, 8; and Joan Tollifson, "Comment: Disabled: We Are No Longer Invisible," July 2, 1977, 2, 12.

40 "Protest Systematic Exclusion: Disabled Sue A.C. Transit," *Black Panther*, July 2, 1977, 14; and "Disabled Score Victory over Supermarket Barriers: Blind Mother Fights Bias for Custody of Children," *Black Panther*, August 13, 1977, 10.

41 The number of people who received or read the paper can only be estimated. In May 1978, the editor of the *Black Panther* estimated they printed approximately 5,500 copies of the paper per issue. Spencer, *Revolution Has Come*, 192. It is

reasonable to assume, therefore, that about that number were being printed and distributed during the period discussed here.

42 "Rights for Disabled at Issue," 4.

43 "Rights for Disabled at Issue," 20.

44 A version of the social model was explicitly included in a quote from a protester who stated, "If they'd take away the handicaps (like stairs, and others barriers for wheelchair-confined and otherwise disabled people), then we wouldn't be handicapped." "Rights for Disabled at Issue," 20.

45 Shakespeare, "Social Model of Disability."

46 Quoted in "Rights for Disabled at Issue," 20.

47 See "Medical Malpractice as Methods of Torture at Niantic State Farm for Women," *Black Panther*, November 21, 1970, 17.

48 Quoted in "Pressure Forces Califano," 6.

49 For more on oppression analogies, see Schalk, "Interpreting Disability Metaphor and Race"; Sherry, "(Post)Colonising Disability"; and Samuels, "My Body, My Closet."

50 For examples of other articles in major national papers that focused much more on cost, see Nancy Hicks, "Equity for Disabled Likely to Be Costly," *New York Times*, May 1, 1977, 29; or Bill Peterson, "Schools Hit Cost of Ending Bias against Disabled," *Washington Post*, July 5, 1977, A8.

51 "Editorial: What Price Freedom," 2.

52 "Comment: The Harder You Look," 12.

53 "Comment: The Harder You Look," 2.

54 "BPP Members Interviewed," 5, 8.

55 "BPP Members Interviewed," 8; and "Delegation to Go to Washington," 12.

56 "BPP Members Interviewed," 5.

57 Beal, "Double Jeopardy"; and Bambara, *Black Woman*.

58 Combahee River Collective, "The Combahee River Collective Statement."

59 K.-Y. Taylor, *How We Get Free*, 8.

60 Phillips, "Feminist Leadership of Ericka Huggins."

61 "Carter, HEW Secretary Califano Snub," 10; "Delegation to Go to Washington," 4; and "Pressure Forces Califano," 6. Across the ten articles (approximately ten thousand words total) covering the 504 demonstration in the *Black Panther*, the words *inspiring* or *inspiration* were used six times total, the word *poignant* was used twice, and the words *victimized* or *victim* were used four times (all four in reference to Lomax's multiple sclerosis).

62 Schweik, "Lomax's Matrix."

63 For more on this argument, see Schalk, "Black Disability Gone Viral."

64 "Carter, HEW Secretary Califano Snub," 10; "Editorial: What Price Freedom," 2; and "BPP Members Interviewed," 5.

65 "Pressure Forces Califano," 1.

66 Shapiro, *No Pity*, 66.

67   For more on the history of the Intercommunal Youth Institute and its evolution into the OCS, see C. Jones and Gayles, "'The World Is a Child's Classroom'"; and Williamson, "Community Control with a Black Nationalist Twist."

68   Huggins and LeBlanc-Ernest, "Revolutionary Women, Revolutionary Education," 173.

69   Huggins and LeBlanc-Ernest, "Revolutionary Women, Revolutionary Education," 168, 170.

70   Huggins and LeBlanc-Ernest, "Revolutionary Women, Revolutionary Education," 177.

71   In an audio interview, former OCS teacher M. Gayle "Asali" Dickson provides an anecdote about a preschool-aged girl who was "very hard to understand" in her verbal communication excitedly using clearer language with her mother after Dickson created a large-scale visual representation of a class field trip. This is potentially another example of a student with a disability at the OCS. Tammerlin Drummond, "Black Panther School a Legend in Its Time," *East Bay Times*, October 6, 2016, https://www.eastbaytimes.com/2016/10/06/black -panther-school-ahead-of-its-time/.

72   Huggins and LeBlanc-Ernest, "Revolutionary Women, Revolutionary Education," 172, 177; emphasis added.

73   Huggins and LeBlanc-Ernest, "Revolutionary Women, Revolutionary Education," 176.

74   Huggins and LeBlanc-Ernest, "Revolutionary Women, Revolutionary Education," 162.

75   Abron, "Reflections of a Former Oakland Public School Parent," 15.

76   Huggins and LeBlanc-Ernest, "Revolutionary Women, Revolutionary Education," 176; and "Closing Arguments Heard in I.Q. Lawsuit," *Black Panther*, June 3, 1978, 3, 15. See also Abron, "Reflections of a Former Oakland Public School Parent," 18; and "Lester Lewis Unjustly Placed in E.M.R. Class for 5 Years: Black Youth Testifies at I.Q. Bias Trial," *Black Panther*, November 5, 1977, 4.

77   See, for example, the following *Black Panther* articles: "Lawsuit to Stop Racist Placement in Schools: Biased I.Q. Tests Label Black Children Mentally Retarded," October 8, 1977, 1, 6; "Demand End to Use in Labeling Black Children as Mentally-Retarded: Top Psychologists Testify on I.Q. Test Bias," October 22, 1977, 3, 8; "Lester Lewis Unjustly Placed"; "I.Q. Test Bias Trial: Educator Links Reading Skills and E.M.R. Placement," December 24, 1977, 4; and "I.Q. Bias Trial: Still Too Many Blacks in Classes for Retarded," January 21, 1978, 11, 26.

78   See Ahram, Fergus, and Noguera, "Addressing Racial/Ethnic Disproportionality in Special Education"; Erevelles, "Crippin' Jim Crow"; and Annamma, *Pedagogy of Pathologization*.

79   Ericka Huggins, "An Oral History with Ericka Huggins," interview by Fiona Thompson in 2007, Oral History Center, Bancroft Library, University of California Berkeley, 2010, https://digitalassets.lib.berkeley.edu/roho/ucb/text /huggins_ericka.pdf.

80 "Biography," Ericka Huggins, accessed January 8, 2017, https://www
.erickahuggins.com/bio.

81 "Ericka Huggins Reviews First Year on the Alameda County Board of Education (Part 2)," *Black Panther*, August 6, 1977, 20.

82 "Ericka Huggins Reviews (Part 2)," 4, 20.

83 "Ericka Huggins Reviews First Year on the Alameda County Board of Education (Conclusion)," *Black Panther*, August 13, 1977, 4, 20.

Chapter Two: Fighting Psychiatric Abuse

1 Claude Steiner, "Principles of Radical Psychiatry," *Black Panther*, December 31,
1977, 2, 6.

2 Steiner, "Principles of Radical Psychiatry," 6.

3 See the following *Black Panther* articles: "NY's Tombs of Torture," August 30,
1969, 8; "Queens Copy Acquitted in Murder of 10-Year-Old; Brooklyn Officer
Indicted for Killing Sickle Cell Victim," June 22, 1974, 7; and "Blowing Off
Steam—a Necessity for Good Health," March 10, 1980, 7.

4 Steiner, "Principles of Radical Psychiatry," 6.

5 Steiner, "Principles of Radical Psychiatry," 6.

6 E. Brown, "Leader of the Black Panther Party."

7 Price, *Mad at School*, 7.

8 Occasionally, the *Black Panther* misnamed the NAPA in articles as the Network
against Psychiatric Abuse. For more on the NAPA, see their website: http://
networkagainstpsychiatricassault.org.

9 See the following *Black Panther* articles: "Chemical Zombies," April 24, 1976,
8; "Sit-In: N.A.P.A. Protests 'Human Slavery' of Mental Patients," July 10, 1976,
9, 25; "Suit Filed against Involuntary Confinement in Mental Institutions,"
July 17, 1976, 10; "At Calif Governor's Office: NAPA Ends Month Long Sit-
In," August 7, 1976, 6; "People's Perspective: Millions Denied Mental Health,"
September 24, 1977, 8; and "Suit Seeks Rights for Mental Patients," January 21,
1978, 11, 26.

10 For more on the history of the deinstitutionalization movement, see Grob,
From Asylum to Community.

11 See the following *Black Panther* articles: "Oppression Is Alive and Running
Amuck at Cuyahoga County Nursing Home," October 17, 1970, 15; "Mental
Hospital Sued for Violating Rights of Black Children," April 12, 1975, 8;
"Probe Deaths in Calif Mental Hospitals," October 23, 1976, 11; "373 'Ques-
tionable' Deaths Uncovered in Calif. Mental Hospitals," November 27, 1976,
9, 25; "An Inside Look at Napa State Mental Hospital: Warehousing Society's
Casualties," February 12, 1977, 5, 10; "Cruelty to Nursing Home Patients, Il-
legal Transfers Charged," May 7, 1977, 8; and "Bias against Retarded Banned,"
December 31, 1977, 4.

12 A. Nelson, *Body and Soul*, 158.

13 J. Johnson, *American Lobotomy*, 2; see also Pressman, *Last Resort*.

14 J. Johnson, *American Lobotomy*, 2, 17–18.

15 J. Johnson, *American Lobotomy*, 112.

16 As mentioned in the previous chapter, in the 1970s approximately 5,500 copies of the paper were being printed per issue and were distributed primarily in California but also in select cities nationwide. Spencer, *Revolution Has Come*, 192.

17 See Ben-Moshe and Carey, *Disability Incarcerated*; and the following *Black Panther* articles: "San Quentin Prisoners Kept Heavily Drugged," February 9, 1974, 3; "Regional Prisons for Disruptive Inmates Planned," February 9, 1974, 7, 10; "Inmates Expose Forced Drug Treatments," August 7, 1976, 9; "Forced Drugging of Mentally Ill California Inmates Probed," November 6, 1976, 10; and "Bill Seeks Ban on Prison Druggings," December 18, 1976, 5.

18 "Vacaville—America's Headquarters for Medical Genocide," *Black Panther*, June 26, 1971, 14. For historical context, Harriet A. Washington explains, "During World War II, prisoners had been commonly used as research subjects, and after the war, the United States was the only nation in the world continuing to legally use prisoners in clinical trials. Federal, pharmaceutical, and cosmetic companies' money catalyzed a thirty-year boom in research with prisoners" (*Medical Apartheid*, 249). These experiments occurred despite the American Medical Association's 1952 public disapproval of such practices. Washington writes that news coverage of prison medical, pharmaceutical and cosmetic research was generally lauded in the US until the reforms were passed in the 1970s (256, 265). By the time the Panthers were writing on the subject, prison research was supposed to be limited to therapeutic medical treatments with minimal risk, but as their articles suggest, even purportedly therapeutic medicine, especially psychiatric drugs, can be abused, especially when specifically applied to incarcerated racialized populations.

19 See, for example, "New Federal Prison for 'Behavior Modification' to Open," *Black Panther*, July 6, 1974, 5, 6.

20 For more on the concept of able-mindedness and its racial, gender, and class norms, see A. Taylor, "Discourse of Pathology"; or Schalk, *Bodyminds Reimagined*, chap. 2.

21 "Right to Refuse Psychosurgery Promoted," *Black Panther*, March 13, 1976, 7; and "Psychosurgery Given Ok," *Black Panther*, September 18, 1976, 7. Johnson provides more detailed information about the psychosurgery laws eventually passed in California and Oregon as well as on the congressional hearings on psychosurgery. J. Johnson, *American Lobotomy*, 122–31.

22 Kevin Crockett, "Patients Legal Defense Protests Forced Medication," *Black Panther*, January 24, 1976, sec. Letters to the Editor, 25.

23 K. Crockett, "Patients Legal Defense Protests Forced Medication," 25.

24 K. Crockett. "Patients Legal Defense Protests Forced Medication," 25.

25 Note that in the first letter the author is listed as Kevin Crockett, and in the second letter the author is listed as Calvin Crockett. It is unclear which

of these is correct, though it is reasonable to assume, given the content and origin of both letters, that the author is the same in each case, but the name was mistyped in one of the printings of the letters (which were likely handwritten).

26 Calvin Crockett, "Appeal from Chester Mental Health Center," *Black Panther*, May 1, 1976, 25.

27 C. Crockett, "Appeal from Chester Mental Health Center," 25.

28 "Vacaville—America's Headquarters for Medical Genocide," 14.

29 E. Kim, *Curative Violence*, 14.

30 Rayford Anderson, "Voice from Mental Institution," *Black Panther*, August 7, 1976, 25.

31 Crockett specifically mentions reading another issue of the *Black Panther* and requests additional political education materials in his January 24, 1976, letter.

32 For example, Judi Chamberlin's foundational 1978 book, *On Our Own: Patient-Controlled Alternatives to the Mental Health System*, mentions the presence of a Black woman on a psychiatric ward with her but does not engage the intersection of race and psychiatric disability (44). The most robust example I could find is an extended quote from an interview with Jennifer Reid, a mixed-race Black and Native lesbian, in which Reid explicitly discusses the intersection of the prison industrial complex, racism, and the psychiatric industrial complex based on her experiences in Canada. Everett, *Fragile Revolution*, 83–87.

33 Morrison, *Talking Back to Psychiatry*, 78 79.

34 For more on Black experiences with psychiatric institutions, see Vanessa Jackson, "In Our Own Voice: African-American Stories of Oppression, Survival and Recovery in Mental Health Systems."

35 For more on race and disability metaphors and oppression analogies, see either Schalk, *Bodyminds Reimagined*, chap. 1; or Schalk, "Interpreting Disability Metaphor and Race."

36 "History of the Black Panther Party"; emphasis added.

37 J. Johnson, *American Lobotomy*, 114.

38 J. Johnson, *American Lobotomy*, 114.

39 "Vacaville 'Medical' Facility," *Black Panther*, October 28, 1972, 12.

40 "Burn Your Brains Out," *Black Panther*, January 1, 1972, 3, 18.

41 J. Johnson, *American Lobotomy*, 114.

42 In addition to "Burn Your Brains Out," see also "On Eldridge Cleaver by Kathleen Cleaver," *Black Panther*, August 9, 1969, 5.

43 Hilliard and Cole, *This Side of Glory*, 356.

44 Hilliard and Cole, *This Side of Glory*, 358–59.

45 "Tearing Out Our Thoughts: Psychosurgery and the Black Community," *Black Panther*, January 6, 1973, 6, 13.

46 "Tearing Out Our Thoughts," 13; emphasis added.

47 See, for example, "v.a. Admits 16 Psychosurgery Operations," *Black Panther*, July 7, 1973, 6; and "Human Experimentation at Holmesburg Prison Exposed," *Black Panther*, October 27, 1973, 6, 12.

48 A. Nelson, *Body and Soul*, 161–73.

49 "Brain Operation Performed without Permission: Oakland Youth Victim of Psychosurgery," *Black Panther*, April 30, 1977, 10, 12.

50 Quoted in "Brain Operation Performed without Permission," 10.

51 "Brain Operation Performed without Permission," 10.

52 "Brain Operation Performed without Permission," 10.

53 "Brain Operation Performed without Permission," 10; and "v.a. Hospital Pays for Human Guinea Pigs: Performs Psychosurgery on Black Oakland Youth," *Black Panther*, May 28, 1977, 7.

54 "Brain Operation Performed without Permission," 10.

55 "Brain Operation Performed without Permission," 10.

56 "Brain Operation Performed without Permission," 12.

57 "Brain Operation Performed without Permission," 12.

58 "Mother of Psychosurgery Victim Appeals for Community Help," *Black Panther*, May 7, 1977, 12.

59 "Mother of Psychosurgery Victim Appeals for Community Help," *Black Panther*, May 7, 1977, 26.

60 Utsey et al., "Cultural, Sociofamilial, and Psychological Resources"; and Kwate and Goodman, "Cross-Sectional and Longitudinal Effects of Racism on Mental Health."

61 "v.a. Hospital Pays for Human Guinea Pigs," 7.

62 Washington, *Medical Apartheid*, 349.

63 J. Fisher and Kalbaugh, "Challenging Assumptions about Minority Participation in US Clinical Research"; and J. Fisher, "Expanding the Frame of 'Voluntariness' in Informed Consent." See also Cottingham and Fisher, "Risk and Emotion among Healthy Volunteers in Clinical Trials"; and Monahan and Fisher, "'I'm Still a Hustler.'"

64 Ojanuga, "Medical Ethics of the 'Father of Gynaecology,' Dr J Marion Sims"; Spettel and White, "Portrayal of J. Marion Sims' Controversial Surgical Legacy"; Washington, *Medical Apartheid*, 2, 24–36, 105–8; and Skloot, *Immortal Life of Henrietta Lacks*.

65 Rhodes, *Framing the Black Panthers*.

66 Quoted in, respectively, Erin Strecker, "Rudy Giuliani Says Beyoncé's Super Bowl Performance Was 'Attack' on Police," Billboard, February 8, 2016, https://www.billboard.com/articles/news/super-bowl/6867370/rudy-giuliani-beyonce-super-bowl-performance-attack-police; and "Milwaukee County Sheriff David Clarke Sounds Off on Beyoncé," Fox 32 Chicago, February 10, 2016, https://www.fox32chicago.com/news/milwaukee-county-sheriff-david-clarke-sounds-off-on-beyonce.

67 Proud of the Blues, "Anti-Beyoncé Protest Rally—New York," Eventbrite, 2016, https://www.eventbrite.com/e/anti-beyonce-protest-rally-new-york-tickets -21446744791?aff=efbneb#.

68 Andy Campbell, "The Anti-Beyoncé Protest at NFL Headquarters Had a Dismal Turnout," *Huffington Post*, February 16, 2016, https://www.huffpost .com/entry/anti-beyonce-protest-nfl_n_56c33e36e4b08ffac12676fd; and Spencer Kornhabe, "Why Beyoncé Is Embracing Her Own Backlash," *Atlantic*, April 28, 2016, https://www.theatlantic.com/entertainment /archive/2016/04/boycott-beyonce-merchandise-formation-tour -opposition/480318/.

69 See Nelson, *Body and Soul*; Spencer, *The Revolution Has Come*; Huggins and LeBlanc-Ernest, "Revolutionary Women, Revolutionary Education"; and Bloom and Martin, *Black against Empire*.

70 Federal Bureau of Investigation, Counterterrorism Division, *Black Identity Extremists Likely Motivated to Target Law Enforcement Officers*, 2.

Praxis Interlude One

1 *Oxford English Dictionary Online*, s.v. "vegetable," accessed November 29, 2021, https://www-oed-com.ezproxy.library.wisc.edu/view/Entry/221872?rskey =ijcppT&result=1&isAdvanced=false.

2 Jennett and Plum, "Persistent Vegetative State after Brain Damage." See also Jennett, *Vegetative State*.

3 Examples of this early use of *vegetable* or *human vegetable* to describe the effects of psychosurgery are cited in J. Johnson, *American Lobotomy*, 96; and Diefenbach et al., "Portrayal of Lobotomy in the Popular Press."

4 Interestingly, *vegetable* is an example of how the social reception and use of medical language can result in changes to medical terminology and practices. This has occurred previously in regard to words like *idiot, imbecile, moron,* and *retarded,* which were all at one time official medical terms for what we would now call *developmental* or *intellectual disabilities* but are no longer used as such, in part owing to how these words were taken up as insults in wider society. Tammy Reynolds, c.e. Zupanick, and Mark Dombeck, "History of Stigmatizing Names for Intellectual Disabilities," accessed December 18, 2017, https://www.mentalhelp.net/intellectual-disabilities/history-of -stigmatizing-names/.

   In regard to *vegetable* and *vegetative state*, in 2010 a group of doctors affiliated with the European Task Force on Disorders of Consciousness argued for changing the name of this condition to *unresponsive wakefulness syndrome*. In their rationale for why the name should be changed, Steven Laureys and colleagues provide both social and medical reasons, arguing that for "most of the lay public and media *vegetative state* has a pejorative connotation" that reduces the humanity of the person involved, and that *vegetative state* as a descriptor misrepresents the condition in multiple ways.

The misleading nature of the term *vegetative state*, the authors argue, can potentially lead to a misunderstanding of prognosis by loved ones (because *state* implies permanence) and/or misrecognition of consciousness and awareness in patients "without behavioral responses to command." So although part of the rationale for changing the term *vegetative state* to *unresponsive wakefulness syndrome* is based in medical practice and diagnosis, a significant portion is also based on the negative social connotations of the term and its derivative social insult of *vegetable,* which was used in the Panthers' articles on psychiatric abuse and continues to be used today. Laureys et al., "Unresponsive Wakefulness Syndrome," 711.

5   "Tearing Out Our Thoughts," 13.

6   *Vegetable* continues to be used today as an ableist term to disparagingly describe people with a number of disabilities, particularly those with limited movement and communication capacities. The top two definitions for *vegetable* on the Urban Dictionary website in 2017, for example, were "a person who is brain-dead" and "something that is living, but their brain is not working, they have no personality, they're stupid." Urban Dictionary, s.v. "vegetable," accessed December 14, 2017, https://www.urbandictionary.com/define.php?term =vegetable. The latter definition also includes the hashtags "#coma #stupid #retard #no-lifer."

7   Increasingly, the disabled poster child in US, Canadian, and European contexts is becoming the "foreign" racialized disabled poster child for charity and nonprofit organizations. For more on this particular use of disabled bodyminds for supposedly positive social justice purposes, see Barker, *Postcolonial Fiction and Disability*, 7–15; and Talley, *Saving Face*, chap. 5.

8   Kafer, *Feminist, Queer, Crip*, 158–59.

9   Clare, *Brilliant Imperfection*, 56.

10 J. Johnson, *American Lobotomy*; and Metzl, *The Protest Psychosis*.

11 Erevelles, *Disability and Difference in Global Contexts*, 17. See also Puar, *Right to Maim*.

12 Clare, *Brilliant Imperfection*, 62.

13 Aisha I. Jefferson, "7 Shots in the Back: How 3 Minutes with Police Ripped Apart Jacob Blake's Life and Rekindled His Family's Push for Justice," *Insider*, June 13, 2021, https://www.insider.com/jacob-blake-profile-family-history-civil -rights-2021-6.

14 Jacob Blake, "Jacob Blake Speaks Out for 1st Time since Near-Fatal Shooting in Exclusive Interview," interview by Michael Strahan, *ABC News*, January 14, 2021, https://abcnews.go.com/US/abc-news-exclusive-jacob-blake-speaks-1st -time/story?id=75244637.

15 Blake, "Jacob Blake Speaks Out"; and Jefferson, "7 Shots in the Back."

16 Jefferson, "7 Shots in the Back"; and Christina Morales, "What We Know about the Shooting of Jacob Blake," *New York Times*, March 26, 2021, https:// www.nytimes.com/article/jacob-blake-shooting-kenosha.html.

17 Blake, "Jacob Blake Speaks Out."

18 During the Kenosha protests, two men, Joseph Rosenbaum and Anthony Huber, were shot and killed by Kyle Rittenhouse, a white teenager from Illinois. Rittenhouse was found not guilty of all charges on November 19, 2021 by a nearly all white jury.

19 Morales, "What We Know."

20 Jefferson, "7 Shots in the Back."

21 Clare Proctor, "Jacob Blake Handcuffed to Hospital Bed, Father Says," *Chicago Sun Times*, August 27, 2020, https://chicago.suntimes.com/2020 /8/27/21404463/jacob-blake-father-kenosha-police-shooting-hospital-bed -handcuffs; and Disability Rights Wisconsin, "DRW Condemns Use of Restraints on Jacob Blake," August 28, 2020, https://www.disabilityrightswi.org /wp-content/uploads/2020/08/DRW-Press-Release-Statement-on-Treatment -of-Jacob-Blake-082820-acc.pdf.

22 Meg Wagner and Mike Hayes, "August 25 Jacob Blake Protests News," CNN, August 26, 2020, https://www.cnn.com/us/live-news/jacob-blake-kenosha -wisconsin-shooting-08-25-2020/h_a1b64cca97f5e27f97856dcffc428a60.

23 Ben Crump (@AttorneyCrump), "#JacobBlake released this powerful video message from his hospital bed today, reminding everyone just how precious life is. #JusticeForJacobBlake," Twitter, September 5, 2020, 7:11 p.m., https:// twitter.com/AttorneyCrump/status/1302398977938161667?ref_src=twsrc% 5Etfw%7Ctwcamp%5Etweetembed%7Ctwterm%5E1302398977938161667% 7Ctwgr%5E%7Ctwcon%5Es1_&ref_url=https%3A%2F%2Fwww.news8000 .com%2Fnothing-but-pain-jacob-blake-speaks-about-shooting-from-hospital -bed%2F.

24 Quoted in "Wisconsin DOJ Reveals New Details Surrounding Jacob Blake's Shooting by Kenosha Police," NBC *Chicago*, August 26, 2020, https://www .nbcchicago.com/news/local/wisconsin-doj-reveals-new-details-surrounding -jacob-blakes-shooting-by-kenosha-police/2329213/.

25 Rhea Boyd, "Jacob Blake's Police Shooting Highlights the Hidden Victims of Police Violence," NBC *News*, August 29, 2020, https://www.nbcnews.com /think/opinion/jacob-blake-s-police-shooting-highlights-hidden-victims -police-violence-ncna1238574.

26 "New Vacaville Drug Control Program Makes Vegetables out of Inmates," *Black Panther*, August 31, 1974, 8.

27 "Tearing Out Our Thoughts," 13; "Mother of Psychosurgery Victim," 12; and "V.A. Hospital Pays for Human Guinea Pigs," 7.

28 "Mother of Psychosurgery Victim," 12; and "V.A. Hospital Pays for Human Guinea Pigs," 7.

29 "Tearing Out Our Thoughts," 13; "New Vacaville Drug Control Program," 8; and "V.A. Admits 16 Psychosurgery Operations," 6.

30 "Mother of Psychosurgery Victim," 12; and "V.A. Hospital Pays for Human Guinea Pigs," 7.

1 Black Women's Health Project, "First National Conference on Black Women's Health Issues," 1983, 8, 10, 14, 19, Black Women's Health Imperative Records, Sophia Smith Collection, Smith College, Northampton, MA. Unless otherwise noted, all documents by the NBWHP are from this collection.

2 Lillie Allen, "Black and Female: What Is the Reality?" in "First National Conference on Black Women's Health Issues," 42.

3 Valerie Boyd describes the workshop as follows: "The 'Black & Female' workshop seeks to help us recognize and purge ourselves of internalized oppression. The workshop teaches us to engage in confirmation rather than in condemnation. To appreciate our diversity rather than scorn our differences. To validate our own beauty, our own strength, our own ability and right to give and take. The workshop teaches us to overcome fear of relationships that require genuine self-exposure. To pursue our longing for each other/ourselves." Boyd, "Where Is the Love?," 2.

4 For histories of progressive health movements generally, see Hoffman, *Politics of Knowledge*; Dittmer, *Good Doctors*; and Loyd, *Health Rights Are Civil Rights*. For histories of feminist health activism, see Ruzek, *Women's Health Movement*; Morgen, *Into Our Own Hands*; and J. Nelson, *More Than Medicine*. For histories of Black health activism, see S. Smith, *Sick and Tired of Being Sick and Tired*; and A. Nelson, *Body and Soul*.

5 Avery, "Empowerment through Wellness."

6 A. Nelson, *Body and Soul*, 96.

7 Evan Hart notes that "in 1986, a group of Latina women founded the National Latina Health Organization (NLHO). The Native American Women's Health Education Resource Center (NAWHERC) opened its doors in 1986, and Asian activists founded the National Asian Women's Health Organization (NAWHO) in 1993. These groups and their founders all pointed to Avery and the NBWHP as inspirations and models for organizing themselves." Hart, "Building a More Inclusive Women's Health Movement," 11.

8 NBWHP, *Lasting Legacy*, 30.

9 NBWHP, "Self-Help Booklet," 1985, 1–2.

10 Byllye Avery, "Byllye Y. Avery," interview by Loretta Ross, July 21–22, 2005, Provincetown, MA, Voices of Feminism Oral History Project, box 6, Sophia Smith Collection, Smith College, Northampton, MA.

11 Avery, "Byllye Y. Avery," 11.

12 Russell, *Black Genius and the American Experience*, 393.

13 For more on Avery's personal history, see Hart, "Building a More Inclusive Women's Health Movement."

14 See, for example, NBWHP, "The National Black Women's Health Project Self-Help Developers' Manual," 1990, vol. 13; and Hoytt, Beard, and Black Women's Health Imperative, *Health First!*, 198.

15 Quoted in NBWHP, *Lasting Legacy*, 8.

16 Hart, "Building a More Inclusive Women's Health Movement," 75–76; and NBWHP, "Project Proposal 1994–1995 Submitted to Public Welfare Foundation," 1994, 19.

17 For instance, the 1991 evaluation report of the Center for Black Women's Wellness states "that all staff members are expected to participate in the self-help group process," and the 1996 national organization bylaws require that 51 percent of the board members be active members of a self-help group in good standing with the organization. NBWHP, "Center for Black Women's Wellness Evaluation Report," 1991, vol. 4; and NBWHP, "Amended and Restated Bylaws of the National Black Women's Health Project, Inc.," 1996, vol. 5.

18 NBWHP, "Project Proposal to Ford Foundation," 1989, 13; and NBWHP, "Organization Briefing Material," 2000.

19 NBWHP, "Annual Report," 1989, 3.

20 NBWHP, "Eight Week Self-Help Group Meeting Guide Draft," ca. 2000, 24. This sentiment is also expressed earlier in the organization's history in the 1989 annual report, which states, "Self-help groups provide a supportive environment for women to build self-esteem and develop coping and problem-solving skills, the basis for a commitment to wellness. Groups raise awareness about controllable factors associated with major health problems, and offer basic information on family life and educational skills within a framework of empowerment. Self-help groups create a bridge to community resources, new pathways for referrals that have the potential to significantly improve a member's quality of life and, by extension, her family and community.... NBWHP self-help groups provide a time and place for Black women to come together to talk openly and honestly, to be validated for their historic ability to survive despite assaults to self-esteem and self-worth, and to collectively develop solutions to our poor health status. By breaking the conspiracy of silence that threatens individual health, NBWHP self-help groups enable each participant to analyze her life and understand her decision-making within a social context. The empowerment process encourages personal responsibility and a commitment to changing one's life and community for the better." NBWHP, "Annual Report," 1989, 3.

21 NBWHP, "A Proposal for Consideration for Program Funding Continuation Submitted on Behalf of Center for Black Women's Wellness, a Program Component of the National Black Women's Health Project," 1991, 3.

22 NBWHP, "Self-Help Developer's Manual," 15.

23 NBWHP, "Organization Briefing Material," 2000.

24 NBWHP, "Our Bodies, Our Voices, Our Choices," 1998, 1.

25 Grad, "Preamble of the Constitution of the World Health Organization."

26 Villarosa and NBWHP, *Body and Soul*, xvii.

27 See also Boykins, "Wellness Not Medicine, Safeguard for the Year 2000," 16, 63.

28 Parker, "Emotional Aspects of Chronic Illness," 3.

29 Harriet A. Washington writes that "African Americans also suffer far more devastating but equally preventable disease complications, such as blindness,

confinement to wheelchairs, and limb loss. Studies continue to demonstrate that, far from sharing in the bounty of American medical technology, African Americans are often bereft of high-technology care, even for life-threatening conditions such as heart disease." Washington, *Medical Apartheid*, 20. See also Smedley, Stith, and Nelson, *Unequal Treatment*.

30 Shakespeare, "Social Model of Disability," 199; and Kafer, *Feminist, Queer, Crip*, 6–10.

31 See Wendell, "Unhealthy Disabled"; Deal, "Disabled People's Attitudes toward Other Impairment Groups"; and Shakespeare, *Disability Rights and Wrongs*, 75.

32 See Price, "Bodymind Problem and the Possibilities of Pain," 280–81; N. Jones and Brown, "Absence of Psychiatric c/s/x Perspectives in Academic Discourse"; and Kafer, *Feminist, Queer, Crip*.

33 Puar, *The Right to Maim*.

34 See, for example, Wilson, "Reclaiming Our Spiritual Health"; Crichlow, "Queen Afua"; Estes, "Choosing to Live in a Time of AIDS"; and Helem, "Little Pentecostal Lesbian That Sat on the Pew."

35 Villarosa and NBWHP, *Body and Soul*, 395.

36 Villarosa and NBWHP, *Body and Soul*, 397.

37 Hawkins, "'… I Wanted to Live' Dialysis," 6.

38 See Cort, "Spiritual Sexuality"; or Avery, "Self-Help Is the Best Help."

39 See, for example, the articles in the "Religion and Spirituality" themed section of *Disability Studies Quarterly* 26, nos. 3 and 4 in 2006; as well as Avalos, Melcher, and Schipper, *This Abled Body*; and Olyan, *Disability in the Hebrew Bible*.

40 See, for example, King, "Beam in Thine Own Eye"; or Rogers-Dulan and Blacher, "African American Families, Religion, and Disability."

41 Tinu Abayomi-Paul, interview by Sami Schalk, September 12, 2019.

42 T. S. Banks, interview by Sami Schalk, October 29, 2019.

43 Minich, *Accessible Citizenships*, 99–104.

44 See, for example, McClain, "Tai Chie for Older Women"; Zimbabwe, "Wonders of Herbs"; Crichlow, "Queen Afua"; Carruthers, "Herbs"; Crichlow, "Holistic Healing for a Whole You"; Crichlow, "Healing Ourselves, Healing Each Other"; M. Brown, "Understanding Islamic Medicine"; and Villarosa and NBWHP, *Body and Soul*, chap. 20, "Alternative Healing."

45 For more about healing justice, see Piepzna-Samarasinha, "Not-So-Brief Personal History of the Healing Justice Movement"; BadAss Visionary Healers, "Babe-ilicious Healing Justice Statement"; and Prentis Hemphill, "Healing Justice Is How We Can Sustain Black Lives," *Huffington Post*, February 7, 2017, https://www.huffpost.com/entry/healing-justice_b _5899e8ade4b0c1284f282ffe.

46 Minich, *Accessible Citizenships*, 104.

47 NBWHP, "Project Proposal to Ford Foundation," 10. The phrase *conspiracy of silence* is used frequently as a shorthand for the effects on Black women of

internalized oppression that keeps us silent about our experiences and separate from one another. As Valerie Boyd explains, "When we dare to break the conspiracy of silence, we begin our journey back to connectedness, our journey back to our self. When we dare to break the conspiracy of silence, we allow ourselves to provoke and cherish each other's rich, uninhibited laughter. When we dare to break the conspiracy of silence, we allow ourselves with curious minds, responsive eyes and slightly timid hearts, to revel in self-revelation. When we dare to break the conspiracy of silence, we allow ourselves, with little surprise, to recognize each other as the treasures that we are." Boyd, "Where Is the Love?," 2.

48 Banks-Wallace, "Tell Your Story," 9.

49 Moreau, "If Looks Could Kill."

50 Richardson, "My Life with Lupus," 4.

51 NBWHP, "A Proposal for Consideration for Program Funding Continuation," 11.

52 Braxton, "Wellbeing Is Our Birthright," 10.

53 NBWHP, "Eight Week Self-Help Group Meeting Guide," 5.

54 For more on the strong Black woman stereotype, see Wallace, *Black Macho and the Myth of the Superwoman*; Beauboeuf-Lafontant, *Behind the Mask of the Strong Black Woman*; and Parks, *Fierce Angels*.

55 M. Fisher, "Slavery Still in Effect," 34.

56 M. Fisher, "Slavery Still in Effect," 34.

57 M. Fisher, "Slavery Still in Effect," 34–35.

58 See, for example, Davis, "Roots of Black Women's Oppression"; Braxton, "And a Little Child Shall Lead Us"; and Villarosa and NBWHP, *Body and Soul*, 429–32.

59 Villarosa and NBWHP, *Body and Soul*, 115.

60 Villarosa and NBWHP, *Body and Soul*, 119–20.

61 Villarosa and NBWHP, *Body and Soul*, 115. Simi Linton's *Claiming Disability: Knowledge and Identity*, first published in 1998, is an example of where the mainstream movement was in terms of language around disability in the 1990s, particularly in regard to what she terms "nice words" like *physically challenged*, which were used in *Body and Soul* alongside the more commonly accepted terms of the period, *disability* and *handicapped*. Linton, *Claiming Disability*, 9–14.

62 Bell, "Introducing White Disability Studies."

63 NBWHP, "Our Bodies, Our Voices, Our Choices," 1.

64 I use the term *fat* as opposed to *obese* or *overweight* in alignment with the politics of the body positivity, Health at Every Size, and anti-fatphobia movements, in which *fat* is a neutral description of bodyminds that are above the average size or above the social ideal/norm. I do not use *fat* as an insult or as an indicator of health and well-being. For more information, see Kirkland, *Fat Rights*; or Rothblum and Solovay, *Fat Studies Reader*. For the specific relationship of fatphobia, anti-Black racism, and ableism, see Mollow, "Unvictimizable." Notably,

the NBWHP's approach to fatness varied widely, sometimes acknowledging fatphobia and at other times seeming to perpetuate it. See, for example, Janice S. Vaughn, "Obesity and the Black Woman," in First National Conference on Black Women's Health Issues, 1983, Atlanta Lesbian Feminist Alliance Archives, Duke University Libraries, Durham, NC, box 8; and Hoytt, Beard, and Black Women's Health Imperative, *Health First!*, 193–95, 198, 258–59.

65 Avery, "Breathing Life into Ourselves," 150.

66 Goldstraw, "Social Security Benefits for People with HIV/AIDS," 50; and NBWHP, "Social Security Disability and HIV."

67 See, for example, Spoonie Living (http://www.spoonieliving.com/) or the Chronic Illness Bloggers Directory (https://chronicillnessbloggers.com /bloggerdirectory/).

68 NBWHP, "National Black Women's Health Project Information Sheet."

69 Jammott-Dory, "Internal Politics of Black Women's Health," 12.

70 NBWHP, "Project Proposal 1994–1995," 7.

71 NBWHP, "Body and Soul: The Black Women's Health Agenda 2000; the National Black Women's Health Project 7th Annual Conference Schedule," 1993, 6. The 1992 and 1994 conferences included related workshops entitled "Our Piece of the Pie: How to Impact Public Policy" and "Black Women: A Powerful Force in the Public Policy Arena," respectively. NBWHP, "Healing: The Essence of Health; the National Black Women's Health Project Sixth Annual Meeting and Conference," 1992; and NBWHP, "The National Black Women's Health Project 10th Anniversary Conference Homecoming Celebration: 'We Are the Ones We've Been Waiting For,'" 1994, vol. 64.

72 NBWHP, *Our Bodies, Our Voices, Our Choices*, 5.

73 See Hart, "Building a More Inclusive Women's Health Movement," 207–12.

Chapter Four: More Than Just Prevention

1 New York NBWHP, "Untitled," 1989, 1–2.

2 New York NBWHP, "Untitled," 1.

3 New York NBWHP, "Untitled," 1; emphasis added.

4 New York NBWHP, "Untitled," 2.

5 See Shilts, *And the Band Played On*; Schneider and Stoller, *Women Resisting AIDS*; Stoller, *Lessons from the Damned*; Cohen, *Boundaries of Blackness*; Engel, *Epidemic*; Bayer and Oppenheimer, *AIDS Doctors*; Berger, *Workable Sisterhood*; Gillett, *Grassroots History of the HIV/AIDS Epidemic in North America*; and US Department of Health and Human Services, "A Timeline of HIV and AIDS," HIV.gov, accessed September 17, 2018, https://www.hiv.gov/sites/default/files /aidsgov-timeline.pdf.

6 US Department of Health and Human Services, "Timeline of HIV and AIDS."

7 Stoller, *Lessons from the Damned*, 13, 157–58.

8 Berger, *Workable Sisterhood*, 102–3; and Stoller, *Lessons from the Damned*, 10.

9   US Department of Health and Human Services, "Timeline of HIV and AIDS."

10 Cohen, *Boundaries of Blackness*, 21–22.

11 McRuer, "Critical Investments," 222.

12 Shapiro, *No Pity*, 136–37; and Colker, *Disability Pendulum*, 41, 51, 53–54.

13 Colker, *Disability Pendulum*, 65.

14 For more on the role of HIV/AIDS in the development of the ADA, see Colker, *Disability Pendulum*, 26–68.

15 McRuer, "Critical Investments," 225.

16 For existing disability studies scholarship on HIV/AIDS, see R. McRuer "Critical Investments"; and A. Day "Resisting Disability, Claiming HIV."

17 Kafer, *Feminist, Queer, Crip*, 12; and Minich, "Enabling Whom?"

18 McRuer, "Critical Investments," 231.

19 For instance, almost all of the histories of HIV/AIDS I've read for this research don't even include *disability* as an index keyword, let alone as a political issue or intellectual/theoretical perspective.

20 NBWHP, "AIDS Education Project Proposal," 1988, 4.

21 NBWHP, "AIDS Education Project Final Report," 1988.

22 See, for example, Washington, *Medical Apartheid*; Kline, *Building a Better Race*; and Stern, *Eugenic Nation*.

23 Clare, *Brilliant Imperfection*, 76.

24 For examples of work in disability studies that explore pain or push against simplistic approaches to cure and prevention, see Wendell, "Unhealthy Disabled"; and Price, "Bodymind Problem and the Possibilities of Pain."

25 In the many social, cultural, and political histories of the AIDS crisis, there are many other organizations, such as SisterLove, with whom the NBWHP partnered or with whom their work overlapped or intersected. I am not aiming to present the project's work as wholly unique; rather, I intend to highlight how their approach can be understood as a Black disability political one that is applicable beyond HIV/AIDS specifically.

26 NBWHP, "AIDS Education Project Proposal," 4.

27 NBWHP, "AIDS Education Project Proposal," 1.

28 See, for example, the chapter on HIV/AIDS in Villarosa and NBWHP, *Body and Soul*, 535–54.

29 Avery, "A Question of Survival/a Conspiracy of Silence," 79. The concept of "the conspiracy of silence" is related to Darlene Clark Hine's "culture of dissemblance." See Hine, "Rape and the Inner Lives of Black Women in the Middle West"; and Schalk, "Contextualizing Black Disability and the Culture of Dissemblance."

30 Dixon, "African American Women and HIV," 17.

31 Dixon, "Black Women and AIDS 2000," 10.

32 NBWHP, "AIDS Education Project Proposal," 2.

33 Dixon, "African American Women and HIV," 17.

34 NBWHP, "From Cries and Whispers to Action: African-American Women Respond to AIDS," 1988.

35 NBWHP, "From Cries and Whispers to Action," 11; and Villarosa and NBWHP, *Body and Soul*, 544–45.

36 NBWHP, "From Cries and Whispers to Action," 11.

37 See, for example, Abofraa, "Taking Control of Our Health"; Saran, "Love in the Time of AIDS"; Goldstraw, "Social Security Benefits for People with HIV/AIDS"; Estes, "Choosing to Live in a Time of AIDS"; and Young, "Black and Woman in the Age of AIDS."

38 Poteat, "AIDS and Black Lesbians," 8, 44.

39 NBWHP, "From Cries and Whispers to Action," 1.

40 NBWHP, "From Cries and Whispers to Action," 10.

41 NBWHP, "From Cries and Whispers to Action," 10.

42 Lorde, *Cancer Journals*, 42–44.

43 Lorde, *Cancer Journals*, 49–51, 56–57.

44 NBWHP, "AIDS Education Project Proposal," 1.

45 NBWHP, "AIDS Education Project Proposal," 1.

46 Andresen, "Public Health Education, Research, and Disability Studies."

47 Hayward, "Slowly Evolving Paradigm of Disability in Public Health Education."

Praxis Interlude Two

1 NBWHP, *Lasting Legacy*, 28.

2 "Timeline of the Americans with Disabilities Act," ADA National Network, accessed June 17, 2021, https://adata.org/ada-timeline.

3 Villarosa and NBWHP, *Body and Soul*, 115. For other examples of ways Black disabled people receive less legal protection and accommodation, see Carolyn Thompson, "Civil Rights Panel: Disabled Students of Color Punished More," *AP News*, July 23, 2019, https://apnews.com/article/discrimination-education -politics-united-states-school-discipline-aa1d0514e886442382d09a086f923359; and ChrisTiana ObeySumner, "#DisabilitySoWhite: Reflections on Race and Disability on ADA Day," Epiphanies of Equity LLC, July 26, 2019, https://www .christianaobeysumner.com/blog/2019/7/26/disabilitysowhite-reflections-on -race-and-disability-on-ada-day.

4 Goldstraw, "Social Security Benefits for People with HIV/AIDS," 50.

5 NBWHP, "Social Security Disability and HIV."

6 See, for example, Thomas, "Socializing in the Age of HIV/AIDS"; and Parker, "Emotional Aspects of Chronic Illness."

7 Banks, interview, 2019. Unless noted otherwise, all quotes from Banks in this interlude are from this interview.

8 Lewis, interview, 2019. Unless noted otherwise, all quotes from Lewis in this interlude are from this interview.

9   Tinu Abayomi Paul, interview by Sami Schalk, September 12, 2019. Unless noted otherwise, all quotes from Cokley in this interlude are from this interview.

10   Patrick Cokley, interview by Sami Schalk, October 1, 2019. Unless noted otherwise, all quotes from Cokley in this interlude are from this interview.

11   Dustin Gibson, interview by Sami Schalk, September 3, 2019. Unless noted otherwise, all quotes from Gibson in this interlude are from this interview.

12   Vilissa Thompson, interview by Sami Schalk, July 30, 2019. Unless noted otherwise, all quotes from Thompson in this interlude are from this interview.

13   Candace Coleman, interview by Sami Schalk, September 23, 2019. Unless noted otherwise, all quotes from Coleman in this interlude are from this interview.

14   Kayla Smith, interview by Sami Schalk, September 18, 2019. Unless noted otherwise, all quotes from Smith in this interlude are from this interview.

15   Here Lewis is referencing, in part, the Say the Word campaign. See Barbara King, "'Disabled': Just #SayTheWord," *NPR*, February 25, 2016, https://www .npr.org/sections/13.7/2016/02/25/468073722/disabled-just-saytheword.

16   For related scholarly arguments on the ways in which disability, as legally defined, excludes certain disabled people in order to function, see Puar, *Right to Maim*.

17   Villarosa and NBWHP, *Body and Soul*, 119–20.

18   Nefert-irie, "What It Means to Belong to a Black Woman's Self-Help Support Group," 5.

Chapter Five: Black Disability Politics Now

1   Movement for Black Lives, "A Vision for Black Lives: Policy Demands for Black Power, Freedom, and Justice," August 1, 2016. The original platform has since been removed, and only the updated platform is now publicly available online at https://cjc.net/wp-content/uploads/2017/04/A-Vision-For-Black -Lives-Policy-Demands-For-Black-Power-Freedom-and-Justice.pdf.

2   According to the Harriet Tubman Collective, the Movement for Black Lives did not connect with many self-identified Black Disabled/Deaf advocates, community builders, or organizers in the drafting process. "This led to the Movement's overall failure to adequately address the disparities and specific violence and oppression that exist at the intersection of Blackness and Disability/Deafness." Harriet Tubman Collective, "Disability Solidarity: Completing the 'Vision for Black Lives,'" Medium, September 7, 2016, https://medium .com/@harriettubmancollective/disability-solidarity-completing-the-vision -for-black-lives-119ee03e9822.

3   In my 2019 interview with Dustin Gibson, he explained that the phrase *disability solidarity* originated in 2014 with Ki'tay D. Davidson, Talila "TL" Lewis, and Allie Cannington as a hashtag on Twitter "just a few weeks after Mike Brown was killed as a call for the disability community to be in solidarity

with folks fighting for racial justice" and has continued to be used to call for disability communities to be invested in intersectional, collective liberation. Davidson, Lewis, and Cannington hosted a Twitter chat on August 22, 2014, where hundreds of people joined to discuss. At the time, Davidson said, the three defined disability solidarity as that which holds the disability community accountable for intersectional justice and holds all communities accountable for disability justice. See Talila "TL" Lewis (@talilalewis), "@KitayDavidson, @AllieCannington & I hosted the 1st #DisabilitySolidarity chat," Twitter, August 22, 2019, 9:14 p.m., https://twitter.com/talilalewis/status/1164722603619160064.

4 Audism is discrimination against people who are D/deaf or hard of hearing, which includes devaluing or discriminating against D/deaf modes of communication and literacy (such as banning sign language) and overvaluing hearing and hearing people's methods of communication and literacy. Audism also includes lack of recognition of Deaf cultures and languages as distinct cultures and languages.

5 HTC, "Disability Solidarity."

6 HTC, "Disability Solidarity."

7 The names of the people on the HTC's "Disability Solidarity" statement are Patricia Berne, Kylie Brooks, Neal Carter, Patrick Cokley, Candace Coleman, Dustin Gibson, Timotheus Gordon Jr., Keri Gray, Christopher DeAngelo Huff, Cyree Jarelle Johnson, Lorrell D. Kilpatrick, Carolyn Lazard, Talila A. Lewis, Leroy F. Moore Jr., Vilissa Thompson, Alexis Toliver, and Heather Watkins.

8 I am unable to find out the exact date of the changes or if the changes occurred over time.

9 "Platform," Movement for Black Lives, accessed January 23, 2020, https://m4bl.org/policy-platforms/.

10 See the following pages on the Movement for Black Lives website, accessed January 23, 2020: "End the War on Black People" (https://m4bl.org/end-the-war-on-black-people/); "Invest-Divest" (https://m4bl.org/policy-platforms/invest-divest/); "Economic Justice" (https://m4bl.org/policy-platforms/economic-justice/); and "Political Power" (https://m4bl.org/policy-platforms/political-power/).

11 See the following statements available on Tumblr from the HTC, accessed January 23, 2020: "#ProtectHarriet: The Harriet Tubman Collective's Response to RespectAbility's Racism and Ford Foundation Enabling the Same," January 19, 2017, https://harriettubmancollective-blog.tumblr.com/post/156079791938/protectharriet; "Accountable Reporting on Disability, Race, and Police Violence: A Community Response to the 'Ruderman White Paper on the Media Coverage of Use of Force and Disability,'" June 1, 2018, https://harriettubmancollective-blog.tumblr.com/post/174479075753/accountable-reporting-on-disability-race-and; and "In Defense of No New Jails: An Open Letter on Disability Justice to Darren Walker, President of the Ford Founda-

tion," October 1, 2019, https://harriettubmancollective-blog.tumblr.com/post
/188063892118/in-defense-of-no-new-jails-open-letter-to-darren.

12 Coleman, interview, 2019. Unless noted otherwise, all quotes from Coleman in
this chapter are from this interview.

13 Abayomi-Paul, interview, 2019.

14 Heather Watkins, interview by Sami Schalk, September 5, 2019.

15 Gibson, interview, 2019. Unless noted otherwise, all quotes from Gibson in this
chapter are from this interview.

16 Cokley, interview, 2019. Unless noted otherwise, all quotes from Cokley in this
chapter are from this interview.

17 Lewis, interview, 2019. Unless noted otherwise, all quotes from Lewis in this
chapter are from this interview.

18 Talila "TL" Lewis, "Updated Working Definition of Ableism," Face-
book, January 25, 2020, https://www.facebook.com/photo.php?fbid
=10102728588169305&set=a.10101262893458255&type=3&theater.

19 Thompson, interview, 2019.

20 Combahee River Collective, "The Combahee River Collective Statement."

21 Banks, interview, 2019. Unless noted otherwise, all quotes from Banks in this
chapter are from this interview.

22 Sins Invalid, *Skin, Tooth, and Bone*, 16.

23 For more on care webs, including within organizing spaces, see Piepzna-
Samarasinha, *Care Work*.

24 Lorrell Kilpatrick, interview by Sami Schalk, July 31, 2019. Unless noted
otherwise, all quotes from Kilpatrick in this chapter are from this
interview.

25 Participants identified a wide range of issues as Black disability political concerns. The most commonly named issues (mentioned by at least three of the
eleven interviewees) were health care/medicine, education, police violence, and
incarceration/institutionalization. Other issues mentioned include economics/
employment, housing, sexual violence, and environmental racism.

26 In the interview, for example, Lewis noted that in the work of HEARD, lawyers
often want to go in and sue for accommodations like TTY telephones and
interpreting services for Deaf and disabled people but that lawsuits often result
in punishment and retaliation against Deaf and disabled inmates; therefore,
attempting to bring about change without a lawsuit is often what most benefits
the people most impacted by this particular injustice of the prison industrial
complex.

27 "History," Black Youth Project, accessed February 1, 2020, http://
blackyouthproject.com/about-us/history/.

28 Jade Perry, "Chills down My Spinal Degeneration: Why We Need Black Queer
Disabled Kink," Black Youth Project, March 27, 2019, http://blackyouthproject
.com/chills-down-my-spinal-degeneration-why-we-need-black-queer-disabled
-kink/; Hari Ziyad, "Black People Aren't Resistant to Mental Health Treatment.

We're Resistant to Framing It as a Cure," Black Youth Project, January 27, 2020, http://blackyouthproject.com/black-people-arent-resistant-to-mental-health -treatment-were-resistant-to-framing-it-as-a-cure/; and Amber Butts, "Yup. Non-profit Culture and Performative Activism Perpetuate Ableism and Anti-Blackness," Black Youth Project, January 30, 2020, http://blackyouthproject .com/yup-non-profit-culture-and-performative-activism-perpetuate-ableism -and-anti-blackness/.

29 S. Taylor, *Body Is Not an Apology*.

(Not a) Conclusion

1 Shout-out to my Twitter followers, who donated over $20,000 in a month to allow these supplies to be freely provided to so many people, as well as to the many Madison locals who donated supplies and made masks.

2 The COVID Tracking Project, "The Covid Racial Data Tracker," March 7, 2021, https://covidtracking.com/race.

BIBLIOGRAPHY

Archives

Atlanta Lesbian Feminist Alliance Archives. Duke University Libraries, Durham, NC.
Black Women's Health Imperative Records. Sophia Smith Collection. Smith College, Northampton, MA.
Dr. Huey P. Newton Foundation Inc. Collection. M0864. Department of Special Collections, Stanford University Libraries, Stanford, CA.

Published Works

Abofraa, Yaa A. "Taking Control of Our Health: Educating Ourselves about AIDS." *Vital Signs* 6, no. 1 (1989): 2.
Abron, JoNina M. "Reflections of a Former Oakland Public School Parent." *Black Scholar* 27, no. 2 (2015): 15–20.
Ahram, Roey, Edward Fergus, and Pedro Noguera. "Addressing Racial/Ethnic Disproportionality in Special Education: Case Studies of Suburban School Districts." *Teachers College Record* 113, no. 10 (2011): 2233–66.
Alameen-Shavers, Antwanisha. "The Woman Question: Gender Dynamics within the Black Panther Party." *Spectrum: A Journal on Black Men* 5, no. 1 (2016): 33–62.
Andresen, Elena M. "Public Health Education, Research, and Disability Studies: A View from Epidemiology." *Disability Studies Quarterly* 24, no. 4 (2004). https://dsq-sds.org/article/view/889/1064.
Annamma, Subini A. *The Pedagogy of Pathologization: Dis/abled Girls of Color in the School-Prison Nexus*. New York: Routledge, 2017.
Austin, Curtis J. *Up against the Wall: Violence in the Making and Unmaking of the Black Panther Party*. Fayetteville: University of Arkansas Press, 2008.
Avalos, Hector, Sarah J. Melcher, and Jeremy Schipper. *This Abled Body: Rethinking Disabilities in Biblical Studies*. Atlanta: Society of Biblical Literature, 2007.
Avery, Byllye. "Breathing Life into Ourselves: The Evolution of the National Black Women's Health Project." In *Feminism and Community*, edited by Penny A. Weiss and Marilyn Friedman, 147–53. Philadelphia: Temple University Press, 1995.

Avery, Byllye. "Empowerment through Wellness." *Yale Journal of Law and Feminism* 4, no. 1 (1991): 147–54.

Avery, Byllye. "A Question of Survival/a Conspiracy of Silence: Abortion and Black Women's Health." In *From Abortion to Reproductive Freedom: Transforming a Movement*, edited by Marlene Gerber Fried, 75–80. Boston: South End, 1990.

Avery, Byllye. "Self-Help Is the Best Help." *Vital Signs* 10, no. 2 (1994): 5.

Bad Ass Visionary Healers. "A Babe-ilicious Healing Justice Statement." *nineteen sixty nine: an ethnic studies journal* 2, no. 1 (2013). https://escholarship.org/uc/item /1z61z54j.

Bailey, Moya. "Race and Disability in the Academy." *Sociological Review*, November 9, 2017. https://thesociologicalreview.org/collections/chronic-academics /race-and-disability-in-the-academy/.

Bambara, Toni Cade. *The Black Woman: An Anthology*. 1970. Reprint, New York: Washington Square, 2005.

Banks-Wallace, JoAnne. "Tell Your Story." *Sister Ink* 2, no. 2 (2000): 9.

Barclay, Jenifer L. "'The Greatest Degree of Perfection': Disability and the Construction of Race in American Slave Law." *South Carolina Review* 46, no. 2 (2014): 27–43.

Barclay, Jenifer L. *The Mark of Slavery: Disability, Race, and Gender in Antebellum America*. Champaign: University of Illinois Press, 2021.

Barclay, Jenifer L. "Mothering the 'Useless': Black Motherhood, Disability, and Slavery." *Women, Gender, and Families of Color* 2, no. 2 (2014): 115–40.

Barker, Clare. *Postcolonial Fiction and Disability: Exceptional Children, Metaphor and Materiality*. New York: Palgrave Macmillan, 2011.

Bayer, Ronald, and Gerald M. Oppenheimer. *AIDS Doctors: Voices from the Epidemic; An Oral History*. New York: Oxford University Press, 2002.

Baynton, Douglas. "Disability and the Justification of Inequality in American History." In *The New Disability History: American Perspectives*, edited by Paul Longmore and Lauri Umansky, 33–57. New York: New York University Press, 2001.

Beal, Frances M. "Double Jeopardy: To Be Black and Female." *Meridians: Feminism, Race, Transnationalism* 8, no. 2 (2008): 166–76.

Beauboeuf-Lafontant, Tamara. *Behind the Mask of the Strong Black Woman: Voice and the Embodiment of a Costly Performance*. Philadelphia: Temple University Press, 2009.

Bell, Chris. "Introducing White Disability Studies: A Modest Proposal." In *The Disability Studies Reader*, edited by Lennard J. Davis, 275–82. New York: Routledge, 2006.

Ben-Moshe, Liat, and Allison C. Carey. *Disability Incarcerated: Imprisonment and Disability in the United States and Canada*. New York: Palgrave Macmillan, 2014.

Berger, Michele Tracy. *Workable Sisterhood: The Political Journey of Stigmatized Women with HIV/AIDS*. Princeton, NJ: Princeton University Press, 2010.

Berne, Patty. "Disability Justice—a Working Draft." *Sins Invalid: An Unshamed Claim to Beauty in the Face of Invisibility* (blog), June 9, 2015. https://www .sinsinvalid.org/blog/disability-justice-a-working-draft-by-patty-berne.

Bloom, Joshua, and Waldo E. Martin. *Black against Empire: The History and Politics of the Black Panther Party*. Berkeley: University of California Press, 2013.

Boster, Dea H. *African American Slavery and Disability: Bodies, Property, and Power in the Antebellum South, 1800–1860*. New York: Routledge, 2013.

Boyd, Valerie. "Where Is the Love? Black Women Renewing Ties That Bind." *Vital Signs* 4, no. 1 (1987): 2.

Boykins, Cheryl Y. "Wellness Not Medicine, Safeguard for the Year 2000." *Vital Signs* 2, no. 3 (1993): 16, 63.

Braxton, Gwen. "And a Little Child Shall Lead Us." *Vital Signs* 4, no. 1 (1987): 8–10.

Braxton, Gwen. "Wellbeing Is Our Birthright: The Meaning of Empowerment for Women of Color." *Health PAC Bulletin* 4 (1991): 8–10.

brown, adrienne maree. *Pleasure Activism: The Politics of Feeling Good*. Oakland, CA: AK Press, 2019.

Brown, Malaika. "Understanding Islamic Medicine." *Vital Signs* 2, no. 2 (1993): 46.

Carruthers, Marsha. "Herbs: Healing Agents." *Vital Signs* 2, no. 2 (1993): 53.

Chamberlin, Judi. *On Our Own: Patient-Controlled Alternatives to the Mental Health System*. New York: McGraw-Hill, 1978.

Charlton, James I. *Nothing about Us without Us: Disability Oppression and Empowerment*. Berkeley: University of California Press, 1998.

Clare, Eli. *Brilliant Imperfection: Grappling with Cure*. Durham, NC: Duke University Press, 2017.

Cohen, Cathy J. *The Boundaries of Blackness: AIDS and the Breakdown of Black Politics*. Chicago: University of Chicago Press, 1999.

Colker, Ruth. *The Disability Pendulum: The First Decade of the Americans with Disabilities Act*. New York: New York University Press, 2005.

Combahee River Collective. "The Combahee River Collective Statement." In *Home Girls: A Black Feminist Anthology*, edited by Barbara Smith, 264–74. New York: Kitchen Table Press, 1983.

Cort, Sheila. "Spiritual Sexuality." *Vital Signs* 10, no. 1 (1994): 68.

Cottingham, Marci D., and Jill A. Fisher. "Risk and Emotion among Healthy Volunteers in Clinical Trials." *Social Psychology Quarterly* 79, no. 3 (2016): 222–42.

Crichlow, Vena. "Healing Ourselves, Healing Each Other: Talking with the Healing Drum." *Vital Signs* 2, no. 2 (1993): 19.

Crichlow, Vena. "Holistic Healing for a Whole You." *Vital Signs* 2, no. 2 (1993): 44–45.

Crichlow, Vena. "Queen Afua: Healing Our People." *Vital Signs* 2, no. 3 (1993): 28–29.

D'Lil, HolLynn. *Becoming Real in 24 Days: One Participant's Story of the 1977 Section 504 Demonstrations for Disability Rights*. N.p.: Hallevaland Productions, 2015.

Davis, Angela Y. "The Roots of Black Women's Oppression." *Vital Signs* 4, no. 1 (1987): 3.

Day, Ally. "Resisting Disability, Claiming HIV: Introducing the Ability Contract and Conceptualizations of Liberal Citizenship." *Canadian Journal of Disability Studies* 3, no. 3 (2014): 104–21.

Deal, Mark. "Disabled People's Attitudes toward Other Impairment Groups: A Hierarchy of Impairments." *Disability and Society* 18, no. 7 (2003): 897–910.

Diefenbach, Gretchen J., Donald Diefenbach, Alan Baumeister, and Mark West. "Portrayal of Lobotomy in the Popular Press: 1935–1960." *Journal of the History of the Neurosciences* 8, no. 1 (2010): 60–69.

Dittmer, John. *The Good Doctors: The Medical Committee for Human Rights and the Struggle for Social Justice in Health Care*. New York: Bloomsbury, 2009.

Dixon, Dazon. "African American Women and HIV: Not Just Another Brick Wall." *Vital Signs* (Summer 1991): 7, 17.

Dixon, Dazon. "Black Women and AIDS 2000: 'When the Tides Turn.'" *Vital Signs* 2, no. 3 (1993): 10, 60.

Dolmage, Jay. "Disabled upon Arrival: The Rhetorical Construction of Disability and Race at Ellis Island." *Cultural Critique*, no. 77 (2011): 24–69.

Engel, Jonathan. *The Epidemic: A Global History of AIDS*. New York: Smithsonian Books/Collins, 2006.

Erevelles, Nirmala. "Crippin' Jim Crow: Disability, Dis-location, and the School-to-Prison Pipeline." In *Disability Incarcerated: Imprisonment and Disability in the United States and Canada*, edited by Liat Ben-Moshe, Chris Chapman, and Allison C. Carey, 81–99. New York: Palgrave Macmillan, 2014.

Erevelles, Nirmala. *Disability and Difference in Global Contexts: Enabling a Transformative Body Politic*. New York: Palgrave Macmillan, 2011.

Estes, Valjeanne. "Choosing to Live in a Time of AIDS." *Vital Signs* 10, no. 4 (1994): 31–32.

Everett, Barbara. *A Fragile Revolution: Consumers and Psychiatric Survivors Confront the Power of the Mental Health System*. Waterloo, Canada: Wilfrid Laurier University Press, 2000.

Federal Bureau of Investigation, Counterterrorism Division. *Black Identity Extremists Likely Motivated to Target Law Enforcement Officers*. Department of Homeland Security, 2017. https://www.politico.com/f/?id=0000015f-11c2-d01e-a35f-f7c641380000.

Fisher, Jill A. "Expanding the Frame of 'Voluntariness' in Informed Consent: Structural Coercion and the Power of Social and Economic Context." *Kennedy Institute Ethics Journal* 23, no. 4 (2013): 355–79.

Fisher, Jill A., and Corey A. Kalbaugh. "Challenging Assumptions about Minority Participation in US Clinical Research." *American Journal of Public Health* 101, no. 12 (2011): 2217–22.

Fisher, Marlene Braxton. "Slavery Still in Effect: Lamentables of a Women's Health Advocates." *Vital Signs* 2, no. 3 (1993): 34–35.

Fleischer, Doris Zames, and Frieda Zames. *The Disability Rights Movement: From Charity to Confrontation*. Philadelphia: Temple University Press, 2001.

Gillett, James. *A Grassroots History of the HIV/AIDS Epidemic in North America*. Spokane, WA: Marquette Books, 2011.

Goldstraw, Robert G. "Social Security Benefits for People with HIV/AIDS." *Vital Signs*, no. 2 (1993): 50.

Grad, Frank P. "The Preamble of the Constitution of the World Health Organization." *Bulletin of the World Health Organization: The International Journal of Public Health* 80, no. 12 (2002): 981–84.

Grob, Gerald N. *From Asylum to Community: Mental Health Policy in Modern America*. Princeton, NJ: Princeton University Press, 1991.

Guy-Sheftall, Beverly, ed. *Words of Fire: An Anthology of African-American Feminist Thought*. New York: New Press, 1995.

Hart, Evan. "Building a More Inclusive Women's Health Movement: Byllye Avery and the Development of the National Black Women's Health Project, 1981–1990." PhD diss., University of Cincinnati, 2012.

Hawkins, Berlinda. "'. . . I Wanted to Live' Dialysis: A Second Chance for Life." *Vital Signs* 3, no. 4 (1986): 6.

Hayward, Katherine. "A Slowly Evolving Paradigm of Disability in Public Health Education." *Disability Studies Quarterly* 24, no. 4 (2004). https://dsq-sds.org /article/view/890/1065.

Helem, Rebecca. "The Little Pentecostal Lesbian That Sat on the Pew: True Tales from the Church 'Hood." *Vital Signs* 11, no. 4 (1999): 12, 33–34.

Hendershot, Gerry E., and Nancy L. Eiesland, eds. "Religion and Spirituality." Themed section of *Disability Studies Quarterly* 26, no. 3 (2006).

Hendershot, Gerry E., and Nancy L. Eiesland, eds. "Religion and Spirituality, Part Two." Themed section of *Disability Studies Quarterly* 26, no. 4 (2006).

Hilliard, David, ed. *The Black Panther Party: Service to the People Programs*. Albuquerque: University of New Mexico Press, 2010.

Hilliard, David, and Lewis Cole. *This Side of Glory: The Autobiography of David Hilliard and the Story of the Black Panther Party*. New York: Little, Brown, 1993.

Hine, Darlene Clark. "Rape and the Inner Lives of Black Women in the Middle West." *Signs: Journal of Women in Culture and Society* 14, no. 4 (1989): 912–20.

Ho, Jennifer, and James Kyung-Jin Lee, eds. "The State of Illness and Disability in Asian America." Special issue, *Amerasia* 39, no. 1 (2013).

Hoffman, Lily M. *The Politics of Knowledge: Activist Movements in Medicine and Planning*. Albany: State University of New York Press, 1989.

Hoytt, Eleanor Hinton, Hilary Beard, and Black Women's Health Imperative. *Health First! The Black Woman's Wellness Guide*. New York: Smiley Books, 2012.

Huggins, Ericka, and Angela D. LeBlanc-Ernest. "Revolutionary Women, Revolutionary Education: The Black Panther Party's Oakland Community School." In *Want to Start a Revolution? Radical Women in the Black Freedom Struggle*, edited by Jeanne Theoharis, Komozi Woodard, and Dayo F. Gore, 161–84. New York: New York University Press, 2009.

Hull, Gloria T., Patricia Bell-Scott, and Barbara Smith, eds. *All the Women Are White, All the Blacks Are Men, but Some of Us Are Brave: Black Women's Studies*. New York: Feminist Press, 1982.

Jackson, Vanessa. "In Our Own Voice: African-American Stories of Oppression, Survival and Recovery in Mental Health Systems." National Empowerment Center, 2017, https://power2u.org/wp-content/uploads/2017/01 /InOurOwnVoiceVanessaJackson.pdf.

Jammott-Dory, Frances. "The Internal Politics of Black Women's Health: Reflections on Issues of Governance." *Vital Signs* (Summer 1991): 12.

Jarman, Michelle. "Coming Up from Underground: Uneasy Dialogues at the Intersections of Race, Mental Illness, and Disability Studies." In *Blackness and Disability:*

Critical Examinations and Cultural Interventions, edited by Chris Bell, 9–30. East Lansing: Michigan State University Press, 2012.

Jarman, Michelle. "Cultural Consumption and Rejection of Precious Jones: Pushing Disability into the Discussion of Sapphire's *Push* and Lee Daniels's *Precious*." *Feminist Formations* 24, no. 2 (2012): 163–85.

Jarman, Michelle. "Dismembering the Lynch Mob: Intersecting Narratives of Disability, Race, and Sexual Menace." In *Sex and Disability*, edited by Robert McRuer and Anna Mollow, 89–107. Durham, NC: Duke University Press, 2012.

Jennett, Bryan. *The Vegetative State: Medical Facts, Ethical and Legal Dilemmas*. New York: Cambridge University Press, 2002.

Jennett, Bryan, and Fred Plum. "Persistent Vegetative State after Brain Damage." *Lancet* 299, no. 7753 (1972): 734–37.

Johnson, Jenell M. *American Lobotomy: A Rhetorical History*. Ann Arbor: University of Michigan Press, 2014.

Johnson, Merri, and Robert McRuer. "Cripistemologies: Introduction." *Journal of Literary and Cultural Disability Studies* 8, no. 2 (2014): 127–47.

Johnson, Ollie A., III. "Explaining the Demise of the Black Panther Party: The Role of Internal Factors." In *The Black Panther Party (Reconsidered)*, edited by Charles E. Jones, 391–414. Baltimore: Black Classic, 1998.

Jones, Charles E., and Jonathan Gayles. "'The World Is a Child's Classroom': An Analysis of the Black Panther Party's Oakland Community School." In *Teach Freedom: Education for Liberation in the African-American Tradition*, edited by Charles M. Payne and Carol Sills Strickland, 100–116. New York: Teachers College Press, 2008.

Jones, Nev, and Robyn Brown. "The Absence of Psychiatric C/S/X Perspectives in Academic Discourse: Consequences and Implications." *Disability Studies Quarterly* 33, no. 1 (2013). https://dsq-sds.org/article/view/3433/3198.

Kafer, Alison. *Feminist, Queer, Crip*. Bloomington: Indiana University Press, 2013.

Khúc, Mimi, ed. "Open in Emergency: A Special Issue on Asian American Mental Health." Special issue, *Asian American Literary Review* 7, no. 2 (2016).

Kim, Eunjung. *Curative Violence: Rehabilitating Disability, Gender, and Sexuality in Modern Korea*. Durham, NC: Duke University Press, 2017.

Kim, Jina B. "Cripping East Los Angeles: Enabling Environmental Justice in Helena Maria Viramontes's *Their Dogs Came with Them*." In *Disability Studies and the Environmental Humanities: Toward an Eco-Crip Theory*, edited by Sarah Jaquette Ra and Jay Sibara, 502–30. Lincoln: University of Nebraska Press, 2017.

Kim, Jina B. "Toward a Crip-of-Color Critique: Thinking with Minich's 'Enabling Whom?'" *Lateral* 6, no. 1 (2017). https://csalateral.org/issue/6-1/forum-alt-humanities-critical-disability-studies-crip-of-color-critique-kim/.

King, Sharon V. "The Beam in Thine Own Eye: Disability and the Black Church." *Western Journal of Black Studies* 22, no. 1 (1998): 37–48.

Kirkland, Anna Rutherford. *Fat Rights: Dilemmas of Difference and Personhood*. New York: New York University Press, 2008.

Kline, Wendy. *Building a Better Race: Gender, Sexuality, and Eugenics from the Turn of the Century to the Baby Boom*. Berkeley: University of California Press, 2001.

Knadler, Stephen. "Dis-abled Citizenship: Narrating the Extraordinary Body in Racial Uplift." *Arizona Quarterly: A Journal of American Literature, Culture, and Theory* 69, no. 3 (2013): 99–128.

Knadler, Stephen. *Vitality Politics: Health, Debility, and the Limits of Black Emancipation*. Ann Arbor: University of Michigan Press, 2019.

Kwate, Naa Oyo A., and Melody S. Goodman. "Cross-Sectional and Longitudinal Effects of Racism on Mental Health among Residents of Black Neighborhoods in New York City." *American Journal of Public Health* 105, no. 4 (2015): 711–18.

Laureys, Steven, Gastone Celesia, Francois Cohadon, Jan Lavrijsen, Jose Leon-Carrion, Walter Sannita, Leon Sazbon, et al. "Unresponsive Wakefulness Syndrome: A New Name for the Vegetative State or Apallic Syndrome." BMC *Medicine* 8, no. 1 (2010): 711–18.

Linton, Simi. *Claiming Disability: Knowledge and Identity*. New York: New York University Press, 1998.

Livingston, Julie. *Debility and the Moral Imagination in Botswana*. Bloomington: Indiana University Press, 2005.

Longmore, Paul K. *Why I Burned My Book and Other Essays on Disability*. Philadelphia: Temple University Press, 2003.

Lorde, Audre. *The Cancer Journals*. San Francisco: Aunt Lute Books, 1997.

Loyd, Jenna M. *Health Rights Are Civil Rights: Peace and Justice Activism in Los Angeles, 1963–1978*. Minneapolis: University of Minnesota Press, 2014.

McClain, Mildred. "Tai Chi for Older Women." *Vital Signs* 1, no. 2 (1984): 3.

McRuer, Robert. *Crip Theory: Cultural Signs of Queerness and Disability*. New York: New York University Press, 2006.

McRuer, Robert. "Critical Investments: AIDS, Christopher Reeve, and Queer/Disability Studies." *Journal of Medical Humanities* 23, no. 3–4 (2002): 221–37.

Meade, Teresa, and David Serlin. "Editors' Introduction." *Radical History Review* 2006, no. 94 (2006): 1–8.

Metzl, Jonathan M. *The Protest Psychosis: How Schizophrenia Became a Black Disease*. New York: Beacon Press, 2010.

Mingus, Mia. "Reflection toward Practice: Some Questions on Disability Justice." In *Criptiques*, edited by Caitlin Wood, 107–14. Minneapolis: May Day, 2014.

Minich, Julie Avril. *Accessible Citizenships: Disability, Nation, and the Cultural Politics of Greater Mexico*. Philadelphia: Temple University Press, 2014.

Minich, Julie Avril. "Enabling Whom? Critical Disability Studies Now." *Lateral* 5, no. 1 (2016). http://csalateral.org/wp/issue/5-1/forum-alt-humanities-critical-disability-studies-now-minich.

Mollow, Anna. "Unvictimizable: Toward a Fat Black Disability Studies." *African American Review* 50, no. 2 (2017): 105–21.

Monahan, Torin, and Jill A. Fisher. "'I'm Still a Hustler': Entrepreneurial Responses to Precarity by Participants in Phase I Clinical Trials." *Economy and Society* 44, no. 4 (2015): 545–66.

Moreau-Morgan, A. D. "If Looks Could Kill: Lupus." *Vital Signs* 10, no. 3 (1994): 63, 76.

Morgen, Sandra. *Into Our Own Hands: The Women's Health Movement in the United States, 1969–1990*. New Brunswick, NJ: Rutgers University Press, 2002.

Morrison, Linda Joy. *Talking Back to Psychiatry: The Psychiatric Consumer/Survivor/Ex-Patient Movement*. New York: Routledge, 2013.

Nash, Jennifer C. *Black Feminism Reimagined: After Intersectionality*. Durham, NC: Duke University Press, 2018.

National Black Women's Health Project (NBWHP). *Lasting Legacy: The National Black Women's Health Project; An Oral History*. Washington, DC: National Black Women's Health Project, 2003.

National Black Women's Health Project (NBWHP). "National Black Women's Health Project Information Sheet." *Vital Signs* 11, no. 3 (1995): 7.

National Black Women's Health Project (NBWHP). "Social Security Disability and HIV." *Vital Signs* 10, no. 4 (1994): 59, 76.

Nefert-irie, Ptah. "What It Means to Belong to a Black Woman's Self-Help Support Group." *Health Talk*, NBWHP New York Chapter, no. 1 (1988): 5–6.

Nelson, Alondra. *Body and Soul: The Black Panther Party and the Fight against Medical Discrimination*. Minneapolis: University of Minnesota Press, 2011.

Nelson, Jennifer. *More Than Medicine: A History of the Feminist Women's Health Movement*. New York: New York University Press, 2015.

Nelson, Stanley. *The Black Panthers: Vanguard of the Revolution*. PBS, February 16, 2016. https://www.pbs.org/independentlens/documentaries/the-black-panthers -vanguard-of-the-revolution/.

Nishida, Akemi. "Understanding Political Development through an Intersectionality Framework: Life Stories of Disability Activists." *Disability Studies Quarterly* 36, no. 2 (2016). https://dsq-sds.org/article/view/4449/4302.

Ojanuga, Durrenda. "The Medical Ethics of the 'Father of Gynaecology,' Dr J Marion Sims." *Journal of Medical Ethics* 19, no. 1 (1993): 28–31.

Olyan, Saul M. *Disability in the Hebrew Bible: Interpreting Mental and Physical Differences*. New York: Cambridge University Press, 2008.

O'Toole, Corbett. *Fading Scars: My Queer Disability History*. N.p.: Autonomous Press, 2015.

Parker, Lorraine Greene. "Emotional Aspects of Chronic Illness." *Vital Signs* 3, no. 4 (1986): 3.

Parks, Sheri. *Fierce Angels: The Strong Black Woman in American Life and Culture*. New York: One World/Ballantine Books, 2010.

Pelka, Fred. *What We Have Done: An Oral History of the Disability Rights Movement*. Amherst: University of Massachusetts Press, 2012.

Phillips, Mary. "The Feminist Leadership of Ericka Huggins in the Black Panther Party." *Black Diaspora Review* 4, no. 1 (2014): 187–218.

Piepzna-Samarasinha, Leah Lakshmi. *Care Work: Dreaming Disability Justice*. Vancouver, BC: Arsenal Pulp, 2018.

Piepzna-Samarasinha, Leah Lakshmi. "A Not-So-Brief Personal History of the Healing Justice Movement, 2010–2016." *MICE Magazine*, last accessed July 19, 2018. https://micemagazine.ca/issue-two/not-so-brief-personal-history-healing-justice -movement-2010%E2%80%932016.

Poteat, Tonia. "AIDS and Black Lesbians." *Vital Signs* 9, no. 1 (1993): 8, 44.

Pressman, Jack David. *Last Resort: Psychosurgery and the Limits of Medicine*. New York: Cambridge University Press, 1998.

Price, Margaret. "The Bodymind Problem and the Possibilities of Pain." *Hypatia* 30, no. 1 (2015): 268–84.

Price, Margaret. *Mad at School: Rhetorics of Mental Disability and Academic Life*. Ann Arbor: University of Michigan Press, 2011.

Puar, Jasbir K. *The Right to Maim: Debility, Capacity, Disability*. Durham, NC: Duke University Press, 2017.

Rhodes, Jane. *Framing the Black Panthers: The Spectacular Rise of a Black Power Icon*. Champaign: University of Illinois Press, 2017.

Richardson, Angela Ducker. "My Life with Lupus." *Vital Signs* 1, no. 3 (1984): 4.

Robnett, Belinda. "African-American Women in the Civil Rights Movement, 1954–1965: Gender, Leadership, and Micromobilization." *American Journal of Sociology* 101, no. 6 (1996): 1661–93.

Rogers-Dulan, Jeannette, and Jan Blacher. "African American Families, Religion, and Disability: A Conceptual Framework." *Mental Retardation* 33, no. 4 (1995): 226–38.

Rosenthal, Keith. "The Intersections and Divergences of Disability and Race: From the 504 Sit-in to the Present." *Spectre Journal* (2021). https://spectrejournal.com /the-intersections-and-divergences-of-disability-and-race/.

Rothblum, Esther D., and Sondra Solovay. *The Fat Studies Reader*. New York: New York University Press, 2009.

Russell, Dick. *Black Genius and the American Experience*. New York: Carroll and Graf, 1998.

Ruzek, Sheryl Burt. *The Women's Health Movement: Feminist Alternatives to Medical Control*. New York: Praeger, 1978.

Samuels, Ellen. "Examining Millie and Christine McKoy: Where Enslavement and Enfreakment Meet." *Signs* 37, no. 1 (2011): 53–81.

Samuels, Ellen. *Fantasies of Identification: Disability, Gender, Race*. New York: New York University Press, 2014.

Samuels, Ellen. "My Body, My Closet: Invisible Disability and the Limits of Coming-Out Discourse." *GLQ: A Journal of Lesbian and Gay Studies* 9, nos. 1–2 (2003): 233–55.

Saran, Ama R. "Love in the Time of AIDS." *Vital Signs* (Summer 1991): 13.

Schalk, Sami. "Black Disability Gone Viral: A Critical Race Approach to Inspiration Porn." *CLA Journal* 64, no. 1 (2021): 100–120.

Schalk, Sami. *Bodyminds Reimagined: (Dis)ability, Race, and Gender in Black Women's Speculative Fiction*. Durham, NC: Duke University Press, 2018.

Schalk, Sami. "Contextualizing Black Disability and the Culture of Dissemblance." *Signs* 45, no. 3 (2020): 1–6.

Schalk, Sami. "Critical Disability Studies as Methodology." *Lateral* 6, no. 1 (2017). https://csalateral.org/issue/6-1/forum-alt-humanities-critical-disability-studies -methodology-schalk/.

Schalk, Sami. "Experience, Research, and Writing: Octavia E. Butler as Author of Disability Literature." *Palimpsest: A Journal on Women, Gender, and the Black International* 6, no. 2 (2017): 153–77.

Schalk, Sami. "Interpreting Disability Metaphor and Race in Octavia E. Butler's 'The Evening and the Morning and the Night.'" *African American Review* 50, no. 2 (2016): 139–51.

Schneider, Beth E., and Nancy E. Stoller. *Women Resisting AIDS: Feminist Strategies of Empowerment*. Philadelphia: Temple University Press, 1995.

Schweik, Susan. "Lomax's Matrix: Disability, Solidarity, and the Black Power of 504." *Disability Studies Quarterly* 31, no. 1 (2011). https://dsq-sds.org/article/view/1371 /1539.

Scotch, Richard K. *From Good Will to Civil Rights: Transforming Federal Disability Policy*. 2nd ed. Philadelphia: Temple University Press, 2001.

Shakespeare, Tom. *Disability Rights and Wrongs*. New York: Routledge, 2006.

Shakespeare, Tom. "The Social Model of Disability." In *The Disability Studies Reader*, edited by Lennard J. Davis, 197–204. 2nd ed. New York: Routledge, 2006.

Shapiro, Joseph P. *No Pity: People with Disabilities Forging a New Civil Rights Movement*. New York: Times Books, 1994.

Shaw, Randy. *The Activist's Handbook: A Primer for the 1990s and Beyond*. Berkeley: University of California Press, 1996.

Sherry, Mark. "(Post)Colonising Disability." *Wagadu* 4 (2007): 10–22.

Shilts, Randy. *And the Band Played On: Politics, People, and the AIDS Epidemic*. New York: Penguin Books, 1988.

Sins Invalid. *Skin, Tooth, and Bone: The Basis of Movement Is Our People; A Disability Justice Primer*. Berkeley, CA: Sins Invalid, 2016.

Skloot, Rebecca. *The Immortal Life of Henrietta Lacks*. New York: Crown, 2010.

Smedley, Brian D., Adrienne Y. Stith, and Alan R. Nelson, eds. *Unequal Treatment: Confronting Racial and Ethnic Disparities in Health Care*. Washington, DC: National Academies Press, 2003.

Smith, Barbara, ed. *Home Girls: A Black Feminist Anthology*. 1st ed. New York: Kitchen Table: Women of Color Press, 1983.

Smith, Susan Lynn. *Sick and Tired of Being Sick and Tired: Black Women's Health Activism in America, 1890–1950*. Philadelphia: University of Pennsylvania Press, 1995.

Spencer, Robyn C. *The Revolution Has Come: Black Power, Gender, and the Black Panther Party in Oakland*. Durham, NC: Duke University Press, 2016.

Spettel, Sara, and Mark Donald White. "The Portrayal of J. Marion Sims' Controversial Surgical Legacy." *Journal of Urology* 185, no. 6 (2011): 2424–27.

Springer, Kimberly. *Living for the Revolution: Black Feminist Organizations, 1968–1980*. Durham, NC: Duke University Press, 2005.

Stern, Alexandra. *Eugenic Nation: Faults and Frontiers of Better Breeding in Modern America*. Berkeley: University of California Press, 2005.

Stoller, Nancy E. *Lessons from the Damned: Queers, Whores, and Junkies Respond to AIDS*. East Sussex, UK: Psychology Press, 1998.

Talley, Heather Laine. *Saving Face: Disfigurement and the Politics of Appearance*. New York: New York University Press, 2014.

Taylor, Ashley. "The Discourse of Pathology: Reproducing the Able Mind through Bodies of Color." *Hypatia* 30, no. 1 (2015): 181–98.

Taylor, Keeanga-Yamahtta. *How We Get Free: Black Feminism and the Combahee River Collective*. Chicago: Haymarket Books, 2017.

Taylor, Sonya Renee. *The Body Is Not an Apology: The Power of Radical Self-Love*. Oakland, CA: Berrett-Koehler, 2018.

Thomas, Debbie. "Socializing in the Age of HIV/AIDS." *Vital Signs* 10, no. 4 (1994): 58, 75.

Tyler, Dennis, Jr. "Jim Crow's Disabilities: Racial Injury, Immobility, and the 'Terrible Handicap' in the Literature of James Weldon Johnson." *African American Review* 50, no. 2 (2017): 185–201.

Utsey, Shawn O., Norman Giesbrecht, Joshua Hook, and Pia M. Stanard. "Cultural, Sociofamilial, and Psychological Resources That Inhibit Psychological Distress in African Americans Exposed to Stressful Life Events and Race-Related Stress." *Journal of Counseling Psychology* 55, no. 1 (2008): 49–62.

Villarosa, Linda, and National Black Women's Health Project (NBWHP), eds. *Body and Soul: The Black Women's Guide to Physical Health and Emotional Well-Being*. New York: HarperPerennial, 1994.

Waggoner, Jess. "'My Most Humiliating Jim Crow Experience': Afro-Modernist Critiques of Eugenics and Medical Segregation." *Modernism/Modernity* 24, no. 3 (2017): 507–25.

Wallace, Michele. *Black Macho and the Myth of the Superwoman*. New York: Dial, 1979.

Washington, Harriet A. *Medical Apartheid: The Dark History of Medical Experimentation on Black Americans from Colonial Times to the Present*. New York: Doubleday, 2006.

Wendell, Susan. "Unhealthy Disabled: Treating Chronic Illnesses as Disabilities." *Hypatia* 16, no. 4 (2001): 17–33.

Williamson, Joy Ann. "Community Control with a Black Nationalist Twist: The Black Panther Party's Educational Programs." In *Black Protest Thought and Education*, edited by William H. Watkins, 137–58. New York: Peter Lang, 2005.

Wilson, Sylvia. "Reclaiming Our Spiritual Health." *Vital Signs* 4, no. 1 (1987): 9.

Young, Toni. "Black and Woman in the Age of AIDS." *Vital Signs* 11, no. 3 (1995): 34–35.

Zimbabwe, Nehanda. "The Wonders of Herbs." *Vital Signs* 9, no. 1 (1993): 29.

Banks-Wallace, JoAnne, 98
Banyton, Douglas, 6
Beal, Frances M., 37
behavior, 41, 53
Bell, Alicia, 4
Bell, Christopher, 6
Berne, Patty, 7, 147–48
Beyoncé, 67
bipolar disorder, 94
birth control, 107
birth defects, 71
bisexuals, 108
Black activists and activism: ableism and, 79; Black disability politics and, 2, 6, 9, 19; Black Panther Party, 27; psychiatric abuse and, 68; psychosurgery and, 60. *See also* Black cultural workers; Black feminist health activism
Black cultural workers: approaches to health, 101; Black disability politics and, 1, 6, 11–21, 128; Black Panther Party and, 27, 46, 52, 68; contemporary praxis, 143–51; disability identity and, 131–39; disabling violence and, 80; intersectionality and, 13; Oakland Community School and, 42, 45; psychiatric abuse and, 57. *See also* Black activists and activism
Black disability politics: the 504 sit-in, 23–40; Black feminist health activism, 80–89, 108–9; Black Health Matters and, 1–5; Black Panther Party and, 23–28, 46–47; contemporary praxis, 143–51; contextualization and historicization in, 14–15; cultural approaches, 95–102; disability identity and, 13–14, 129–39; disabling violence and, 69–80; fields and frameworks, 5–12; futures of, 154–57; health and wellness and, 89–92; HIV/AIDS and, 110–17, 125–28; as holistic, 15–18; holistic approaches, 92–95; intersectionality and, 12–13; Oakland Community School and, 40–46; political approaches, 102–8; prevention and, 117–21; prisons and mental institutions and, 52–58; psychiatric abuse and, 48–52,

66–68; psychosurgery and, 58–66; social justice movements and, 151–53; support and, 121–25; uprisings of 2020 and, 157–60
Black disability studies, 5–11
Black feminism, 5, 21, 37, 71–72, 141, 147, 152
Black feminist health activism: Black disability politics and, 18–19, 81–83, 108–9; cultural approaches, 95–102; disability identity and, 129–39; health and wellness and, 89–92; HIV/AIDS and, 110–17, 125–28; holistic, 92–95; National Black Women's Health Project and, 84–89; political approaches, 102–3; prevention and, 117–21; support, 121–25
Black Health Matters, 1, 3–4
"black identity extremists," 68
Black liberation, 1–3, 8, 11–12, 21, 79–80, 97, 159–60. *See also* collective liberation
Black Lives Matter, 68, 148–49
Black men, 17, 23–24, 30, 53, 57, 67
Blackness and Black people: the 504 sit-in and, 35; Black disability politics and, 1–3, 5, 10, 140–43; disability identity and, 13–14, 129–39; intersectionality and, 12–13. *See also* Black women
Black Panther (newspaper): the 504 sit-in and the, 29–30, 33, 35–38; ableist language and the, 69–72, 77–78; Black disability politics and the, 23–24, 26–27, 46; Oakland Community School and the, 42, 44–45; psychiatric abuse and the, 48–53, 56, 58; psychosurgery and, 58–63, 65–66
Black Panther Party: the 504 sit-in, 28–40; ableist language and the, 69–77; Black disability politics and the, 1, 7, 15–18, 23–28, 46–47, 127, 140–44, 149–51, 155, 165n31; disability identity and the, 131, 137; disabling violence and the, 77–80; holistic health and the, 94; Oakland Community School and the, 40–46; prisons and mental institutions and the, 52–58; psychiatric

abuse and the, 48–52, 66–68; psycho-surgery and the, 58–66. *See also Black Panther* (newspaper)

Black Panther Party v. Kehoe, 51

Black.Seed, 3–5

Black studies, 18, 26–27, 38, 46, 109, 114

Black Thoughts (newspaper), 61–62, 70

Black Woman, The (Bambara), 37

Black women: Black disability politics and, 5, 18–19; Black feminist health activism, 80–89, 108–9; cultural approaches to health, 95–102; disability identity and, 130; health and wellness, 89–92; HIV/AIDS and, 110–17; holistic approaches to health, 92–95; political approaches to health, 102–8; prevention and, 117–21; support and, 121–25

Black Women with Disabilities Alliance, 104, 138–39

Black Youth Project, 148–49, 152

Blake, Jacob, 73–77, 79–80

blindness and blind people, 104

Bloom, Joshua, 68

bodies, 8–9, 15

body and soul, 16, 49. *See also* bodyminds; spirituality and spiritual health

Body and Soul (NBWHP), 90–92, 96, 98, 103–4, 106, 115, 130, 138

Body and Soul (Nelson), 61

Body Is Not an Apology, The (Taylor), 153

bodyminds: Black disability politics and, 15–16; Black feminist health activism and, 88, 90, 94–95; Black Panther Party and, 34, 49; cultural approaches to health and, 97, 101; disability identity and, 132, 134; HIV/AIDS and, 116, 125; psychosurgery and, 64–65

botánicas, 98

Boyd, Rhea, 76

brain injuries, 50, 126

Braxton, Gwen, 101

breast cancer, 94

brown, adrienne marie, 152

Brown, Elaine, 24, 30–31, 49–50, 68

Byers, Lou, 61–66, 69–79

CAFT. *See* Coalition against Forced Treatment (CAFT)

Califano, Joseph, 28–30

California Mental Health Coordinating Council, 50, 58, 61, 66

cancer, 71, 73, 81, 94, 104

Cancer Journals, The (Lorde), 124

capitalism and anti-capitalism: the 504 sit-in and, 30; Black disability politics and, 7, 9, 18, 146, 155; Black Panther Party and, 23–24, 49; disabling violence and, 72–73; intersectionality and, 12–13

carceral institutions. *See* prisons and the prison industrial complex; psychiatric hospitals

care, 8–9

caretaking, 106, 125, 127

Caribbean spiritual practices, 97

Carter, Jimmy, 28, 30, 35

Cartesian dualism, 15

Center for Black Women's Wellness, 85–86, 88, 100

Center for Independent Living, 30–31

Center for the Study and Reduction of Violence, 61, 67

Chester Mental Health Center, 54–56, 61

child abuse, 93

children: Black disability politics and, 16, 25, 136–37, 150; Black feminist health activism and, 85, 106, 115; Black Panther Party and, 41–46, 163n2, 165n31; police violence and, 74–76, 79–80

Christianity, 96–97

chronic disease, 88, 109

chronic fatigue syndrome, 94, 104

chronic illness, 9, 55, 59, 71–73, 93–94, 106, 114, 117, 130, 133–35, 138

chronic pain, 2. *See also* pain

citizenship, 6–7

civil disobedience, 5

civil rights: Black disability politics and, 5, 7, 76, 82, 96, 113, 127–29; Black Panther Party, 28–29, 33, 38, 53

Clare, Eli, 71, 73, 79, 116

Clarke, David A., Jr., 67

disability justice: ableist language and, 72; Black disability politics and, 5–11, 15, 20–21, 50; Black feminist health activism and, 125

Disability Justice Collective, 7

disability pride, 2, 5–6, 72

Disability Pride Madison, 19

disability rights: the 504 sit-in and, 29, 31, 33, 35, 37; Black disability politics and, 5, 7, 9–10, 15–16, 220; Black feminist health activism and, 83, 91, 94; Black Panther Party and, 27, 46, 49; Oakland Community School and, 45; political approaches to health and, 105; psychiatric abuse and, 56; psychosurgery and, 61. See also Black disability politics; white mainstream disability rights movement

Disability Rights Wisconsin, 74

"Disability Solidarity" (The Harriet Tubman Collective), 140–41

Disability solidarity praxis, 20

disability-specific communities, 13–14, 125

disability studies: ableist language and, 38–39, 71; Black disability politics and, 5–11, 13, 15, 18; Black feminist health activism and, 94–95, 125–26; Black Panther Party and, 26, 68; cultural approaches to health and, 98; HIV/AIDS and, 114, 116; political approaches to health and, 105; prisons and mental institutions and, 52; psychiatric abuse and, 56, 58; race and, 47; religion and, 96–97. See also Black disability studies

disability symbolism, 71, 79, 112, 127

Disabled Lives Matter, 140

disabling violence, 18, 69–80, 92. See also racial violence

discipline, 53

discrimination, 6, 26–28, 79, 104, 123, 129, 184n4

disease: Black disability politics and, 10, 14, 16, 19; Black feminist health activism and, 85, 88–89, 91, 94–95, 111; Black Panther Party and, 48–49; Black women and, 83; cultural approaches to health and, 96, 99, 101;

HIV/AIDS and, 115–16, 124; political approaches to health and, 103–4; psychosurgery and, 65. See also illness; sickness

disordered eating, 2

Dixon, Dazon, 118–20

D'Lil, HolLynn, 29

domestic violence, 81, 93, 107, 118–19

drunk driving, 126

eating disorders. See disordered eating

education: Black feminist health activism and, 84–85, 99–100; Black Panther Party and, 25–26, 30, 46, 49; disability identity and, 129; HIV/AIDS and, 118, 121, 123, 125–26; Oakland Community School and, 40–46; political approaches to health and, 105–8. See also sex education

elders, 25, 86, 89. See also age and aging

electroshock therapy, 50

emotional disabilities, 33

emotional health, 85–87, 90–95, 99, 103, 110–11

employment, 26, 30, 35, 65, 129, 185n25

empowerment, 35

English as a second language, 42

environmental racism and activism, 9, 71–73, 79, 93–94, 103, 185n25

Erevelles, Nirmala, 6, 72–73

ethnicity, 40–41

eugenics, 126, 146

#EverywhereAccessible, 20

exercise, 105, 110–11

experimental procedures and research, 51–53, 59, 61, 65–66, 78, 115, 131, 170n18. See also clinical trials

faith, 83, 94, 97. See also spirituality and spiritual health

family, 87, 107, 125, 136–1367

fatness and fatphobia, 2, 86, 114, 152

FBI, 24–25, 68

feminism, 7, 12, 82–83, 102. See also Black feminism

feminist studies, 5

fibroids, 94

financial support. *See* support
Fisher, Marlene Braxton, 103
504 Emergency Coalition, 29
the 504 sit-in, 18, 23, 27–40, 46–47, 49,
  61, 67, 69
Floyd, George, 74
Folsom State Prison, 59
food and food access, 25, 28–29, 32, 40, 50,
  110–11, 147, 157–59. *See also* nutrition
forced sterilization, 103
forced treatment, 44, 50–60, 66, 69, 72, 78
Ford, Gerald, 28, 35
"Formation" (Beyoncé), 67
fossil fuels, 73
Fox News, 67
Frazier, Demita, 37
free clinics, 46, 82, 92. *See also* clinics
freedom. *See* collective liberation; libera-
  tion ideology
Freedom Inc., 157
Free Legal Aid and Education Program
  (BPP), 78
From Cries and Whispers to Action
  (NBWHP), 120–22
Fultz, Michael, 30

Galloway, Donald, 30
Garry, Charles, 78
gay people and gay rights, 29–30, 112–13,
  118. *See also* queerness and queer
  people
gender: the 504 sit-in and, 35; Black
  disability politics and, 2, 7, 14, 47;
  Black feminist health activism, 88;
  Black Panther Party and, 46; cultural
  approaches to health and, 99, 101;
  HIV/AIDS and, 112, 115, 124; political
  approaches to health and, 103; psychiatric abuse and, 58. *See also* sexism
gender studies, 114
genocide, 58, 60
gentrification, 3
Gibson, Dustin, 20, 132, 134–35, 138, 144,
  146, 149
Giuliani, Rudy, 67
grassroots organizing, 83, 87, 107–8, 165
grief, 93

Guy-Sheftall, Beverly, 83
gynecology, 65

Haitians, 112, 123
Hamer, Fannie Lou, 144
Hampton, Fred, 145
handicapped, 38, 104
harassment, 25
harm reduction, 152
Harriet's Apothecary, 98
Harriet Tubman Collective (HTC), 19–20,
  140–42, 147–49
Hawkins, Berlinda, 96
Hayward, Katharine, 126
healing and healing justice, 7, 10, 91; Black
  feminist health activism and, 98,
  108–9
Health, Education, and Welfare (HEW),
  23, 28, 30, 36, 39. *See also* the 504 sit-in
health activism. *See* Black feminist health
  activism
health and health care: Black disability
  politics and, 9–10, 16; Black feminist
  health activism and, 84, 87, 89–92,
  108–9; Black Panther Party and,
  25–27, 42, 46, 50; cultural approaches
  to, 95–102; disabling violence and, 76;
  HIV/AIDS and, 114–15, 120–21; holistic approaches to, 92–95; political approaches to, 102–8; psychiatric abuse
  and, 58. *See also* well-being; wellness
health-care workers, 124–35
health code violations, 51, 55
heart disease, 85, 94
Helping Educate to Advance the Rights of
  Deaf communities (HEARD), 20, 150
heteropatriarchy, 9, 94
Heumann, Judy, 31, 36
HEW. *See* Health, Education, and Welfare
  (HEW)
hierarchy. *See* disability hierarchy
Hiestand, Fred J., 51, 60–61
Hilliard, David, 59–60
historically Black colleges and universities,
  81, 101
historicization. *See* contextualization and
  historicization

HIV/AIDS: Black disability politics and, 18–19, 110–12, 125–28; Black feminist health activism and, 83–85, 91–94, 101, 106, 109, 114–17; disability identity and, 130, 133–34, 138–39; history of, 112–14; prevention and, 117–21; support and, 121–25
holistic, 12, 18, 67, 92–95, 115, 127
homelessness, 88
homophobia, 2, 30, 86, 114, 121
Hooks, Mary, 1, 22
Hoover, J. Edgar, 24–25
hospitals, 46
housing, 3, 25–26, 50, 90, 124, 185n25
Huggins, Erica, 24, 31, 34–35, 40, 43, 45–46, 68
human rights, 29–30, 33, 35
hypertension, 85, 92, 94, 104, 127

identity: the 504 sit-in and, 39–40; Black disability politics and, 6, 8, 19; disability, 13–14, 33, 97; intersectionality and, 12. *See also* disability identity
illness: Black disability politics and, 8–10, 16; Black feminist health activism and, 89, 94–95, 111; Black Panther Party and, 48–49; cultural approaches to health and, 96–97, 99; disability identity and, 13; HIV/AIDS and, 115–16; psychiatric abuse and, 55; psychosurgery and, 65. *See also* disease; sickness
immigrants, 6
impairments, 34, 65
imperialism and anti-imperialism, 12, 18, 23–24, 49
incarceration: Black Panther Party and, 25, 34, 44, 50; disabling violence and, 70–72, 77; HIV/AIDS and, 115; psychiatric abuse and, 52, 54; psychosurgery and, 62. *See also* mental institutions; prisons and the prison industrial complex
incest, 93
inclusion, 14, 21
Indigenous people, 76, 132, 162n18. *See also* Native people
insanity, 72

inspiration, 37–39, 69
institutionalization. *See* incarceration; mental institutions; prisons and the prison industrial complex; psychiatric hospitals
intellectual disabilities, 50, 94–95
Intercommunal Youth Institute, 40
internalized oppression, 13, 17, 49, 79, 82, 86–88, 91, 103, 122, 132
interpersonal violence, 9
intersectionality: Black disability politics and, 7, 12–13, 47, 127, 146, 155, 162n20; Black feminist health activism and, 84, 86, 112; Black Panther Party and, 36–37, 46, 50, 58, 67; Black women and, 82; disabling violence and, 72, 76; political approaches to health and, 104, 108. *See also* multiply marginalized people
intersex people, 147
involuntary commitment, 50–51
IQ testing, 41–42
isolation, 50

Jackson, Chuck, 23, 30
Jackson, Janice, 103–4
Johnson, Jenell M., 51, 53, 72

Kafer, Alison, 9, 11, 79, 114
kidney disease, 94
Kilpatrick, Lorrell, 20, 148–50
Kim, Eunjung, 55
Kindred Southern Healing Justice, 98
King Jr., Dr. Martin Luther, 4, 96, 145
Ku Klu Klan, 64, 67

labor, 50–51
Larry P. v. Riles, 42
Latinx people, 76, 98, 112, 114, 162n18, 176n7
law and legal systems, 46–47, 129–30, 136. *See also* legal definitions of disability
leadership, 105, 107
Lead on Update, 19
lead poisoning, 80
learning disabilities, 71
LeBlanc-Ernest, Angela D., 40, 68

veterans, 62–66

victims and victimization, 37, 39, 64

Vietnam War, 65

Villarosa, Linda, 92

violence: Black disability politics and, 4, 14–16, 18; Black feminist health activism and, 94–95, 112; Black Panther Party and, 25, 49; disability identity and, 133; psychiatric abuse and, 51–52, 55, 58, 67; psychosurgery and, 59–61, 64. *See also* disabling violence; racial violence

Vital Signs (newsletter), 86, 92–99, 102–3, 106–7, 115–22, 129–30, 138

vocational training, 86

Walking for Wellness, 85

Wallace, Margarite, 62–64, 78

Washington, Harriet A., 65

water, 80

Watkins, Heather, 20, 144

welfare reform, 107

well-being, 4–5, 16, 25, 49, 85, 89–95, 105–8, 115, 127. *See also* health and health care; wellness

wellness: Black feminist health activism and, 89–92, 108–9; cultural approaches to, 95–102; holistic approaches to, 92–95; political approaches to, 102–8. *See also* health and health care; well-being

"We Shall Overcome" (song), 38

wheelchairs and people who use wheelchairs, 31, 95, 104

White, Ellis, 29–30

white activists and activism, 6, 13, 56; psychiatric abuse and, 56, 66. *See also* disability activism; white mainstream disability rights movement

white mainstream disability rights movement, 2, 13, 26, 38–39, 45, 47, 57, 80, 127, 131. *See also* white activists and activism; whiteness

whiteness: Black disability politics and, 6, 57, 95; Black feminist health activism and, 94–95, 99, 124; disability identity and, 132–33, 135–36; psychosurgery and, 60. *See also* white supremacy

white supremacy, 5, 7, 9–11, 50, 72, 132–33, 135–36, 155. *See also* whiteness

Williams-Muhammed, Deborah, 86

women: the 504 sit-in and, 30–31; Black disability politics and, 6, 15; Black Panther Party and, 24–25, 163n2; psychosurgery and, 61, 65. *See also* Black women

women's liberation, 29, 86. *See also* women's rights movement

women's rights movement, 30. *See also* women's liberation

World Health Organization (WHO), 89–90

Yoruba traditions, 96